AN ADMINISTRATOR'S GUIDEBOOK TO EARLY CARE AND EDUCATION PROGRAMS

DOROTHY W. HEWES

San Diego State University

JANE MILLER LEATHERMAN

Indiana University–Purdue University Fort Wayne

PEARSON

Boston   New York   San Francisco
Mexico City   Montreal   Toronto   London   Madrid   Munich   Paris
Hong Kong   Singapore   Tokyo   Cape Town   Sydney

Series Editor: *Traci Mueller*
Editorial Assistant: *Janice Hackenberg*
Senior Marketing Manager: *Krista Groshong*
Editorial-Production Service: *Omegatype Typography, Inc.*
Electronic Composition: *Omegatype Typography, Inc.*
Composition Buyer: *Linda Cox*
Cover Administrator: *Joel Gendron*

For related titles and support materials, visit our online catalog at www.ablongman.com.

Between the time Website information is gathered and then published, it is not unusual for some sites to have closed. Also, the transcription of URLs can result in typographical errors. The publisher would appreciate notification where these errors occur so that they may be corrected in subsequent editions.

ISBN: 0-205-42058-3

Printed in the United States of America

10   9   8   7   6   5   4   3   2   1   09   08   07   06   05   04

CONTENTS

CHAPTER ELEVEN
Working with Families   167

SECTION III EVALUATING   185

CHAPTER TWELVE
Evaluating the Program   185

This guidebook reflects the history of preschool administration as a profession. Prior to the 1950s, directors had come from home economics, elementary education, or other fields of study. Some were mothers with diverse backgrounds who had developed an interest in the field when they participated in classes for their own children. They might have had child psychology courses or participated in some laboratory school observations, but there was no preparation for the management aspects of the director's position. During the 1950s, the impetus for specialized courses developed when it was finally recognized that specific college courses in these areas were required. By the 1960s, there were a few classes in administration, usually not in regular academic programs but through university extension programs.

By the early 1970s, nursery school administration classes were taught in some community colleges and universities, usually in departments of child development or education. There is now a nationwide emphasis on director accreditation and an increased demand for strict licensing requirements. In addition, there is global recognition that properly managed preschools and child care centers are an essential component of workforce support and a basis for later education.

I co-authored the 1972 first edition of *Early Childhood Education: A Workbook for Administrators* with Barbara Hartman. Both of us had home economics backgrounds and had been involved with cooperative preschools as directors and as participating mothers for twenty years. We had been teaching those new university extension classes in preschool administration with ditto handouts because there was no appropriate textbook. The obvious solution was to collaborate to remedy that situation. Major publishers were not interested in such a lowly topic, but Robert Reed of R and E Research Associates took a gamble. He photocopied that 1972 edition from our typed pages, stapled them together, and distributed the resulting book for classes across the United States and in other countries.

Three more editions of the original workbook were published in 1974, 1979, and 1988 before R and E closed. Each one reflected the progress made in word processing and duplication. The revised editions included changes that reflected new technologies and management theories as they related to children's programs. For example, the original section on financial systems began by stating, "Accounting is the language of commerce" and assumed that directors would do their own bookkeeping. In 1974, we kept that opening sentence and added a short glossary of such terms as *accounts receivable* and *balance sheet*. We included a brief overview of systems appropriate for various types of sponsorship, pointing out that "In most schools, amateurs will keep the books as one of their many duties" and that "Federally funded programs have their own multitudinous reports." A technological advancement was included by 1979: "Centers affiliated with colleges and public schools often have their funds handled through a centralized computer, and others may want to buy or lease small computers for accounting and other records." By 1988, it was suggested that directors choose the computer programs best suited for their centers. The comparable chapter in this current workbook reflects the reliance on computers that permeates society today and is but one aspect of change in the profession. In 1988, we could not envision the proliferation of websites that relate to all aspects of our field or their ease of access.

With this first edition published by Allyn and Bacon, there are many new features. One of the most obvious changes is in the title. "Early Care and Education" has taken over the "ECE" acronym from the "Early Childhood Education" in recognition of the dual purpose of preschool programs. Although the entire guidebook has been revised, its essential philosophy, described in the orientation, remains the same.

Barbara Hartman, one of the original co-authors, is recently deceased. Jane Leatherman, the new co-author, presently at Indiana University–Purdue University Fort Wayne, was an ECE teacher, director, and community college and university instructor for fifteen years. While on the faculty at San Diego State University, she taught the introductory and advanced administration classes that I developed and taught from 1974 until retirement in 1992. Now, as professor emeritus, I continue as faculty liaison to our campus child care center and am involved with professional organizations. One of the joys of early care and education lies in the bonds that develop among those who work with young children and to the constantly evolving research that shows us how important we are to society. Welcome to the field! May you enjoy it as much as I do.

D. W. H.

ACKNOWLEDGMENTS

We thank the reviewers for this edition for their helpful suggestions: Jeanne W. Barker, Tallahassee Community College; Susan Gimilaro, College for Lifelong Learning; and Renee Moore, Southwest Missouri State University–West Plains.

ORIENTATION TO THE GUIDEBOOK

What one tries to represent or do he begins to understand.
Friedrich Froebel (1782–1852)

OBJECTIVES

At the completion of this guidebook, you should be able to

1. Recognize your own personal administrative style.
2. Formulate and communicate to others the standards, purposes, and mission statement of early care and education.
3. Write and communicate to others the general, operating, and personnel policies for a specific school or program.
4. Develop a teacher recruitment program and interview applicants.
5. Use differentiated staffing, including aides, parents, and other volunteers, as well as teachers from varied backgrounds.
6. Plan and conduct meaningful staff meetings, including orientation.
7. Set up and supervise a children's program that combines understanding from the past with recent research findings.
8. Participate meaningfully in professional organizations that act on behalf of young children and their welfare.
9. Develop an efficient and effective system for records and reports, including computer software programs.
10. Develop efficient and effective procedures for educational programs, including health, safety, and nutrition.
11. Apply common principles of communication when dealing with staff and the public; be aware of the principles of human relationships.
12. Plan effective parent orientation and educational opportunities, recognizing parents' diverse needs.
13. Understand basic dynamics of working with parents who have unique family values and expectations.
14. Appraise skills and techniques in evaluation of children, staff, program, and self.

This guidebook applies business management principles to the administration of early care and education programs. We recognize that any writings about early care and education programs have limitations. In this field that is rapidly developing and changing its emphasis, in which legislative priorities shift frequently and judicial decisions may be enacted at any time, in which public sentiment mingles with scientific research, information can become obsolete before it gets into print. There is diversity of structure and of regulations from one geographic area to another and from one type of program to another. Even the terminology is not standardized, so that a *director* may instead be a *principal,* a *manager,* a *coordinator,* or a *leader.* Whatever title you hold, the work is essentially that of a leader. In the 1972 edition, it was stated that a standard textbook is premature, ostentatious, and authoritarian. We believe this even more firmly in this edition. This guidebook identifies basic knowledge, principles, and processes, and then guides you to adapt them to fit your own situations. We purposely refrain from advocating one correct way to manage all programs because that method doesn't exist.

We believe in active learning and view the process of developing your unique and personal enterprise as the best way to learn how to be a children's program administrator. Sequenced worksheets provide the structure to develop a real or simulated center. The worksheets can be done in class as a group activity or can be assigned as homework to be an extension of the material covered in the text. The worksheets are varied to meet differing needs, and instructors should use the worksheets that meet their course objectives. After a brief survey of historical background and current curriculum approaches, information and guidance are given to help plan, operate, and evaluate any one of a wide variety of possible programs.

The guidebook is designed primarily for use in college classes. However, it could be of value to directors of established preschools, to committees and individuals preparing grant proposals, and to groups establishing senior citizen and after-school or other human service programs. The material is designed to be covered in one semester, but a two-semester sequence might present planning and licensing requirements during the first term, with operating and evaluating sections during the second.

The guidebook is intended to be a resource and discussion guide. Completed worksheets can be put into file folders or a resource file. Materials from class should be supplemented by a growing collection of newspaper clippings, information downloaded from websites, articles from business and other periodicals, notes from books and professional journals, reports from conferences and workshops, and brochures from early childhood organizations. Videotapes, audiotapes, and compact discs on child development and business topics add another dimension. An abundance of materials is readily and inexpensively available, needing only organization to provide a dynamic and individualized resource library or portfolio. References and resources are included at the end of each chapter. You will not have time to read all of them, but simply noting the titles can acquaint you with available ideas and information. Websites are included for each related topic. These websites were current at the time of publication, although they frequently change.

It has been our experience that a major factor in the successful operation of an early care and education program is the conviction of its administrator that certain decisions are right for a particular school or center at a particular time, a conviction based on a broad knowledge of child development and early childhood education, coupled with a continued desire to learn more.

CLASS DISCUSSION

Brainstorm and discuss the characteristics that make any enterprise successful. As an extension to the discussion, each student might review a different business management book or journal article and then share the salient points.

REFERENCES AND RESOURCES

Chapman, E. N., & Goodwin, C. (2002). *Supervisor's survival kit.* Upper Saddle River, NJ: Prentice Hall.

Culkin, M. (Ed.). (2000). *Managing quality in young children's programs.* New York: Teachers College Press.

Decker, C. A., & Decker, J. R. (2001). *Planning and administering early childhood programs.* Upper Saddle River, NJ: Prentice Hall.

Hearron, P. F., & Hildebrand, V. F. (2003). *Management of child development centers.* Upper Saddle River, NJ: Prentice Hall.

Hoyle, J., English, F., & Steffy, B. (1998). *Skills for successful twenty-first century school leaders.* Lanham, MD: Scarecrow Press, Education Division.

Jensen, M. A., & Hannibal, M. A. (2000). *Issues, advocacy, and leadership in early childhood.* Boston: Allyn & Bacon.

Kagan, S. L., & Hallmark, L. G. (2001). Cultivating leadership in early childhood care and education: Reaping the harvest of a new approach to leadership. *Child Care Information Exchange, 140,* 7–10, 12.

Lowell, S. (2001). *The Harvard Business School guide to careers in the nonprofit sector* [electronic reproduction]. Boulder, CO: NetLibrary 2000.

Patterson, J. (2000). *The anguish of leadership.* Lanham, MD: Scarecrow Press, Education Division.

Rodd, J. (1998). *Leadership in Early childhood.* New York: Teachers College Press.

Schwahn, C. J., & Spady, W. G. (1998). *Total leaders: Applying the best of future-focused change strategies to education.* Lanham, MD: Scarecrow Press, Education Division.

Schweinhart, L. J. (1999). *A school administrator's guide to early childhood program.* Ypsilanti, MI: High/Scope Press.

Sciarra, D. J., & Dorsey, A. G. (2002). *Leaders and supervisors in child care programs.* Albany, NY: Delmar.

Sciarra, D. J., & Dorsey, A. G. (2003). *Developing and administering a child care center.* Albany, NY: Delmar.

Stephens, K. (2003). How to prepare a business plan. *The art of leadership: Managing early childhood organizations.* Redmond, WA: Child Care Information Exchange.

Wellington, S., & Spence, B. (2001). *Be your own mentor: Strategies from top women on the secret of success.* New York: Random House.

JOURNALS WITH ADMINISTRATION COMPONENTS

American Education
Child Care Information Exchange
Child Care Quarterly
Early Child Development and Care
Early Childhood Education Journal
Early Childhood Research Quarterly
Early Years
Education Administration Quarterly
Educational Leadership
Journal of Educational Psychology
School Review
Zero to Three

WEBSITE RESOURCES

Administration of Children and Families: www.acf.hhs.gov
American Association of School Administrators: www.aasa.org
American Management Association (AMA):   www.amanet.org
American Marketing Association: www.marketingpower.com
American Society of Association Executives (ASAE):   www.asaenet.org
Association for Supervision and Curriculum Development: www.ascd.org
Child Care Information Exchange: www.ccie.com
Early Childhood News: www.earlychildhoodnews.com
Journal of Child Care Administration: www.jccajournal.com
National Association of Elementary School Principals: www.naesp.org
National Education Association: www.nea.org

Recognizing Our Roots

BRIEF HISTORY OF EARLY CARE AND EDUCATION

To make plans for an endeavor without knowing its historical background is like trying to grow a rosebush by taking a bouquet out of its vase and sticking it into a hole in the ground. You will begin to establish "roots" for the administration of an early care and education (ECE) program through a review of historical highlights. Recognition of how today's ideas originated will be helpful in understanding your own philosophy and in planning your center.

One aspect to keep in mind is that children have been essentially the same throughout the eons. Archeologists have found ancient footprints that showed two adults walking in a straight line while children zigzagged and circled nearby. They have also found dolls and other playthings. As Osborne (1991) emphasized, today's children are innately very similar to those of prehistoric times. What has changed is society as a whole and the way it influences family structures and economic systems.

Brief sketches are provided for some of the outstanding educators who influenced the educational systems of today. Because education in the United States is traditionally Eurocentric, the following account only traces the thread of influence that has determined our present attitudes toward young children's education and out-of-home care. Suggestions for reading about other cultural influences are included in later chapters.

The Ancient Period

Many of today's beliefs are founded on those of great writers who lived and taught during the classical periods of Greece and Rome. Citizens of Greece and Italy encouraged the playtime of young children and recognized that informal playgroups would facilitate the learning of social skills. Toys included dolls and wheeled vehicles for acting out adult activities. Members of the household were children's primary educators. As Lascarides and Hinitz (2000) and other historians have shown, some of the concepts of these early Greek and Roman writers about the education of young children are still with us. Socrates (470–399 B.C.) wrote that he could not teach anybody anything; he could only make students think. This philosophy is basic to the structure of this guidebook and to many activities of today's preschool centers. Plato (427–347 B.C.) pointed out that training started at birth, with children "straightened like a piece of warped wood" by the threats and blows from parents and servants before they were passed on for school discipline at about age seven. Despite this attitude, he wrote, "nothing learned under compulsion stays in the mind" and spontaneously invented games were the ideal educational devices for young children. He also believed that children's welfare was the responsibility of the entire community. For older children, Greek education at that time included literature, science, and the appreciation of art and music taught through active participation.

Quintilian (A.D. 34–95) recognized a series of developmental levels beginning at birth and believed that education related to a child's interests should start with the ability to speak. For ages three to seven, praise for desired behavior and the good examples of adults developed proper moral standards. For those slightly older, he developed letters carved from ivory and other manipulative materials to help teach reading. His writings, lost for a thousand years and rediscovered at the end of the fifteenth century, expounded the benefits of rewards and the ineffectiveness of corporal punishment.

In much of northern Europe at the beginning of the first millennium, the general population was illiterate, with oral legends and ballads the primary means of passing on shared knowledge. Children were expected to assist adults as soon as they could understand what was to be done. Later, when the Roman Catholic Church sent out missionary monks to convert them to Christianity, young men educated in monasteries learned enough Latin to read and copy religious papers. Young children were still viewed as innocents who were allowed freedom to play. Their learning came from observing adults in their families.

About 1425, the printing press with movable type was introduced to Europeans. Before this, books were reproduced by copying, letter by letter. The idea of enabling women and the lower classes to read was highly controversial. It has been suggested that awareness of childhood developed during these years, but many historians believe that it was the concept of adulthood that evolved with the spread of literacy. Desiderius Erasmus (1466–1536) wrote *Cevilitus Movum* in 1530, a book defining proper behavior in children. He specified that exterior actions can come only from a well-educated inner spirit.

The greatest changes directly affecting American education began in 1517 when Martin Luther (1483–1546) initiated a movement known as the Protestant Reformation. Although he was a monk, he rejected the Roman Catholic idea that communication with God could come only through giving money to the clergy. Because he believed that children were born full of sin and must study the Bible to reach salvation, he advocated that the Scriptures needed to be translated from Latin into the language of the common people. Boys and girls, rich and poor, must learn to read. Public schools and libraries were essential. One result was that America's colonial period, dating from the settlement of Plymouth Colony in 1620, emphasized early reading skills. This is reflected in educational policies today (Beatty, 1995).

Jan Amos Comenius (1592–1670) is known as the inventor of early childhood education. Among his accomplishments were the first picture book for children (*Orbis Pictus,* 1658), a curriculum guide for mothers (*School for Infancy,* 1633), and a description of the stages of child development in a book that he hoped would promote a united education for all people (*The Great Didactic,* 1657). Comenius believed that education should begin during the first six years of life, before the child's mind could become corrupted. Nature study and geography would furnish the materials of thought. Symbols would be provided by drawing and writing. Parents should encourage children to play with others their own age, using constructive and sense-stimulating materials. He wrote about a natural order of "learning by doing" similar to that of Jean Piaget. Fundamental to his philosophy was the idea that children at all economic levels were essentially good and that their education should be filled with joy, but his ideas were ignored for almost two centuries.

Jean Jacques Rousseau (1712–1788) proposed that the goals of education should be based on liberty, romantic naturalism, and the development of the body. He changed the course of educational history. After *Emile* (1762) and his subsequent works were read and discussed by the intellectuals of his time, three great principles of contemporary education were established: (1) the principle of growth through natural unfolding, (2) the principle of a pupil's active involvement in education, and (3) the principle of individuality. He proposed general rules, such as sensory training for young children and using real objects for study instead of symbols, but emphasized that these rules should be presented only when there were indications from the child of readiness.

Johann Pestalozzi (1746–1827) believed that the head, hand, and heart must develop harmoniously; that children must love and be loved; and that they must educate their senses and their sensibilities. Educators from all over Europe, and even from the United States, spent time at his school in Switzerland observing his techniques. Although he believed that the home was the best place for those younger than six or seven years old, his ideas laid the groundwork for early childhood education. In *How Gertrude Teaches Her Children* (1801), he dealt with methods to be used by mothers. Some of Pestalozzi's admirers developed Infant Schools for younger children, but they tried to improve on his methods by systematizing them. Instead of letting children wander in a natural environment to explore and discover, some British and American Infant Schools of the 1820s were designed as galleries for as many as one hundred children, with three year olds at the front and older children seated in the higher back rows. All were taught rote phrases and songs. Their observations of nature consisted of chanted, learned responses about objects held up by the teacher. By the 1830s, these Infant Schools were closed because, according to doctors, early learning made children's little brains pulpy, and the general public began insisting that mothers should be responsible for their own children (De Guimps, 1890). However, some of Pestalozzi's ideas had permeated the elementary grades and the teacher training programs, making acceptance of his ideas easier for the kindergartens that came later.

Friedrich Froebel (1782–1852) is remembered as the Father of the Kindergarten for devising the original early education programs that included children from about age two to seven. He wrote that children old enough to leave their mothers' knees should begin to attend the neighborhood kindergarten for short periods. He also provided inspiration for John Dewey and other exponents of what has come to be called progressive education. At seventeen, while at the University of Jena, he read the newly translated Persian scripture *Zendavesta*. It confirmed his belief in the common characteristics of all living creatures, with the entire universe viewed as an evolving organism. After attending several other universities, spending time with Pestalozzi, and experimenting with a variety of occupations, he opened an elementary-level boarding school for boys and girls, which he operated from 1816 to 1838. He recognized that the children came to him at age seven poorly prepared for their studies, and in his long search for a remedy he discovered the forgotten writings of Comenius.

They became the inspiration for kindergartens that he experimented with for several years before he officially opened the first one in 1840.

Froebel incorporated his former studies in the new science of crystallography into the children's block play and other activities. In addition, he based his system on observations of what boys and girls really enjoyed and how they learned. He also corresponded with leading educators, former students, and others who were interested in early learning (Heineman, 1893). Froebel stressed the importance of play and he worked out the first sequenced educational materials, called the Gifts and Occupations. Construction with wooden building blocks, creative activities with clay and other natural materials, circle time fingerplays and musical activity games, and gardens and pets made up the curriculum (Hewes, 2001).

These early kindergartens emphasized skills now considered important in cognitive development. Froebel believed that rote counting and recitation did not contribute to problem solving. He advocated such activities as collecting and sorting pebbles, comparing the sizes and shapes of leaf collections, building dams in brooks, and tracing letters or shapes in the sandbox to enhance children's educations. The teacher's major function was to help clarify and organize the learning experiences of each individual child. Froebel involved mothers as teacher aides and instigated the custom of children addressing their teachers as "Auntie" to indicate a familial relationship.

One of Froebel's revolutionary ideas was the training of women to be teachers. This was seen by the Prussian government as a socialist plot and led to an official order in 1851 to close all of that country's kindergartens. By that time, their value had become accepted across Europe, and those outside Prussia continued to function and to train teachers. Within the next fifty years, Froebel's system and the concept of women as teachers had spread to North America and Asia. As Wollons (2000) has documented, Froebel's ideas continue to underlie early child care and education programs throughout the world.

The Kindergarten in America

Contemporary preschool centers retain their Froebelian roots. However, just as transplanted flowers grow differently when their environments are changed, so did the kindergartens in America. As they developed in the United States, Froebelian methods took divergent routes to popularity. One followed his original teachings about learning through play, encouraging modifications and materials that fit into his ideas of socialization and creative freedom within limits. The other saw his teachings as a method to get children to conform.

Elizabeth Peabody, who started the first kindergarten for English-speaking children in 1860, was one of the most enthusiastic converts to Froebel's system. Although she rejected physical force to discipline children and curb their wills, there are repeated references in her writings to teachers affecting the very souls of their students by using specific words to direct block-building and paper-folding exercises. She inspired other leaders of the U.S. kindergarten movement of the late 1800s, particularly those in New England, to believe that by knowing the laws of order, children were set upon the paths of righteousness so that they would never stray. Of course, this also meant that the teacher's reward would come in the Hereafter and that monetary compensation was unimportant, which is one of our problems today (Hewes,1990).

Under Peabody's influence, as in the earlier rigid version of Pestalozzian Infant Schools, all children in the kindergarten room followed the teacher's directions or responded to rote questioning. The translations and interpretations of Froebel's writings were given mystical interpretations and his sequenced activities called Gifts and Occupations became standardized and commercialized. At her urging, Milton Bradley began to manufacture the Gifts and Occupations that Froebel's followers had standardized following his death. Other manufacturers soon recognized the potential profits, and they began to print pamphlets with specific directions that teachers should give to children for the construction of identical products.

In contrast to Peabody's teacher-dominated kindergartens, the basic ideas that had come from Pestalozzi and Froebel were passed on by educators who had either grown up in Europe or were predisposed to its orientation before studying there. The same political pressures that forced closure of the Prussian kindergartens and the teacher training schools also led to the arrival in the United States of liberal German educators during the 1850s. Although they first opened schools in which children were taught in their native language, these teachers who had learned the system as it was originally designed, soon influenced the American kindergarten movement. They viewed the teacher as a facilitator rather than an authoritarian. Some of Froebel's equipment and activities, including the sandbox and circle time, remained. Others were modified and developed as he had intended. For example, one adaptation of Froebel's wooden blocks became the colored beads strung by generations of kindergartners and another became the large unit blocks of today. There were child-size group activity tables and dollhouses. Teachers recycled paper and enjoyed using what we now call "scrounge" materials for the children's creative activities.

Froebel had advocated "the union of intelligent families blessed with children of the proper age" to establish "institutions in which under the guidance of one trained for the purpose, the activity of the children should be carefully fostered and nourished." Parent education was part of his plan, but, again, there were two different versions of the kindergarten. In Elizabeth Peabody's opinion, when parents understood that the aim was to develop the child's mind, they "would not go so far as to hinder the kindergarten teacher, who ought to follow out her method without being interrupted." In contrast, German-trained Maria Krause-Boelte told members of the National Education Association (NEA) Kindergarten Department in 1873, "To the mothers goes my mission; they must become my allies and confederates if I shall be heard and understood." Swiss–German William Hailmann, in an 1880 lecture, spoke about discussion groups at which mothers who had been participating in the kindergarten classroom talked about their immediate concerns and said, "the successes, the difficulties, or failures of some child; the best means for enhancing improving the one, or overcoming the other, or avoiding the third for the future;—and so deep, so earnest is the interest manifested, that you are tempted to assume all these are own mothers of the child in question" (Hewes, 2001).

Two examples will show how the German version of the kindergarten was spread. Emma Marwedel, who opened a kindergarten training school in Los Angeles in 1876, had studied with Froebel's widow. She had no qualms about developing new materials or encouraging innovative ideas. Kate Douglas Wiggin was in Marwedel's first class. Although Wiggin is better known as the author of *Rebecca of Sunnybrook Farm* (1903) and other fiction, her young adult years were devoted to a kindergarten in San Francisco's toughest neighborhood. It became so famous that a slogan was created for it: "When you come to California, see Yosemite first, and then visit the Silver Street kindergarten." Between its opening in 1879 and its destruction in the 1906 earthquake, 400 young women graduated as teachers. One was Jane Ledyard, who married and moved to San Jose. The kindergarten that she developed in 1880 was merged with the new normal school when it opened seven years later. Now San Jose State University, it continues to build on those origins, with the child development

CLASS ACTIVITY

Research the history of preschool education in your own community. How does it compare with the national history of preschool education? What factors affected your local programs? How do you think a historian fifty years from now will regard today's early care and education programs?

program director receiving an award in 1996 from Delta Phi Upsilon, an organization that proudly retains its Froebelian origins.

There are countless similar stories about how European educators spread the original Froebelian system; its transplanted roots are directly related to the child care and education programs in the United States today. Anna Bryan, after her own training with one of the German immigrant teachers, opened the Louisville Free Kindergarten and its training school in 1887. Patty Smith Hill was in Bryan's first class and then joined her as a teacher. Together they attended Froebelian conferences and gained national attention for their advocacy of learning through play. In 1888, they were the only two participants to remain in the audience when psychologist G. Stanley Hall criticized the sentimentality and rigidity of traditional kindergartens. Hall had studied children's individual differences using scientific research, which he believed was the way Froebel would have wanted it done. At this time, the three developed an ideal plan for early childhood education that was not implemented for three decades.

By 1920, public school kindergarten enrollments were approaching half a million, but two- to four-year-olds were no longer admitted. Patty Smith Hill had become a faculty member at Teachers College, Columbia University. She decided to implement the plan from 1888. After visiting England's new nursery schools in 1924, she invited two of their teachers to demonstrate methods appropriate for prekindergarten children. This was the beginning of American nursery schools. It should be noted that some nursery schools enrolled infants and toddlers, and that observations of their activities were critical in developing child development theory as it is taught today.

Patty Smith Hill did more than introduce nursery schools. In 1925, she gathered together men and women from several professional fields as a committee on nursery schools. In 1931, this became the National Association for Nursery Education (NANE). In 1964, the name changed to the National Association for the Education of Young Children (NAEYC) and the first issues of the journal *Young Children* were published (Hewes, 1976). Patty Smith Hill would be amazed to know about websites such as www.naeyc.org where articles and other resources can be downloaded, and gratified to note that they maintain the principles for which she fought.

For more information, Appendix A contains a timeline of early care and education.

CURRICULUM APPROACHES

It is generally accepted that high-quality early childhood education has a positive effect on a child's later school years and personality characteristics. Many models or philosophical approaches have been developed and have influenced each other since the 1920s. Most have maintained Froebel's admonitions to have self-chosen play with established rules and flexible schedules. It is common to have a "science table" in the preschool classroom with stones and leaves that the children have collected or other manipulatives for them to investigate. Group activities inherited from the kindergartens of a century ago, such as circle time with stories and activities chosen by the teacher, are selected to be developmentally appropriate. Your previous coursework and the references and resources at the end of this chapter describe the most popular curriculum models, and class members may have firsthand knowledge of others. By now, you probably have ideas about the system of early care and education you would like to have for your own center. For Worksheet 1.1, choose elements to integrate into the planning of your center, perhaps by combining two or more different models. For example, a traditional preschool may provide Montessori materials or may use Distar™ for twenty minutes each day for children who will soon enter kindergarten. Consider whether your curriculum will be teacher centered or learner centered and how the theoretical model fits into the overall goals for your program.

worksheet

1.1

p. 13

Traditional/Developmental Interaction/ Developmentally Appropriate Practice

The most common approach, consistent with the NAEYC Developmentally Appropriate Practice (DAP), has sometimes been termed "eclectic" because it draws on many different models for its basic philosophy of children's active learning. The DAP curriculum contains three basic tenets: (1) knowledge of child development; (2) knowledge of each child's strengths, interests, and needs; and (3) awareness of social and cultural aspects of the child. It is considered a traditional approach because its roots lie in the progressive Froebelian kindergartens. Influences in the twentieth century have included recorded observations of children popularized by Gesell's developmental theory, concerns over mental health as seen by Freudian psychoanalysts, constructivist principles of Piaget and others, and behaviorist strategies based on rewards for desired behavior. This is the system that is taught in most classes for persons entering the field of early care and education. Surveys by NAEYC and others have indicated that about four-fifths of American directors believe that they fit into this category. If this is your choice, try to recognize which aspects are of most importance to the program you are developing and consider what you might want to choose from other categories.

High/Scope

David Weikart developed this "constructivist" variation of the traditional approach for Head Start in 1970. He instituted a research process that has demonstrated its effectiveness in preparing children for subsequent education. It is different because directors and teachers have participated in and completed workshops and other training conducted by High/Scope. In more than 7,000 authorized sites in the United States and other nations, its constructivist curriculum features an active learning period distinguished by a "Plan–Do–Review" sequence. Teachers prearrange interest areas in the classroom so that children can choose individual or small-group activities. The teachers then actively encourage problem solving and verbal reflections. There is a consistent daily routine, for example, the children are responsible for preparing and cleaning the lunch tables. Teachers are expected to interact during outdoor games and all aspects of the children's activities. Also recording children's behaviors and ongoing assessment are emphasized. Studies conducted by High/Scope indicate that each dollar per child spent using their approach to early childhood education saves seven dollars in social services costs by the time a child reaches adulthood.

Reggio Emilia

Although educators and others in the Italian city of Reggio Emilia first sponsored schools for young children in the mid-1940s, their methods only began to receive attention in the United States during the 1990s. Based on the writings of Froebel and others who believed in self-activity, the Reggio schools feature a project-based curriculum that evolves from the children's interests. It is made possible through flexible scheduling, with a great deal of parental and community involvement. One result is that children's art and exhibits contribute to colorful and interesting classroom environments. Important aspects include a system of portfolio documentation that traces the accomplishments of children and adults.

Piaget-Derived/Cognitively Oriented

The Piaget-derived, cognitively oriented approach focuses on children's active problem solving. It is based on the developmental stages theory advanced by Jean Piaget in *To Understand Is to Invent,* first published in French in 1948, translated into English in 1973, and further developed by Constance Kamii. Piaget was well acquainted with the writings of Pestalozzi and Froebel and had been chair of the Swiss Montessori Society. Each of these factors influenced his ideas about how children learn. Teachers must determine when children have developed into self-initiating problem solvers and then guide them toward solutions. Teachers ask open-ended questions, such as, "Why do you think your block tower fell down?" rather than instructing students in processes. The emphasis is not on "pushing" children but on strengthening their abilities. Many elements of Piaget's system have been integrated into the cognitively oriented models.

Montessori

Although Dr. Maria Montessori (1870–1952) developed her methods in Italy during the early 1900s and lectured in the United States between 1913 and 1918, her ideas of "scientific pedagogy" were not widespread until reintroduced in 1958. They had, however, spread to many nations around the world. The stated goals are to develop children's senses, practical life skills, self-discipline, moral values, and character. A distinguishing characteristic of Montessori preschools is the use of "didactic materials" for children's independent learning within a prepared environment according to their needs at "sensitive periods" of development. Although children choose the particular activity in which they participate, self-correcting materials must be used in a precise way to teach a particular skill or concept. Directors of Montessori centers should have studied the system in a training program approved by one of the major Montessori associations. Because many preschools use the Montessori materials without uniformity of philosophy or methodology, efforts are underway toward an approval process for the United States.

Waldorf Schools

Rudolph Steiner (1861–1925), a wealthy European businessman concerned about the rigid emphasis on academic education in the late 1890s, developed and promoted the Waldorf system with its emphasis on creativity and imaginative play. The basic philosophy, which extends from infancy through high school, is that children relate what they learn to their own experiences if they are interested and fully engaged.

■■■■■ ▬▬

WHAT WOULD YOU DO?

As part of the pre-K class unit on birds and their nests, the teacher brought a little incubator and five chicken eggs to class. For three weeks, the children waited. Finally, one morning, the chicks were pecking holes in their shells and breaking out. Four of them were already running around, peeping for food, but the fifth had not hatched. All of the other children went outside, but one little girl remained watching. The teacher suggested that she join the others, but she protested, "Oh no, I do *so* hope this one is a lamb." How will your curriculum approach deal with children's question and explorations?

"What they learn becomes their own." In addition to taking courses in storytelling, the arts, and music, teachers are expected to develop self-understanding and cultural growth. Although they are more popular in Europe, about 200 Waldorf schools have been established in the United States since the 1920s, and that number is increasing.

Direct Instruction/Behaviorist/Distar™/Academic

Distar™ was developed in the mid-1960s for use with children of low-income families: The commercially distributed Distar™ method derives from the Direct Instructional System. It has been termed a *cultural transmission* method because it assumes that children must acquire knowledge from outside themselves. Teachers are required to present precisely planned twenty-minute lessons in language, reading, and arithmetic, reinforcing students with praise for correct responses (Bereiter & Engelmann, 1966). These lessons usually take a designated portion of the day, with traditional activities carried out before and afterward. Although they are more commonly used at the kindergarten level and beyond, especially for children with fewer opportunities, Distar™ and similar programs have claimed to raise test scores of children at all economic levels.

REFERENCES AND RESOURCES

Beatty, B. (1995). *Preschool education in America: The culture of young children from the colonial era to the present.* New Haven, CT: Yale University Press.

Bereiter, C., & Engelmann, S. (1966). *Teaching disadvantaged children in the preschool.* Englewood Cliffs, NJ: Prentice Hall.

Bredekamp, S., & Coppel, C. (Eds.). (1997). *Developmentally appropriate practices in early childhood programs.* Washington, DC: National Association for the Education of Young Children.

Brickman, N., & Taylor, L. (Eds.). (1999). *Supporting young learners: Ideas for preschool and day care providers.* Ypsilanti, MI: High/Scope Press.

Brooks-Gunn, J., Fuligni, A. S., & Berlin L. J. (2003). *Early child development in the twenty-first century.* New York: Teachers College Press.

Brosterman, N. (1997). *Inventing kindergarten.* New York: Harry N. Abrams.

Cadwell, L. B. (2003). *Bringing learning to life: The Reggio approach to early childhood education.* New York: Teachers College Press.

Chatin-McNichols, J. (2002). *The Montessori controversy.* New York: American Montessori Society.

Cleverly, J., & Phillips, D. C. (1986). *Visions of childhood: Influential models from Locke to Spock.* New York: Teachers College Press.

Copple, C. E. (Ed.). (2001). *NAEYC at 75—Reflections on the past and challenges for the future.* Washington, DC: National Association for the Education of Young Children.

De Guimps, R. (1874). *Pestalozzi his life and work* (J. Russell, Trans., 1890). New York: Appleton.

Devries, R., Zan, B., Hildebrandt, C., Edmiston, R., & Sales, C. (2002). *Developing constructivist early childhood education: Practical principles and activities.* New York: Teachers College Press.

Earle, A. M. (1899). *Child life in colonial days.* Williamstown, MA: Cornerhouse. (Reprinted 1975)

Engelmann, S., & Carnine, D. (1982). *Theory of instruction: Principles and application.* New York: Irvington.

Evans, R. I. *Jean Piaget: The man and his ideas* (E. Duckworth, Trans., 1973). New York: Dutton.

Fields, M. V., & Boesser, C. C. (1997). *Constructive guidance and discipline: Preschool and primary education.* Upper Saddle River, NJ: Prentice Hall.

Froebel, F. (1826). *The education of man* (W. N. Hailmann, Trans., 1889). D. Appleton reprint 2003. Grand Rapids, MI: Froebel Foundation.

Gandini, L., & Edwards, C. P. (Eds.). (2000). *Bambini: The Italian approach to infant/toddler care.* New York: Teachers College Press.

Gestwicki, C. C. (1999). *Developmentally appropriate practice: Curriculum and development in early education.* Albany, NY: Delmar.

Gutek, G. L. (1997). *Historical and philosophical foundations of education.* Upper Saddle River, NJ: Merrill/Prentice Hall.

Heinemann, A. H. (Ed.). (1893). *Froebel's letters.* Boston: Lee and Shepard.

Helm, J. H., & Beneke, S. (Eds.). (2003). *The power of projects: Meeting contemporary challenges in early childhood classrooms: Strategies and solutions.* New York: Teachers College Press.

Helm, J. H., & Katz, L. G. (2003). *The project approach in the early years.* New York: Teachers College Press.

Hendrick, J. (1997). *First steps toward teaching the Reggio way.* Upper Saddle River, NJ: Prentice Hall.

Hendrick, J. (2003). *Total learning: Developmental curriculum for the young child.* Upper Saddle River, NJ: Prentice Hall.

Hewes, D. W. (1976). Patty Smith Hill: Pioneer for young children and NAEYC's first half century. *Young Children, 31,* 3.

Hewes, D. W. (1990). Historical foundations of early childhood teacher training. In B. Spodek & O. N. Sarancho (Eds.), *Early childhood teacher preparation* (pp. 1–22). New York: Teachers College Press.

Hewes, D. W. (1992). *Pestalozzi: Foster father of early childhood education.* Presentation at NAEYC History Seminar. (ERIC Documentary Reproduction Service No. ED353067 PS 021 037)

Hewes, D. W. (2001). *W. N. Hailmann: Defender of Froebel.* Grand Rapids, MI: The Froebel Foundation.

Hohmann, M., & Weikart, D. P. (1995). *Educating young children: Active learning practices for preschool and child care programs.* Ypsilanti, MI: High/Scope Press.

Hulbert, A. (2003). *Raising America: Experts, parents, and a century of advice about children.* New York: Knopf.

Isenberg, J. P., & Jalongo, M. R. (1997). *Major trends and issues in early childhood education.* New York: Teachers College Press.

Kaiser, B., & Rasminsky, J. S. (2002). *Challenging behavior in young children: Understanding, preventing and responding effectively.* Boston: Allyn & Bacon.

Kamii, C. K., & Housman, L. B. (2000). *Young children reinvent arithmetic: Implications of Piaget's theory.* New York: Teachers College Press.

Kazdin, A. E. (2000). *Behavior modification in applied settings* (6th ed.). Florence, KY: Wadsworth.

Kostelnik, M. J., Soderman, A. K., & Whiren, A. P. (2004). *Developmentally appropriate curriculum.* Upper Saddle River, NJ: Pearson.

Kramer, R. (1983). *Maria Montessori.* Chicago: University of Chicago Press.

Lascarides, V. C., & Hinitz, B. F. (2000). *History of early childhood education.* New York: Palmer Press.

Miltenberger, R. G. (2000). *Behavior modification: Principles and procedures.* Florence, KY: Wadsworth.

Morrison, G. S. (2001). *Early childhood today.* Upper Saddle River, NJ: Merrill.

Orme, N. (2001). *Medieval children.* New Haven, CT: Yale University Press.

Osborn, K. (1991). *Early childhood education in historical perspective.* Athens, GA: Daye Press.

Peltzman, B. R. (1998). *Pioneers of early childhood education: A bio-bibliographical guide.* Westport, CT: Greenwood Press.

Petrash, J., & Gatte, J. T. (2002). *Understanding Waldorf education: Teaching from the inside out.* New York: Gryphon House.

Prochner, L. (1996). Quality of care in historical perspective. *Early Childhood Research Quarterly, 11,* 5–17.

Ronda, B. A. (1984). *Letters of Elizabeth Palmer Peabody.* Middletown, CT: Wesleyan University.

Seefeldt, C. (Ed.). (1990). *Continuing issues in early childhood education.* Columbus, OH: Merrill.

Shapiro, M. S. (1983). *Child's garden: The kindergarten movement from Froebel to Dewey.* University Park: Pennsylvania State University Press.

Snider, A. (1972). *Dauntless women in early childhood education—1856 to 1931.* Washington, DC: Association for Childhood Education International.

Soto, L. D. (Ed.). (2000). *The politics of early childhood education.* New York: Peter Lang.

Staley, L. (1998). Beginning to implement the Reggio philosophy. *Young Children, 53,* 5.

Taylor, B. (2004). *A child goes forth: A curriculum guide for preschool children.* Upper Saddle River, NJ: Pearson.

Weber, E. (1984). *Ideas influencing early childhood education.* New York: Teachers College Press.

Weston, P. (1998). *Friedrich Froebel: His life, times, and significance,* London: Roehampton Institute.

Williams, L. R., & Fromberg, D. P. (1992). *Encyclopedia of early childhood education.* New York: Garland.

Wolfgang, C. H., & Wolfgang, M. E. (1999). *Schools for young children: Developmentally appropriate practices.* Boston: Allyn & Bacon.

Wollons, R. L. (2000). *Kindergartens and cultures.* New Haven, CT: Yale University Press.

Youcha, G. (1995). *Minding the children: Child care in America from colonial times to the present.* New York: Scribner.

WEBSITE RESOURCES

American Educational Research Association, Division F (History) Network: www.aera.net/divisions/f

American Montessori Society: www.amshq.org

Early Childhood: www.earlychildhood.com

Froebel Foundation: www.Froebelfoundation.org

Gesell Institute of Human Development: www.gesellinstitute.org

High/Scope: www.highscope.org

Montessori: www.montessoriconnections.com

National Association for the Education of Young Children: www.naeyc.org

North American Reggio Emilia Alliance: www.reggioalliance.org

The Association of Waldorf Schools of North America: www.awsna.org/education

U.S. National Committee, World Organization for Early Childhood Education (OMEP):   www.omep-usnc.org

CURRICULUM APPROACHES

Name _____ Date _____

Objective: To understand characteristics of different curriculum approaches.

Directions: Consider the dominant characteristics of the curriculum approaches and describe the components that you plan on incorporating into your program.

Structured/unstructured

Cognitive/affective

Content/process

Preplanning/self-discovery

Teacher-directed/child-oriented

Other

CHAPTER TWO

Economic Factors of Early Care and Education Support

CHAPTER OUTLINE

PHILANTHROPIC SUPPORT

PUBLIC-SECTOR FUNDING

FOUNDATIONS

PROGRAM STRUCTURES

There is a bewildering (but never adequate) array of funding sources for early care and education programs. Related to this are public attitudes about families (especially mothers) who use the funds and about those who work in the organizations providing the funds. As in the previous chapter, a brief historical overview will help explain how this situation has developed. A discussion of various types of financial structures follows. Foundations and agencies award funds on the basis of written requests called proposals. The introductory material for Worksheet 2.1 provides details about this funding process, but you should to be aware of financial alternatives as you begin planning for your proposed center.

worksheet

2.1

p. 27

Some critics believe mothers should stay at home with their children. There exists research that can be interpreted as supporting this belief. For example, some studies indicate that children spending time in centers makes them more aggressive in kindergarten. Other opponents insist that it is socialistic because Cuba and other socialist countries provide free or low-cost care for their youngest citizens. Recall that it was a similar accusation by the Prussian government that led to closure of the Froebelian kindergartens and training programs in 1851. One of the greatest blows to early care and education in the United States came in 1971 when President Nixon vetoed the Comprehensive Child Development Bill (Senate Bill 2007) after both houses of Congress had passed it by a strong majority vote. His reasoning was that this legislation promoted communistic approaches to child rearing rather than family-centered approaches. As we look at the various support systems for ECE, we must recognize that negative viewpoints are still held by many Americans.

It is interesting to note that the current practice of giving parents an income tax deduction for licensed child care costs was devised to provide assistance to families while avoiding "sponsorship" protests that would have arisen if the federal government had supported specific centers. Allowing parental choice and payment has also avoided potential problems related to the separation of church and state. The majority of child care centers continue to be fee based, with parents spending a high proportion of their total income on them. However, increasing numbers of previously employed middle-income parents are opting for part-time employment or are choosing not to work while their children are young. This presents the potential for the expansion of half-day nursery schools and parent cooperatives that satisfy the socialization needs of both parents and children.

PHILANTHROPIC SUPPORT

Relatives, nannies, and governesses took over many child rearing functions in the past and they continue to be important, but out-of-home care also has a long tradition. In Colonial New England, widows or spinsters operated "dame schools" for young children. Because children could not attend the public schools until they could read, these literate women were paid a few pennies a day to teach basic reading. The dame schools also served as day care centers. Across the developing nation, similar informal systems developed for children whose mothers were involved with the family business or with household burdens. On the plantations of southern states, where slave mothers were expected to return to their fieldwork soon after giving birth, an older woman cared for their children in a designated location. Many all-day support systems for impoverished families have been affiliated with churches and other religious organizations as part of their community outreach. One of the first day care centers was established in 1798 by Quakers in Philadelphia and others followed. They drew little public attention, but it should be noted that a few of those established in the mid-1800s continue to function as nonprofit charity centers or Head Start sponsors.

For many years there have been programs and institutions that cared for children who had been abandoned or whose families were struggling to support them, but these were primarily orphanages or other residential institutions. Although many kindergartens of the late 1800s were private schools supported by the tuition fees paid by parents, others were philanthropic. Elizabeth Peabody, who considered kindergartening a "Gospel for children" and a way to assimilate immigrant parents into the American way of life, is usually credited with initiating the free kindergarten movement. Inspired by Peabody and other Froebelian leaders, wives of newly affluent businessmen not only contributed thousands of dollars to those programs and institutions but also became involved as volunteers.

The greatest surge in the growth of child care centers was in the 1870s to 1890s when vast crowds of low-income immigrants arrived in the United States. Some free kindergartens stayed open from early morning until night. They also provided food, clothing, and social services. Hull House, established by Jane Addams in 1889, is one of the best known of these programs that were established to assist low-income families.

Supporters of settlement houses believed that the educational and social development in Froebelian kindergartens would change the surrounding neighborhoods. One classic story was about a little boy who took home a plant that he had sprouted in the kindergarten. When he put it on the windowsill, his mother realized that the window was dirty. After she washed it, she recognized that the entire home needed cleaning. The result was that the father decided to stay home from the grog shop, spending his evenings listening to the son singing kindergarten songs. Although this was probably a fantasy, there was a definite effort by teachers and volunteers to educate mothers in all of the skills they needed to purchase and cook foods, do financial planning, and function in the United States, which was so new and different from their homelands.

PUBLIC-SECTOR FUNDING

The first White House Conference on Children and Youth, meeting in 1909 during President Theodore Roosevelt's term in office, was instrumental in acknowledging the problems facing families living in poverty. The subject of child care was discussed, but any action was postponed because of concerns for the sanctity of family privacy. The controversial establishment of the U.S. Children's Bureau in 1912 was a major accomplishment of President Taft. Subsequent White House conferences, in 1919 during Woodrow Wilson's presidency and in 1930 under Herbert Hoover, emphasized child health and protection but nursery schools were given favorable mention (Hewes, 1998a). From that point onward, there was increased interest in early childhood care and education. In 1997, President and Mrs. Clinton, building on their long-time interests in child care and early education, met with leaders of early childhood associations and other interested persons attending their White House Conference on Child Care. They personally discussed the problems presented by those in attendance, who represented a variety of organizations ranging from NAEYC to the Family Home Day Care Association.

Although these White House events during the twentieth century had no legislative power, they helped guide public interest toward supporting positive action for early care and education programs. Public funding support was possible only when a majority of the involved voters believed that the funded programs would benefit the public. Controversies always arise in determining whether an investment is beneficial, and persistence is usually needed to accomplish anything close to the desired results. The largest component of public funding is that for kindergartens, which most states have provided free for so many years that the long struggle to reach that accomplishment has been forgotten.

Froebelians in the National Education Association (NEA) began efforts in the 1860s to persuade public school administrators to incorporate kindergarten classes into their programs, which at that time would have included children ages three to seven. A resolution was finally passed at the NEA 1885 annual conference to recommend the incorporation of kindergartens into public schools, but this usually meant little more than free use of vacant classrooms (Hewes, 1999). Support became more organized in 1892 when a few Froebelian teachers and volunteers formed a committee that became the International Kindergarten Union and is today's Association for Childhood Education International (ACEI).

New concepts from developmental psychology, anthropology, sociology, social work, and domestic science (home economics) supported the concept of public school kindergartens and day care programs for low-income children. Dr. W. T. Harris established the first public school kindergarten in 1873. He believed in punctuality and silence as cardinal virtues, and he thought that with proper discipline and a few apprentices any well-trained teacher could manage a hundred children per classroom. However, because she or he was not really teaching anything, this kindergarten teacher should get a lower salary than those teachers of higher grades. Harris got little support for this idea but it aroused enough indignation to create additional efforts to maintain Froebel's original ideas about children's learning through play and the need for trained teachers who could relate directly with a small group of children.

The Works Progress Administration (WPA) nursery schools were established in the depths of the 1930s depression as part of the Federal Emergency Relief Act. They were the first preschool programs to directly receive federal funds. President Roosevelt signed legislation in 1933 to provide employment for teachers and others who needed jobs, not for the benefit of children. However, Eleanor Roosevelt was a strong advocate for children and families. It was through her efforts that public housing projects built at this time incorporated child care centers.

The WPA announcement of the nursery schools was made three days before the annual NANE conference. Establishing policies and procedures for the newly funded WPA child care centers became the major business at the conference, with the result that all positions on the advisory board were soon filled by experienced individuals in leadership positions. Almost every nursery school teacher and child development specialist in the United States participated. By 1935, with almost 2,000 WPA nursery schools enrolling 72,404 children, nearly 7,000 adults were involved and thousand of parents volunteered. Training programs for teachers, designs for equipment and buildings, and many other elements of today's preschools date to that 1930s depression era. Twenty-three colleges gave short courses to train the WPA teachers in the first year, and 93 the next. These were so well received that most were integrated into the permanent offerings of the colleges, becoming the basis for many ECE departments of today. In addition, a high proportion of those who entered the profession as staff for these programs continued to work with families and young children, some of them going on to get doctoral degrees and positions in the emerging departments of child development, early childhood education, and child psychology.

Under the Lanham Act, child care began when the 1930s depression era merged with that of World War II. Funding for the WPA schools tapered off and then ended. Their success led to further legislation, instigated by Eleanor Roosevelt, known as the 1943 Lanham Act. It provided federal funding for centers to care for children whose parents were employed in wartime industries. At its peak, about 1.6 million children were enrolled in 3,000 of these centers, which were administered through the public elementary school. Some of these centers provided additional services, such as inexpensive family dinners that could be picked up when parents came for their children.

Federal funding ended in 1946, but the Lanham Act centers had spread awareness about out-of-home care and the educational benefits of preschools across the United States. About half of the nursery schools established at the time continued under other auspices, with California the only state to maintain the entire program. Many of the model buildings constructed for the WPA child care centers were turned over to other sponsors, including cooperative preschools and those that were continued by local school districts. Federal sponsorship and public school administration had given "legitimacy'" to preschool education.

The next major involvement of federal funding came when President Lyndon Johnson accepted recommendations of his Office of Economic Opportunity to begin the Head Start program for children of disadvantaged families. The First Lady again was involved; Lady Bird Johnson held a White House tea (with representatives of the press present) to announce that these preschools would break the cycle of poverty. Research projects and theoretical writings from sociologists, psychologists, and other professionals had confirmed the recognition by educators that underprivileged children needed preschool experiences to help them begin their educations. The project received an overwhelming response, with about 40,000 teachers and an equal number of paraprofessionals attending training sessions before the first children's classes. From the beginning, social services, parent involvement, and health care have been seen as critical components of Head Start. Children with special needs have been included since 1975, and programs have been extended to include a wider age range. Parent participation, as volunteers or paraprofessionals and as members of committees that guide their own local centers, has been an integral element since the inception of Head Start.

Now in the twenty-first century, there are about fifty federal programs that directly or indirectly fund child care and preschool programs, including Title XX, Head Start, and the Child Care Food Program. There are many federal agencies involved, including the Department of Agriculture (Child Care Food Program) and the Department of Education (preschools and handicapped programs). Some states also provide tax credits for parents and/or employers who use or provide child care as a benefit to employees. States may support nursery schools that serve as laboratory settings for parent education programs. Municipalities may provide free rent in public buildings or subsidize centers for homeless families. Other federally funded programs have been supportive of preschool children and their families.

FOUNDATIONS

A major source of philanthropic funding today is through foundations. An individual, family, or corporation can establish a foundation. Foundations can provide tax deductions and a positive public image as well as the satisfaction of accomplishing good works for those who establish them. Foundations can be local or national, and their widely diverse areas of interest include programs for young children. As one example, Eleanor Roosevelt's concern for children and their families was recognized in 1988 by the American Association of University Women (AAUW) Fund for Women and Girls. It was established to subsidize research about problems related to programs associated with latchkey children and the conflicting pressures of work and home. Another is the Dr. Seuss Foundation, which provides millions of dollars for a wide variety of child and youth programs.

We must recognize that there were no child development classes and little scientific interest or knowledge in this subject area before 1920. By that time, the teacher training textbooks of the Froebel kindergarten programs were considered outdated and kindergartens were usually taught by normal school graduates who were more oriented toward older children. Financial support of the Laura Spellman Rockefeller Foundation determined the future of early childhood education. When the term *child development* was first used in 1924, it was viewed as the beginning of a broad social movement, a profession that combined the relevant elements of all the social sciences. The foundation's officers, Beardsley Ruml and Lawrence K. Frank, were advocates of Dewey's progressive education who did not want to focus on habit training or raising the intelligence quotient (IQ). Rather than giving funds to psychology departments or schools of education, the foundation funded home economics departments because their faculties would best deal with the whole child within the whole family. The basic rationale for this was similar to that recognized earlier by kindergarten advocates: Teachers and administrators of public schools were not interested in working with families and would not carry out a play curriculum. The American Home Economics Association had been a proponent of family studies programs

CLASS DISCUSSION

As you think about the funding sources for your own center, consider the demographics of its location. Discuss the aspects of the community in which you want to open your program. This would mean such factors as the economic status of families in the community and their configurations, such as two working parents or single mothers with low incomes; the cultural or ethnic groups predominating in the area; new housing developments or corporate expansion that might mean a subsidized program; or other factors.

since its inception in 1908. Educators in these "domestic science" programs were already interested in the work being done by Patty Smith Hill at Teachers College and in reports brought back by Edna Noble White and others who had visited the McMillan nursery schools in England. Support given to the AAUW provided professional consultation to groups of educated women who were setting up new nursery schools. Although others had been concerned with helping needy families, this was recognition of preschools for the benefit of mothers with academic backgrounds but no training in parenthood skills. One result was Children's Community Nursery School in Berkeley, California, which originated with an AAUW group in 1927. It is recognized as the oldest continuously operating cooperative preschool in the United States (although it became a WPA child care center for two years in part to provide free lunches).

One negative result of the Rockefeller funding for programs in home economics departments has been their lower prestige in academia. Despite their vital role in many aspects of today's lifestyle, and even the change in the nomenclature from *domestic science* to *home economics* and then in the 1990s to a variety of names with family and consumer sciences emphasis, graduates in child development still must defend their professional status. This is not new. For example, Mary Tyler Washburn was a feminist of the 1920s and the second woman president of the American Psychological Association. She refused to have a nursery school on her college campus and warned her students against becoming involved with one because they were "sex tainted" like home economics. This attitude still persists and can make fundraising challenging, but as we begin the twenty-first century there is increased recognition that the early years really do provide the foundation for later education and the rest of an individual's life.

PROGRAM STRUCTURES

Early Care and Education Using Public Funds

In some countries, child care programs are fully supported by public funds. In the United States, the only program with a previously consistent allocation in the federal budget and a comprehensive assessment system is Head Start. The federal government also supports a U.S. Department of Agriculture (USDA) program to provide food for children of low-income families in nonprofit centers, teacher training grants, various subsidies through state agencies, centers on U.S. military bases in many countries, and other specialized programs. Most states and many communities provide support systems, the most common being prekindergarten programs for children at risk or with special needs (Neugebauer, 2003b).

There are efforts to develop universal preschool systems in the United States, in which a city, state, or the federal government integrates administration of all types of preschools. Funding is provided, with tuition free or on a sliding scale based on income. The first universal preschool system, established in New York in 1998, delegates planning to advisory boards of local school districts. Standards are developed, but emphasis on reading skills continues to be used to evaluate their effectiveness. Universal preschool programs may extend half-day kindergarten downward by one year or they may provide all-day care from infancy onward.

Private/Sole-Proprietary Programs

The most common type of program is the individual nursery school or child care center. It can be operated as a private business or incorporated as a for-profit venture. It must be licensed according to the standards of the state in which it is located, but its curriculum and policies are determined by the owner(s). Ages of enrolled children are also at the discretion of the owners, sometimes limited to infants and toddlers or including kindergarten, but most often for those ages three to five. Funding comes primarily from fees paid by parents.

Family Child Care Homes

Early childhood care in a private residence is typically for six to twelve children, including those of the provider. Specific age ranges may be designated, such as infant–toddler or prekindergarten. Family day care homes are usually operated as for-profit sole proprietorships, but they may be incorporated. A nonprofit community program in which each home operates independently but shares in a mutual support network having a name used for advertising or to obtain USDA food funds may also coordinate them. Social agencies may provide supervision and training programs. Regulations vary widely from state to state, but the National Association of Family Child Care encourages professionalism through its accreditation program. Note that there are tax deduction benefits, such as partial mortgage payments, reduced insurance premiums, or assistance with meal or equipment costs.

School-Age Programs

Sometimes called "latchkey" or "6 to 6" centers, these are educational and recreational programs organized and maintained as extensions of regular school hours and during vacation periods. They may operate early in the morning and late in the afternoon and are often located in public school buildings. They supplement regular classes through music, art, computer laboratories, and other activities and provide assistance with homework.

Campus-Based or Laboratory Programs

Campus-based or laboratory programs have been used since the 1920s as model programs for training teachers and to provide sites where psychologists and related professionals can observe young children for research purposes. Originally they were half-day nursery schools, but many now provide full-day child care during the academic year for faculty, staff, and students. They are usually located on or near a college campus.

Parent Participation (Co-operative) Preschools

Parent participation preschools are nonprofit organizations in which parents usually participate as classroom aides, assist in administration, establish policies, and determine school procedures. There is a wide variety of parent participation nursery schools. Although most co-ops are completely parent initiated and operated, with parents hiring the director and other staff members, some are administered by community colleges as adult education classes, are provided by a corporation for its employees, or are controlled by the center's worker–owners with parents serving on an advisory committee.

Employer-Sponsored Day Care

Corporate support for child care has slowly been increasing in importance since the early 1970s, although there are reports of corporate-sponsored programs as early as one at the Otis Elevator Company in 1856. Increasingly, child care is being viewed as a means to reduce absenteeism and as an advantage when private-sector companies are recruiting new employees. Centers may be on site or nearby. Some, especially in hospitals, operate seven days a week, twenty-four hours a day. Others are available only on an emergency basis and are limited to a few days a year, to be used by employees whose regular arrangements are disrupted. Several small businesses may join together as a consortium in an office park center to share the responsibility and costs of a child care center. Varied degrees of corporate involvement may include free use of facilities, contributions of materials and services, or part of staff salaries. Centers may be incorporated as nonprofit philanthropies; contracted for with outside corporate management, such as Bright Horizons, operated as parent cooperatives; or otherwise adapted to the general structure of the business. Tax benefits both to employers and employees are an important consideration.

Faith-Based/Church-Affiliated and Community Agency Centers

Faith-based centers have a long history, and most child care centers during the 1800s were affiliated with religious institutions. Since the mid-1900s, centers in this category, in churches, synagogues, or other faith-based locations, have constituted about half of the morning nursery schools, Mothers Day Out programs, or full-day child care. They may be sponsored as a ministry for the members of their own congregations or as nonsectarian community outreach and social service centers. In some states, no license is required. Agencies, such as the Boys' and Girls' Clubs, Young Men's Christian Association (YMCA), and the Young Women's Hebrew Association (YWHA), provide care in their own facilities or in those leased for that purpose. Funding to supplement parent fees may come from donations or from the local United Way. Financial arrangements range from providing free rent and utilities to charging fees that become budgeted income for their sponsors.

Short-Term/Drop-In Centers

Short-term or drop-in centers are sometimes located in shopping malls or recreational sites, such as ski resorts or cruise ships. They can provide temporary care for children who have minor illnesses or other reasons for not going to their regular care givers. Advance registration may be required, but the staffing is often arranged according to "averaging out" the expected attendance. Fees are usually based on the hours of attendance and may be higher or lower than regular child care. Licensing may be required. Currently, there are no organizations that directly relate to this type of program. For further information, contact the sponsors of the program that you are interested in pursuing.

Infant–Toddler Programs

Infant–toddler programs are specifically designed for the care and education of children under the age of three years. Some centers enroll children soon after birth because of limited maternity leave. Most states have separate requirements for the care of children of this age. This type of program requires specific equipment, such as cribs and changing tables, and the child-to-staff ratio is lower than that for older children to accommodate the needs of the younger children.

Inclusive Child Care

Inclusive child care typically refers to centers that enroll children with identified disabilities or special needs. Some programs have mandates that require admittance of children with disabilities. Head Start, for example, has to reserve 10 percent of the enrollment for children with special needs. Other programs enroll children on the basis of space availability. The Americans with Disabilities Act states that centers must accept children with disabilities unless this will cause undue stress on the centers. However, many centers are able to accommodate children with special needs into their regular classrooms.

Intergenerational and Senior Care Programs

With increasing numbers of senior citizens who are unable to cope with the problems of independent living, communities are developing a variety of facilities that include supervised care and appropriate activities. Some of these facilities follow schedules similar to those for children, with participants attending them while other family members are at work. Their administration is similar to that of child care centers. One of the first federal reports recommending intergenerational programs bringing together senior citizens and young children was made by the Intergovernmental Advisory Council on Education in May 1988 (Hanks, 1998). Since that time, intergenerational programs have become important contributions to many communities. For many children whose grandparents live far away "grandfriends" provide another dimension to their lives. The mingling of elderly individuals in residential or recreational facilities and young children in day care programs reflects the traditional role of nurturing grandparent. At times, both generations may share activities, such as bubble blowing, whereas at other times the elders provide additional volunteer staffing for one-on-one activities, such as reading storybooks or sitting in a rocking chair holding a fussy baby. Funding is from a variety of sources, including community subsidies and individual fees.

Considering Your Program

worksheet

2.1

p. 27

Now that we have discussed funding sources and program structures it is time for you to consider your program. Worksheet 2.1 will help you think about the framework of your program. Will your program be federal or state funded, or private or

■ ■ ■ ■ ■

WHAT WOULD YOU DO?

A Southern California student who used the 1974 version of this guidebook dreamed of opening a center in the Northern California mountain town where her family had vacationed. After graduation, she moved there and took a temporary job working in the local coffee shop. One of the regular customers was an elderly man who was always alone. She stopped to chat with him during idle moments, and one day he commented that she seemed overqualified as a waitress. She confided her dream and he asked how much it would cost to open such a center. Her response (this was in the early 1970s) was $6,000. The following morning, he brought in a certified check for that amount and wished her good luck. What would you do if someone offered you money to open your dream program?

corporate? What about the size of your center and the ages of children that you will serve? You should consider the operating schedule, full or part time. In the third part of the worksheet, include your ideas of curriculum approaches for your program. For example, your program may be faith-based, supported by parent tuition and community funds. It may be full-day licensed, with a Reggio Emilia curriculum influence. Remember, this is your program; design it in terms of your vision of a program for young children.

REFERENCES AND RESOURCES

Beauchemin, C. L. (1999). *The daycare provider's guidebook.* West Linn, OR: TCB Enterprises.

Bergen, D., Reid, R., & Torell, L. (2001). *Educating and caring for very young children.* New York: Teachers College Press.

Bordin, J. (2001). Securing and managing child care subsidies—Questions and answers for centers considering participation. *Child Care Information Exchange, 140,* 11–14.

Children's Defense Fund. (2001). *The state of America's children.* Washington, DC: Children's Defense Fund.

Coiner, C., & Hume G. D. (1998). *The family track: Keeping your faculties while you mentor, nurture, teach and serve.* Urbana: University of Illinois Press.

Coontz, E. K. (2003). *Bringing families together: A guide to parent cooperatives.* Davis: University of California Press.

Copeland, T. (1999). *Family child care marketing guide: How to build enrollment and promote your business as a child care professional.* New York: Teachers College Press.

Dionne, E. J., Jr., & Chen, M. H. (2001). *Sacred places, civic purposes.* Washington, DC: Brookings Institute.

Dunlop, K. (2000). *Family empowerment—One outcome of parental participation in cooperative preschool education.* New York: Garland.

Generations United. (2003). *Young and old serving together: Meeting community needs through intergenerational partnerships.* Washington, DC: Author.

Gestwicki, C. C. (1999). *Developmentally appropriate practice: Curriculum and development in early education.* Albany, NY: Delmar.

Gormally, L. (1992). *The dependent elderly: Autonomy, justice and quality of care.* New York: Cambridge University Press.

Halpern, R. (2003). *Making play work: The promise of after-school programs for low-income children.* New York: Teachers College Press.

Hanks, R. (1998). Connecting the generations. *Child Care Information Exchange, 131,* 12–14.

Harms, T., & Clifford, R. M. (1998). *Family day care rating scale.* New York: Teachers College Press.

Harms, T., Cryer, D., & Clifford, R. M. (2002). *Infant/toddler environment rating scale.* New York: Teachers College Press.

Harms, T., Jacobs, E., & White, D. (1998). *School-age care environment rating scale.* New York: Teachers College Press.

Hewes, D. W, (1998a). *"It's the camaraderie"—A history of parent cooperative preschools.* Davis: University of California Center for Cooperatives.

Hewes, D. W. (1998b). Sisterhood and sentimentality—America's earliest preschool centers. *Child Care Information Exchange, 106,* 24–27.

Hewes, D. W. (1999) Issues in early care and education—A rearward view. *Issues in Teacher Education, 8*(2), 27–40.

Hewes, D. W. (2000). Co-ops—Preschools with parents in charge. *Child Care Information Exchange, 133,* 75–78.

Jenson, M. A., & Hannibal, M. A. (2000). *Issues, advocacy, and leadership in early education* (2nd ed.). Boston: Allyn & Bacon.

Kaplan Press. (2000). *Child care center resource and business kit: How to open a child care center.* Lewisville, NC: Author.

Kostelnick, M. J., Onaga, E., Rohde, B., & Whiren, A. (2002). *Children with special needs: Lessons for early childhood professionals.* New York: Teachers College Press

Lascarides, V. C., & Hinitz B. F. (2000). *History of early childhood education.* New York: Palmer Press.

Lombardi, J. (2002). *Time to care: Redesigning child care to promote education, support families, and build communities.* Philadelphia: Temple University Press.

Morgan, G., & Harvey, B. (2002). *New perspectives on compensation strategies for the out-of-school-time workforce.* Boston: Wellesley Centers for Women.

National Association for the Education of Young Children. (1999). *Activities for school age child care.* Washington, DC: Author.

Neugebauer, R. (1998). Congregations that care: Child care in religious institutions. *Child Care Information Exchange, 124,* 22–25.

Neugebauer, R. (2000). Religious organizations taking a proactive role in child care. *Child Care Information Exchange, 133,* 18–20

Neugebauer, R. (2001). Employer child care growth and consolidation continues—Status report 11 on employer child care. *Child Care Information Exchange, 141,* 14–16.

Neugebauer, R. (2002). Employer child care growth slows with the economy. *Child Care Information Exchange, 147,* 58–61.

Neugebauer, R. (2003a). For-profit organizations maintaining status quo: Sixteenth annual status report on for profit. *Child Care Information Exchange, 149,* 17–20.

Neugebauer, R. (2003b). Update on child care in public schools. *Child Care Information Exchange, 150,* 66–71.

Noam, G. G. (2003). *Afterschool education: Approaches to an emerging field.* Cambridge, MA: Harvard Education Press.

Odom, S. (Ed.). (2002). *Widening the circle.* New York: Teachers College Press.

Porter, P. (2001). Intergenerational care in action—Bringing young and old together works for everybody. *Child Care Information Exchange, 140,* 75–79.

Rab, V. Y., & Wood, K. I. (1995). *Child care and the ADA: A handbook for inclusive programs.* Baltimore, MD: Paul H. Brookes.

Ripple, C. H. et al. (1999). Will fifty cooks spoil the broth? The debate over entrusting Head Start to the states. *American Psychologist, 54,* 327–343.

Sandall, S., McLean, M., & Smith, B. (2000). *DEC recommended practices in early intervention/early childhood special education.* Denver, CO: Division for Early Childhood (DEC) of the Council for Exceptional Children (CEC).

Sciarra, D. J., & Dorsey, A. G. (1999). *Opening and operating a successful child care center.* Albany, NY: Delmar.

Soto, L. D. (Ed.). (2000). *The politics of early childhood education.* New York: Peter Lang.

Thomas, J. A. (2000). *Child care and laboratory school on campus: The national picture.* Cedar Falls, IA: National Coalition for Campus Children's Centers.

Thompson, B. A. (2002). *The home daycare complete recordkeeping system.* New York: Datamaster.

U.S. Department of Education. (2002). *Taking care: An employers' guide to child care options.* Washington, DC. Retrieved February 1, 2004, from www.edpubs@inet.ed.gov

Walton, T. (2001). Why inclusion benefits everyone: Insights from a parent. *Child Care Information Exchange, 139,* 76–79.

Williams, L. R., & Fromberg, D. P. (1992). Historical and philosophical roots of early childhood practice. *Encyclopedia of Early Childhood Education.* New York: Garland.

Wyman, A. (1995). The earliest early childhood teachers: Women teachers of America's dame schools. *Young Children, 50*(2), 29–32.

WEBSITE RESOURCES

AARP Grandparent Information Center: www.aarp.org

Child Care: www.childcare.gov

Children's Defense Fund: www.childrensdefense.org

Ecumenical Child Care Network: www.eccn.org

Generations United: www.elderissues.com and www.gu.org

Head Start Bureau: www.acf.dhhs.gov/program/hsb

Internal Revenue Service (IRS):   www.irs.gov/businesses/small/industries/index.html

National Association of Child Care Resource and Referral Agencies: www.naccrra.org

National Child Care Association: www.NCCANet.org

National Coalition for Campus Children's Centers: www.campuschildren.org

National Institute of Out-of-School Time (Wellesley):   www.wcwonline.org

Noodle Soup: www.noodlesoup.org.

Parent Participation Preschools International (PCPI):   www.preschools.coop

The Administration for Child and Families, U.S. Department of Health and Human Services: www.acf.hhs.gov

The National Association for Family Child Care: www.nafcc.org

White House In Focus, Early Childhood: www.whitehouse.gov/infocus/earlychildhood

Zero to Three Organization: www.zerotothree.org

STRUCTURE OF YOUR PROGRAM

Name _____ Date _____

Objective: To consider your program's funding sources and curriculum approaches.

Directions: Describe your program. Think about the funding sources (public, private, etc.) and types of program structure (private, family child care, etc.) presented in this chapter, and the curriculum approaches in Chapter One.

Major funding sources

Operating structure (ages served, number of children, full or part time, family involvement)

Basic components of curriculum approaches

Structured/unstructured

Teacher directed

Child directed

Other

CHAPTER THREE

The Administrative Process

CHAPTER OUTLINE

ADMINISTRATION DEFINED

THE JOB OF THE PROGRAM DIRECTOR

LEADERSHIP SKILLS

ETHICAL DECISION MAKING

THE ORGANIZATION OF THE PROGRAM

THE DECISION PROCESS

As an administrator, you are an important person. Whether positive or negative, any center reflects the capabilities of its director. Your responsibilities are great but so are your opportunities and rewards. An administrator must genuinely enjoy taking responsibility, must be willing to risk possible failure involved with decision making, and must be able to perform well in the varied roles that are expected by parents, staff, and the public.

Skills and knowledge from experience and education, plus organizational capacity and the ability to work with people, are assets that an administrator must have in order to create a nurturing environment in which each staff member and child can function to full potential. There is a direct relationship between the quality of a center and the professional behavior of those who work in it. Professionalism leads to mutual respect that is demonstrated in the trust that each person is doing what is best in any given situation and is working toward a common goal. Also, it results in a working relationship in which inevitable conflicts can be handled in a manner that leads to positive, healthy growth.

The field of early care and education has become a recognized profession. It offers a service that is beneficial to society. It has a specific body of knowledge that must be learned, understood, and used as a basis for judgments and decisions. In addition, the profession demands a high level of ethical performance. There must be certain attitudes, values, and feelings of responsibility (a code of desirable behaviors) to ensure proper functioning of child care professionals. Internal policing is a further responsibility of any profession.

ADMINISTRATION DEFINED

In order to get a clear overall picture of administration and its many responsibilities, we need to define the term and examine the main processes involved in carrying out your diverse responsibilities. So, what is administration? As commonly defined, *administration* is the total of all processes through which the appropriate human and material resources are made available and effective to accomplish the purposes of an enterprise. Administration has been described as a method, as a set of relationships among people, or as the performance of executive duties. The terms *administration* and *management* are frequently used interchangeably. Although people throughout history have recognized leadership and administrative ability, it is only within the past hundred years that a science of management has developed. This guidebook follows a traditional management structure in which the three components of administration are seen as a triangular arrangement that emphasizes their interrelationships. Each component depends on the one preceding it and each is ineffective without the others. Administration is the supervision of an ongoing process, not simply the arrival at some end point, and is depicted in Figure 3.1.

Planning is the process by which you and your co-workers decide in advance on your future activities and accomplishments. Planning influences later events by taking action in the present, determining tasks to be performed and the methods for accomplishing them, as well as developing the organization of a formal structure through which the mission statement and goals of the center will be carried out. Roles and responsibilities are defined and the structure of the center is described in its bylaws or other policy statements. Because legal requirements and professional standards will influence your planning, they are considered early in the planning stage.

Operating includes consideration of your role in directing, which means making the best possible decisions to fulfill your goals and objectives, delegating responsibility and authority effectively, and encouraging involvement and creativity. You will be the leader but your work as coordinator and supervisor will involve communication skills, selection of and working with staff and parents, record keeping, and supervision of the multiple aspects of delivering services to families and to the community.

Evaluating involves the overall appraisal of results in relation to the purposes or objectives that were set up during the planning stage. You may concentrate evaluation on effectiveness or efficiency, but for the most valid evaluation, a cooperative and involved staff can help you assess and analyze in an ongoing process. At this point, you determine what is being done to accomplish your goals and what needs to be changed. You may have to return to the planning process in order to grow as a leader and organization.

Figure 3.2 presents an example of possible tasks involved in the three components.

FIGURE 3.1 **The Administration Process**

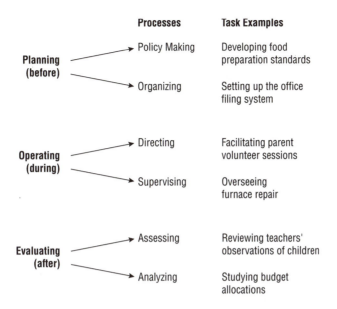

	Processes	Task Examples
Planning (before)	Policy Making	Developing food preparation standards
	Organizing	Setting up the office filing system
Operating (during)	Directing	Facilitating parent volunteer sessions
	Supervising	Overseeing furnace repair
Evaluating (after)	Assessing	Reviewing teachers' observations of children
	Analyzing	Studying budget allocations

FIGURE 3.2   Possible Tasks in the Administration Process

THE JOB OF THE PROGRAM DIRECTOR

What is involved in a typical administrative day? Here is a glimpse of what might happen:

- Work with staff to set up the daily learning environment.
- Give positive reassurance to a new teacher concerning science table.
- Greet children and family members; watch for evidence of concerns.
- State and interpret an operating policy component for a parent.
- Prepare a monthly financial report for the board of directors.
- Outline a tentative agenda for regularly scheduled staff meeting.
- Pull information from files at the request of a local pediatrician.
- Confer with an anxious mother regarding the effects of her divorce.
- Review next month's menu with the food staff.
- Analyze a staff problem related to workload distribution.
- Schedule an observation trip of high school child development students.
- Chat with a "last year's child" and her mother who have come to visit.

Each of these functions fits into one or more of the phases listed in the cycle of planning–operating–evaluating. For example, scheduling an observation of the program by high school students would fall most obviously into the operating segment of the cycle. Prior to that, during planning, policies would have been set up to determine such visitation procedures to the program. Perhaps evaluation would take place at a staff meeting when teachers express their concern about disruption of the program during the trip but agree that this was a worthwhile experience for the high school students. Further planning would then take place to smooth out the next visit by a student group.

CLASS DISCUSSION

What are additional duties of child care directors? Can you think of responsibilities to supplement those previously suggested. Should some of these, such as unplugging the toilet when it overflows, be done by other persons? Why? Why not?

Additionally, there are many responsibilities that are on a cyclical or less-than-daily schedule. These tasks may include planning for next year's budget, setting long-range fund-raising plans for new playground equipment, working on staff performance evaluations, and participating in professional organizations. No matter what the type of program, your participation in professional organizations that promote the quality of child care and education will be a vital component of your level of professionalism and in modeling for your staff. Your interest in the profession will encourage your staff to participate and grow as well. Worksheet 3.1 gives you a chance to address tasks in the three stages of planning, operating, and evaluating.

worksheet

3.1
p. 41

LEADERSHIP SKILLS

As a center director, you will assume a leadership role during all phases of the administrative process. Even in an informal family-style center or in one using collective status-free staff, success seems to depend on having one individual in an acknowledged leadership position. This is important during the planning and evaluating components of management but will be demonstrated most clearly during the operating phases.

Leadership describes someone who has the capacity to coordinate and guide the efforts of others. Here are some of the special qualifications that seem to be required for an early childhood program director:

1. Strength, vitality, good health, and the ability to accelerate output when a crisis demands it.
2. Effective conservation and utilization of energy by recognizing what is important and what is trivial, what must be handled immediately and personally, and what may be delegated to others.
3. A balance between seriousness and a sense of humor.
4. Functional intelligence, the ability to identify problems and their solutions, the willingness to accept ideas from others, and the knack of encouraging them to contribute suggestions to aid in decision-making processes.
5. Self-confidence and strength in the face of conflict. An easily threatened director is inadequate, whether the threats are from superiors, staff, or parents. Conflict is an integral part of a dynamic organization, not something to be avoided. Conflict is as natural in an organization's developmental process as the "terrible two" phase of childhood or an adolescent rebellion.
6. Communication skills, including speech, writing, and body language, must be well developed for two-way problem solving.
7. Ability to clarify and state goals and to keep staff members working toward center objectives while maintaining their individuality.

■ ■ ■ ■ ■ ▬▬▬▬▬▬▬▬▬▬▬▬▬▬▬▬▬▬▬▬▬▬▬▬▬▬▬▬▬▬▬▬▬

CLASS DISCUSSION

Think about the job description for a supervisory position that you are familiar with. What qualities and competencies does that job require? What qualities should be included to incorporate the responsibilities of the supervisor?

Leadership Styles

The traditional management pyramid placed "the boss" at the top, with successive layers of employees below them in status. This structure was accepted by mainstream management until the 1960s, although social psychologists had done pioneering work in the 1930s that identified three main types of leadership as *democratic*, *authoritarian*, and *laissez-faire*.

The democratic leader is a member of the group in spirit, offering choices to the staff and following policies that they have determined together. The democratic leader sets high standards and has clear expectations, helps teachers grow by explaining actions, encourages self-discipline, nurtures teachers and supports their decisions, and believes that cooperation is important.

An authoritarian leader determines policy and dictates what is to be done and how, usually structuring the steps of arriving at goals so that the staff sees only the immediate outcome and not the long-range plan. This type of leader keeps teachers dependent on the leader, strictly enforces policies and procedures, enforces punishment for breaking policies, and believes that compliance is important.

The laissez-faire leader is passive, leaving all decision making up to the group members, offering suggestions only when asked directly, and simply assuming that things will work themselves out. This type of leader ignores policies and procedures, and lets people interpret policies as they want to, leaving teachers unsure of their roles and responsibilities. Because the laissez-faire leader is not in control, unofficial leaders may emerge.

The leadership style of the director influences all that happens within a center. For example, consider a midmorning snack time under the three leadership types just described. An authoritarian might expect all children to stop what they are doing at exactly 9:45 A.M. They would sit quietly at assigned tables to be served two crackers and apple juice while an adult read a story. Under a democratic leader, children would be reminded that it was almost snack time. They could drift to the tables as they finished their activities. As the adults began to cut wedges of red, yellow, and green apples, they would be involved in conversations about the various colors of the outsides of those apples, meanwhile observing that the apples were all white inside. They would pour apple juice from small pitchers and relate that to the taste of the raw apples. Baskets of assorted crackers would be passed. The laissez-faire children could help themselves to crackers whenever they felt hungry, but their beverage would be from a powdered mix because nobody had remembered to order the apple juice.

As a director, you probably will prefer to be a democratic leader. This has traditionally been the role taken by administrators in early childhood programs from Friedrich Froebel to Patty Smith Hill and by most campus laboratory school directors. In 1847, Froebel wrote that he "would never presume to interfere with anything decided by the faculty." In the marginal notes of their plan books, Patty Smith Hill told teachers to "try it out and let me know how it works" (Hewes, 1994).

Further studies of leadership characteristics in relation to their effectiveness, together with emergence of the "hippie generation" and sympathetic researchers, led to the development of *contingency theory,* that became popular in the late 1960s. It was found that most people were primarily task oriented or relationship oriented. Task-oriented administrators were primarily concerned with getting the job done and in accomplishing their goals without much concern for the feelings of the people involved. In contrast, the relationship-oriented administrators were most concerned with the human aspects of their positions and were considerate of the feelings of others even if goals were not reached. Characteristics determining any individual's leadership style appear to lie deep within the personality structure, and awareness of those characteristics determines how situations can best be handled. You may have identified the category that you fit into. However, there are times and situations that require you to lead in different styles. Worksheet 3.2 encourages you to consider different circumstances that may warrant each of the three styles.

worksheet

3.2
p. 43

ETHICAL DECISION MAKING

Your concern for children and parents will not be enough to be good administrator, even though that will be what puts heart into the job. A capacity to view the enterprise as a whole, to grasp new ideas and relate them to practical operations, and to identify relationships of activities to their probable outcomes, will be essential. You will need to feel good about making decisions, whether you make them by yourself or work with staff or board members as a team, and you will need to be comfortable assuming responsibility. You will recognize your own biases and shortcomings and will value differing opinions and views.

During the planning phase of setting up your center, you will formulate the center policies. Those policies should reflect a code of ethics. Your professional code of ethics involves giving children and adults the respect they are due as human beings. The National Association for the Education of Young Children has adopted a professional code of ethics for early childhood educators (Feeney & Freeman, 1999). The core values of the code include understanding child development, supporting the relationships between children and families, recognizing individual children's needs, and helping children achieve their full potential. As you operate your center, you and your staff will maintain these professional standards by avoiding discussions of children in their presence, by respecting the confidential nature of information about children and their families, and by not talking about personal matters while working with the children. The many aspects of the NAEYC Code of Ethical Conduct can be explored in the books and articles listed in the reference and resources section at the end of the chapter.

CLASS DISCUSSION

Investigate the NAEYC Code of Ethical Conduct and how it applies to administration. Classmates can share different dilemmas they have faced and how they made their decisions.

THE ORGANIZATION OF THE PROGRAM

The successful management of an early childhood center means putting together all the processes of planning, operating, and evaluating to achieve a coordinated unit. This is a matter of organization. The ability to organize is perhaps the most critical factor in the success or failure of any program. Management requires the constant input of ideas, facts, and opinions from many sources. Your challenge as a director will be to put them all together, to communicate them to the staff, and to implement them appropriately to attain your predetermined objectives and goals.

Organization affects everyone involved in your program and will simplify management if it is well done. For you, as a director, it means keeping on top of the work to be done rather than being swamped or jumping from crisis to crisis. The logical division of tasks and the specific allocation of duties and responsibilities promotes teamwork and frees the staff from frustrations and mechanical problems so they can concentrate on their assigned duties. Research on stress at the worksite pinpoints inadequate organization as a primary cause of burnout. Organization can mean more flexibility if each staff member understands the functioning of the entire center and is assured of his or her own areas of responsibility and decision making.

Organization provides stability in the environment so that children can concentrate on their work or play curriculum without picking up anxieties from the adults and with the security of knowing what will happen from day to day. There is, of course, no such thing as an unstructured program. At the present time, organizational structure runs the gamut from authoritarian rigidity to chaotic anarchy. Regardless of whether those conditions are planned, they *do* constitute the organizational structure. It is up to you and those who work with you to determine how tightly or loosely the structure is organized. Whatever the mission statement of your program, certain fundamentals of organizational structure may be enumerated:

1. The organization should be consistent with the mission statement, goals, and purposes of the center and should be modified as evaluation indicates.
2. Definite patterns of authority must be established, although these need not be of the conventional up-and-down lines, and all persons involved must know them.
3. There must be impartial placement of duties and responsibilities.
4. There must be regard for all individuals involved, adults and children, paid and unpaid, full time or part time.

Systems for Effective Functioning

Throughout written history, various ideas about operating and organizing have been proposed. How did the pyramids get built? How did ancient Roman armies construct roads and aqueducts hundreds of miles from home? How did the early Christian church function with a hierarchy from pope to village priest and monastery? Using modern terminology, we would say that they developed a viable system. Our business management use of sophisticated system analysis is not much different from everyday talk about the respiratory system or the school system or our recognition that our lives will be simpler once we get everything down to a system. Although scientists and big corporations rely on complicated computer programs to analyze a vast array of variables and execute their planning, philosophers since Plato and Aristotle have advocated a systems approach using a common resource: the human mind. A computer can supplement our thought processes but it cannot replace them.

Like many other terms used in this guidebook, systems can mean different things to different people or under different circumstances. As we use it here, a *system* is any set of elements that forms a unified whole. There must be two or more components to make a system and they must interact or interrelate in some way. Their unity comes through their interdependence. Your job is to create an orderly relationship between all of the elements involved with your center. As you think about its operations, you will begin to set up subsystems that function within it—systems for office procedures, for mealtimes, for communications, for programming. You will ask yourself many questions. How will I collect tuition? How will supplies be ordered, delivered, and stored? What will I do if parents ask me to give medicine to a sick child? You will find the answers through logical problem solving with your mission statement, your program goals, and your regulatory requirements in mind. Your answers will involve looking at complex situations and then breaking them down into parts that can be analyzed. Analysis involves studying how the system is put together, what it implies, what the alternatives are, and how you can get everything and everyone working smoothly so that your work gets done. Then you will have time to listen fully to a parent who needs to talk and energy to become involved in professional organizations. You then avoid the situation of the sign painter who neatly lettered

> THINK AHEA
> D

Total Quality Management

Do you or individuals close to you drive a car of Japanese origin? If so, it is the tangible result of a system called Total Quality Management (TQM). This has become one of the most popular systems in U.S. management since its introduction by Dr. W. Edwards Deming in the 1960s. When he was sent to Japan to help that country's reconstruction following World War II, he worked out the basics of TQM so well that the American auto industry felt threatened. They began to study his plan and enthusiasm quickly spread to all areas of management (Hewes, 1994). The basic principles are as follows, with their application to ECE programs following in parentheses.

1. Focus is on the needs of customers and on the needs of employees. (The needs of families and children in the center as well as the staff are of top concern, but sponsor's or community group's needs should also be considered.)

2. High-quality performance is built into the way things are done through innovation, research, and education. (Staff members are encouraged to take classes, attend conferences and workshops, and read professional journals.) Benchmarking implies a systematic search for the best way to do things. (In ECE, this can mean visiting other centers or talking with their staff members.)

3. Problems are identified and dealt with in an appropriate manner. (Rather than waiting for complaints from parents, accidents on the playground, or other areas of potential problems, take a proactive approach. Instead of having parents pull their children from your center because you close too early in the afternoon, plan a way to combine children of different ages in one room for additional hours.)

4. Staff members, individually and in teams, are empowered to make changes and are recognized for improvements. (Teachers, aides, parents, and volunteers know that their ideas are valued and are comfortable working within the center's structure to accomplish them. This has led to added services in some centers, such as providing children's haircuts one afternoon a week, setting up a magazine or coupon exchange, or even providing ready-to-serve packaged dinners.)

5. Success is measured by indications of an increase in quality service and more satisfied customers. (This might mean a waiting list for enrollments, the generally positive attitude expressed by family members, and the comfortable atmosphere in the classrooms. One objective measure would be NAEYC accreditation.)

As a leader, you will benefit from a cooperative system with the entire staff working toward combined goals. Recognizing the differences in people is important. One aspect of the leadership position is to determine who needs special help and not to expect perfection. It is important to recognize that Total Quality Management is an ongoing process, not something that is set up and then ignored. It is sometimes called Continuous Quality Improvement (CQI) on university campuses or at health centers, Quality Improvement Programs (QIP) in Wal-Mart and others in the corporate world, or Total Quality Education (TQE) in public schools. One university preschool coined the acronym of TQC, meaning Total Quality Caring.

THE DECISION PROCESS

The decision process can be defined as a complex series of actions that originates with the discovery of the need for change, determines the best way to accomplish that change, assesses or evaluates the result, and either accepts it or alters it. We make countless decisions everyday. For example, as we go through the daily mail or e-mail, we should deal appropriately with their content, saving some, passing some on to interested individuals, and discarding the rest to avoid an accumulation that bogs down our efficiency. In the next paragraphs we consider situations that apply to major decisions, such as equipment purchases, a change in age levels admitted to a center, or other decisions that affect the program and personnel.

The administrator of an ECE center will probably be judged more by decision style than by any other quality. Sometimes ideas aren't explored or situations aren't dealt with because things have always been done in a certain way and a complacency develops. These "buffers" keep a problem from reaching the point at which it is obvious that a decision must be made. Chronic indecisiveness or delay in picking up cues about a problem situation often lead to concerns of staff or parents about the quality of leadership. They understand a director's inability to make decisions if they have developed a sense of trust, but the trait of chronic procrastination is devastating to the leadership image and should be dealt with if it is a problem.

Simply recognizing that a decision must be made and that a situation must be dealt with is the first step. However, some decisions must be postponed. Perhaps the purchase of new playground equipment will depend on the success of a community organization's fund drive. In preparation, teachers may discuss what they would like to buy, perhaps after visiting the exhibitor area of an ECE conference, in preparation for the actual decision process. In some situations, it is not the director's job to make the decision. If your program site is the property of another organization, such as a church or public school, you may report a leaky roof but not be responsible for choosing the repair service. As the director, you will provide staff and parents with information about progress toward the solution and then coordinate the process to completion.

Written policies and a family handbook will be followed when routine problems arise. For example, if your policy states that half fees can be paid to hold the place of a child who will be absent for one week or more, that policy defines the situation when a parent wants to "withdraw" a child and then "reenter" after a vacation. Because unusual situations occur, there should also be written exceptions to them and a clear description of the process to enact them. There will be times when you solve a problem or make a decision by yourself because it involves privileged (private and confidential) information. There may be other occasions when there is not enough time to consult others. In a crisis situation, attending a preschool where they feel loved and cared for may provide critical support for young children and for other family members.

But let us assume that a standard administrative decision must be made. A situation or problem becomes apparent and must be resolved. Who is involved? Is there a board of directors that meets regularly? Does your sponsoring organization expect to have input into some decisions but not others? If this is a private family child care would a spouse and teenagers want to give input? In a typical child care center with an involved staff, it is appropriate to get input through a discussion group or by delegating some of the planning to individuals who will be affected or who have a particular interest in this situation. Will you need a legal or tax consultant? In some cases, the problem may be an appropriate discussion topic for older children. Recognize that some situations do not allow time for others to act. If you smell smoke coming from the supply closet, you do not poll the teachers to determine who should call 911 or whether you should grab the fire extinguisher yourself. You act! Following are seven steps of major decision making:

1. Analyze the problem that has presented itself. Write down the situation and the final goal that you believe you can accomplish.

2. Include financial and policy restrictions, possible reactions from parents and the community, and your own personal feelings about the situation. Consider the overall goals and objectives of your center.

3. Consider various alternative routes to reach your goals. How many ways can this situation or problem be resolved? Get ideas from others about alternatives. At this point, you can consider options that seem outrageous; there might be some validity to them. Recognize that your intuitive feelings about some aspects of the solution may be of value. One aspect of the process is called the "utility factor" because there are sometimes intangible considerations that make certain solutions important to you, even though they do not matter very much to others.

4. Use a chart or computer program to analyze the costs and benefits of the various alternatives that are suggested. Try to visualize their end results. Determine alternatives that may improve your chance of success.

CLASS DISCUSSION

Think of some position you have held and what decisions you were allowed to make. Did you meet with co-workers as a group? Was your superior giving instructions, asking for help, or reprimanding?

5. At the choice point, a frequently used alternative is called the "satisficing route" because you do what seems to satisfy the situation but leave other options available. This is not the best way to make a decision, but sometimes it works out. It is preferable to choose the best possible alternative based on a sequenced and careful analysis of the problem. As you proceed with this stage, ask yourself if you have considered several viable solutions.

6. Carry out appropriate action to complete the process. Keep a record of your activities to show that you proceeded appropriately. Communicate the decision to all who might be involved or interested. Do they believe in the success of this action, and are they willing to work toward its success?

7. Monitor and evaluate to determine whether the decision was, indeed, proper. If it was not, analyze what could have been improved by reviewing the original process and trying to correct deficiencies.

worksheet

3.3
p. 45

The seven steps can be applied to most big decisions. Worksheet 3.3 provides an opportunity to work through a problem using the seven steps. Possible decision-making suggestions for Worksheet 3.3 follow.

1. Playground equipment needs to be updated to meet new playground regulations. Consider fund-raising for the new playground. What type? How? When?
2. Teachers in one room do not get along. Do you make them work it out or change classrooms and upset the balance in another room?
3. Parents want you to teach a second language to children in the preschool class. Both Spanish and French have been suggested. Which is best? Are two too many?
4. Are pay raises a possibility? If so, how much? When would they be effective? What effects would they have on the budget?

WHAT WOULD YOU DO?

Your program has a waiting list for enrollment. The policy of your program is that there are no preferences given to board members for waiting list placement or enrollment. On your board is a very active and supportive member who requests that you "move" her granddaughter up on the list because her son needs the child care. She offers to make a "generous contribution" to the center if you enroll her granddaughter within the next three months. What would you do?

REFERENCES AND RESOURCES

Bell, A. H., & Smith, D. M. (1997). *Winning with difficult people.* Hong Kong: Barron's.

Blanchard, K., Carlos, J. P., & Randolph, A. (1998). *Empowerment takes more than a minute.* San Francisco, CA: Berrett-Koehler.

Culkin, M. (Ed.). (2000). *Managing quality in young children's programs: The leaders role.* New York: Teachers College Press.

Feeney, S., & Freeman, N. K. (1999). *Ethics and the early childhood educator: Using the NAEYC code.* Washington, DC: National Association for the Education of Young Children.

Feeney, S., & Kipins, K. (1998). *Code of ethical conduct and statement of commitment.* Washington, DC: National Association for the Education of Young Children.

Guzzo, R. A. et al (1995). *Team effectiveness and decision-making.* San Francisco, CA: Jossey-Bass.

Hewes, D. W. (1981). Leadership in child care: What contingency theory can show us. *Child Care Information Exchange, 17,* 11–14.

Hewes, D. W. (1994). TQ what? *Child Care Information Exchange, 98,* 20–24.

Hewes, D. W. (1998). Decision making: A linear process. *Child Care Information Exchange, 124,* 26–29.

Hostetler, K. D., & Hostetler, B. S. (1997). *Ethical judgment in teaching.* Boston: Allyn & Bacon.

Juslin, P., & Montgomery, H. (1999). *Judgment and decision making.* Mahwah, NJ: Erlbaum.

Kagan, S. L., & Bowman, B. T. (Eds.). (1997). *Leadership in early care and education.* Washington, DC: National Association for the Education of Young Children.

Kagan, S. L., & Choen, N. E. (1997). *Not by chance: Creating an early care and education system for America's children.* New Haven, CT: The Bush Center for Child Development and Social Policy, Yale University.

Kouzes, J. M., & Posner, B. Z. (2002). *The leadership challenge.* San Francisco, CA: Jossey-Bass.

Robertson, J., & Talley, K. (2002). Synchronistic leadership. *Child Care Information Exchange, 146,* 7–10.

Rodd, J. (1998). *Leadership in early childhood.* New York: Teachers College Press.

Sciarra, D. J., & Dorsey, A. G. (2002). *Leaders and supervisors in child care programs.* Albany, NY: Delmar.

Wellington, S. (2001). *Be your own mentor: Strategies from top women on the secret of success.* New York: Random House.

WEBSITE RESOURCES

Association for Supervision and Curriculum Development (ASCD):   www.ascd.org

Center for Creative Leadership: www.ccl.org

Ethics Resource Center: www.ethics.org/index.html

Motivation in the Workplace: www.motivation-tools.com/workplace/index.htm

Out of the Box Coaching: www.breakoutofthebox.com/index.htm

ADMINISTRATIVE DUTIES

Name _____ Date _____

Objective: To develop skills in addressing administrative tasks in each of the three stages of administration.

Directions: Consider two tasks that you may perform in your job. On the following chart, divide these tasks into the three components previously considered; provide details as to what you might do in each one.

	EXAMPLE HIRE A NEW TEACHER	TASK 1	TASK 2
The planning stage	Job description Advertisement Handbook Interviews		
The operating stage	Hire teacher; complete paperwork Conduct 　Orientation 　Training Ongoing staff development		
The evaluating stage	Probationary period Staff evaluations Work on professional development		
Further planning as a result of evaluation	Teacher has met requirements for the position; continued employment		

LEADERSHIP STYLES

Name _____ Date _____

Objective: To describe the characteristics of leadership styles.

Directions: Every administrator assumes these three styles at appropriate times. Under what circumstances will you take each of these roles?

Democratic leader

Authoritarian leader

Laissez-faire leader

Which leadership style do you feel is really you? List reasons or give examples to explain your style.

DECISION MAKING

Name _____ Date _____

Objective: To apply the seven steps of decision making to a fictitious situation.

Directions: Identify a decision to be made in your program. Address how you will make the decision based on the seven steps.

1. **Define the problem**

2. **List boundaries/restrictions**

3. **Consider alternative routes**

4. **Determine the costs and benefits of each possible route**

WORKSHEET 3.3   *(continued)*

5. Determine the best route/decision

6. Implement the decision; consider who, what, when, where, how

7. Evaluate the outcome of the decision

CHAPTER FOUR

Standards and Policies

CHAPTER OUTLINE

LEGAL REQUIREMENTS AND PROFESSIONAL STANDARDS

DEVELOPING PURPOSES, GOALS, AND A MISSION STATEMENT

POLICY OPTIONS

POLICY WRITING

OPERATING POLICIES

LEGAL REQUIREMENTS AND PROFESSIONAL STANDARDS

In the orientation to this guidebook, it was pointed out that the administration of early care and education programs is a developing and growing field. Although we have valid research on what is considered best for children in our society, different programs address the standards in a variety of ways, such as the best adult-to-child ratio or the optimal amount of indoor space. There are overlapping and sometimes conflicting regulations as to how standards will be enforced. The same pattern applies to states and localities. You will want to follow these and other aspects of public policy as they relate to your program and to the entire field of early care and education.

Although attempts at uniformity continue, neither you nor today's children can wait for their resolution. Before you can progress further in planning your center, you will need to know just what legal regulations apply to it. If you intend to enroll children for whom federal or state funds will be used, you will need to conform to special requirements. You will also need to consider local zoning, building and fire codes, health and sanitation regulations, and other issues that will apply to your program in your community. Although terminology in this area is often confusing, the following definitions may help as you move toward setting up your program.

Regulations are based on the action of a government agency and are the legal rules you must follow. They may have been developed through a widespread investigation of professional standards and parent needs, or they may have passed through the legislative process. Some, such as prohibition of racial discrimination, have evolved through judicial decisions. Others are part of local codes and may not be relevant to the facility you envision. For example, the built-in fire sprinkler system that makes sense for a hospital would not be needed in a mothers' morning-out program and restaurant food-handler permits should not be imposed on three-year-olds who are preparing snacks. Each state has its own set of regulations for early childhood programs, and you should obtain a copy of all necessary regulations. If you are not familiar with your state's regulations, consult the website www.nrc.uchsc.edu, which contains links to the governing sites of each of the fifty states.

Licensing is the procedure by which an individual, association, corporation, or other legal body obtains the authorization to operate a specific facility. The applicant who asks for permission to operate under the relevant regulations requests the license. Licensing usually implies the absence of harmful surroundings but it does not ensure a high-quality program. Many people believe licenses are simply one more example of government interference with the individual rights of parents and businesspeople, whereas others attempt to make the regulations even more stringent for the protection of children and their families. The National Association for the Education of Young Children (NAEYC) officially endorses licensing for all out-of-home child care (Morgan, 1996).

Registration is closely related to licensing. It usually implies inclusion on a list of facilities but with limited mandatory requirements. Programs that are registered may receive such benefits as referrals from a central office. This system is most often used or suggested for family child care homes.

Accreditation is the establishment of maximum standards of quality through voluntary action by various professional organizations, such as the NAEYC. Criteria are established and mechanisms are set up to identify and recognize programs that are worthy of recognition and respect because they meet those criteria. These criteria are more stringent than licensing regulations, but they are determined essential for a high-quality program. The NAEYC accreditation process is implemented in three phases: (1) The center self-study includes classroom observations, and staff and parental evaluations; (2) validation requires an on-site visit by trained validators who verify that the program meets the criteria; and (3) the commission (a committee of three early childhood experts) reviews the materials to determine accreditation status. The early child care program administrators are encouraged to continually improve the quality of care for children by applying every five years for reaccreditation. NAEYC periodically revises the accreditation process to improve on current knowledge of best practices for young children (National Academy of Early Childhood Programs, 1991).

Standards can be defined as specific statements of measurable performance factors, something used by general agreement to determine whether things are as they should be. The term is sometimes used to mean regulations, which are those requirements you must legally follow. For clarity, we assume that basic professional standards were used in establishing those legal requirements and that you recognize them as the minimum requirements below which you cannot fall. Your own standards may be considerably higher. You may follow standards established by a franchiser; by a professional group, such as the American Academy of Pediatricians; or by a philosophical organization, such as the American Montessori Association or your own religious denomination. However you establish the standards for your own center, they will provide a framework that will serve as a basis for judgments and operating decisions.

Although regulations and licensing or registration policies differ according to geographic location and funding source, standards are professionally and individually determined. For example, standards applied to purchasing will relate directly to your budget. In publicly funded centers or large programs requiring purchase orders, often with competitive bidding, standards are built into the process. In other

CLASS DISCUSSION

How will standards and regulations differ if your center includes school-age children? If you have infants and toddlers?

cases, staff members make purchases using personal value judgments. It will be up to you to apply safety standards for equipment, nutritional standards for snacks and lunches, standards for cleanliness and sanitation, and other standards for all aspects of the program. This includes your own personal standards for the performance of your management function. Even minor decisions will reflect your basis for maintaining established standards. For example, regulations may require that drinking water is available to the children. In your community, you believe that the water is filled with harmful chemicals and you are concerned with reports of lead leaching out of pipes and water cooler tanks. In addition, you have observed that young children drinking from fountains do not actually swallow much water. Mostly, they seem to wash their chins in the stream. Your standards, therefore, specify commercially bottled water and paper cups. This must be included in your annual budget.

worksheet
4.1
p. 59

Your primary sources for Worksheets 4.1 and 4.2 will be regulations relevant to the program you are planning and the state in which you reside. The National Resources Center for Health and Safety in Child Care website (www.nrc.uchsc.edu) has a link for all fifty states for child care regulations and for contact information. Worksheet 4.1 provides the opportunity to compare major components of child care regulations among the states. As you do this worksheet it will help you clarify your values and standards. Then proceed to Worksheet 4.2, which can be used to compare your state requirements with your own standards. Standards are used to determine the high quality of your program.

worksheet
4.2
p. 61

DEVELOPING PURPOSES, GOALS, AND A MISSION STATEMENT

Now that you have considered your standards, the next step is to develop your purposes, goals, and mission statement. Note that the basic process will be the same regardless of the size or complexity of your organization and that this applies to all types of business ventures whether they are for profit or are not for profit, just starting up or well established.

WHAT WOULD YOU DO?

At your center there is no running water because of a major plumbing problem in the neighborhood. There are twenty-two families that you provide child care for and the parents need that care starting at 7:00 A.M. You have been told that the plumbing problem will not be corrected until after 5:00 P.M. today. Your state regulations require that you have running water and operating toilet facilities. What do you do?

An identifiable purpose, well-defined goals, and a clear mission statement will give character to your center and become the foundation on which you base further decisions. They will provide direction for you and your staff. The terms we use mean different things to different people. This guidebook will define *purpose* as "that which one sets before himself as something to be attained." In other words, your purpose is the *reason why* your center exists and what it will encompass. How would you respond to the following: "Why do we need a program like the one you propose? Give me a few good reasons." You might say that it will provide basic child care services for a community that lacks them or you might want to provide educational preparation for children deficient in preacademic skills. You might want to offer an opportunity for parents to develop their skills. Think back to the reasons for operating various types of centers that were discussed in Chapter Two for some ideas. In some cases, a formal needs assessment should be completed before going forward with planning. In others, city or county planning departments or local child care resource and referral agencies might be consulted. Whether you plan to start a new center or to take over an established business, this definition of its purpose or its several interrelated purposes is a necessary first step.

A *goal* is defined as "the end to which a purpose tends." It is what you hope to achieve for the children and families in your program. For example, if your purpose is to provide preparation toward academic skills, your goals might include developing children's language fluency and fostering their positive self-concept. The content and focus of the learning experience will be contained in your statement of goals, which is usually a list of what you want to accomplish over the period of time you will have the children enrolled in your center. You will also have daily and other short-term goals, which will be cumulative. You might think of short-term goals in terms of a field sport, such as football or soccer, in which there are many advances while the teams are trying to get the ball past the goal post. The term *objectives* is often used alternately with goals but, in general, objectives provide a more precise and limited evaluation than is used for this guidebook.

The final phase involves writing down your own mission statement of early care and education: "the how." How do you believe that you and your staff must perform in order to satisfy your purposes and move toward your goals? Your mission statement will reflect your knowledge of the principles of growth and development, your beliefs of how children learn, and your values concerning people and education. There has been a recent emphasis on publishing a program's or agency's mission statement. For example, "The National Association for the Education of Young Children (NAEYC) exists for the purpose of leading and consolidating the efforts of individuals and groups working to achieve healthy development and constructive education for all young children" (www.naeyc.org). An example of a mission statement for a child care center might be, "The program is based on the philosophy that children can learn the skills necessary to succeed in school, that each child learns at his own rate, and that success in learning will develop a child's self-esteem."

CLASS ACTIVITY

Discuss how the mission statement of the director varies according to class members' experiences. How will your proposed program reflect your own background, desires, beliefs, and values?

■ ■ ■ ■ ■

WHAT WOULD YOU DO?

You have been hired as the new director for an existing program with a strong parent advisory board. Before you were hired, you read and understood the mission statement and goals of the center. At the first parent advisory board meeting, the parents request that you change the goals of a developmentally appropriate curriculum to a more rigid academic curriculum so their children will be eligible to go to the private kindergartens in your community. What would you do?

worksheet

4.3
p. 63

Today, although there is virtually unanimous agreement that high-quality early childhood education is valuable, there are still differences in curriculum approaches. Of the several models presented in Chapter One, you may follow only one or you may choose to combine the features that seem to be most attractive from several. Worksheet 4.3 addresses the purposes, goals, and mission statement for your program. You will want to use information from previous worksheets to help develop what your program stands for. Remember that this is your own unique project. There are no "right" or "wrong" answers.

POLICY OPTIONS

You are now ready to establish boundaries within which decisions will be made. The best management is always based on clearly defined principles and procedures. These constitute the policies of your center. They must have a unity of direction and be written to support your purpose, goals, and mission statement within the boundaries set down by licensing and sponsoring agencies.

Because the organizational structure of early childhood programs varies so widely, policies take many forms. A franchised center program conforms to policies established by the corporate office. A private proprietary program would have a set of written guidelines established by the owner. An unincorporated center may have articles of association. Guidance can be obtained in booklets from your regional office of the Internal Revenue Service. However, the owner and/or director will be personally responsible for debts and problems. In either a private proprietary program or a partnership, the owners have complete authority in their operation, although they may choose an advisory committee or board for suggestions in decision making.

You may want to form a corporation, which is the joining together of a group to create a legal organization. You may be able to form a not-for-profit (usually called nonprofit) corporation by providing evidence that you will function for the public benefit and not for private profit. Your salary would be paid as a business expense, as would retirement and other benefits. This type of corporation must have a community board of directors. The advantages of this type of organization lie in lower taxes, the possibility of receiving tax deductible gifts and other funds, and gaining public goodwill. If your aim is to receive a profit, there are several types of small corporations that should be explored with the assistance of an attorney skilled in this area.

Both categories of incorporation file their own income and other tax returns. A major advantage is that the corporation is responsible for debts only to the extent of its assets. Policy making is shared by members of a board of directors and the board members become legally responsible for these policy decisions. A corporation must usually apply for a charter from the Secretary of State by filing Articles of Incorporation and Bylaws. Requirements vary from state to state but the Articles usually include the corporate name, the purpose of the business, and the names of the corporate directors initiating the incorporation. The Bylaws are the regulations and restrictions that have been agreed on for running the business. These are legal documents and must be carefully written so that their intent is clear. An attorney is required to draft the final papers to be filed, however, you should prepare a preliminary draft.

Policy Boards

A board of directors, advisory board, or parent advisory committee should be large enough to carry out its responsibilities but not so large that it is inefficient—from five to twenty persons is customary. Members may be invited or elected but provision for board continuity is important. Half of the members may be chosen in even years and half in odd years; members serve two-year terms, and you thus avoid ever having an all-new group. It is usually not wise, and may not be legal, to have a board member employed as a staff member of the center. However, scheduling staff to attend board meetings on a rotating basis, without voting privileges, is frequently seen as a way to build rapport between the two groups.

Board members may bring a variety of backgrounds; they may include parents, experts in child development or pediatrics, members of a church, or community advisers with no knowledge of early childhood education. Functions of a board of directors usually include the following:

- Defining the scope and the service of the center
- Establishing and approving all policies
- Adopting and supporting the annual budget
- Appointing the director; hiring and approving other staff
- Playing an active role in public relations
- Conferring with the director on all major problems
- Developing criteria and processes for evaluating the center and staff
- Specifying areas in which the director can make decisions

The program administrator (director) should regularly attend board meetings as an advisory, nonvoting member to:

- Furnish information relevant to the business of the meeting
- State probable consequences of actions being discussed
- Keep the board up-to-date on changes in methods, legislation, and so on
- Point out conflicts with previously established policies
- Report center activities that correlate board business with educational and other goals of the program

In order to carry out the policies of the center, responsibilities of the board should be specified. An orientation plan for new board members is important, including a prepared packet of informative materials. In parent-participation schools, parent members assume major responsibilities. For example, one may be treasurer, another may be in charge of admissions, and a third will schedule parent-participation days. Each becomes an authority on some aspect of the school and feels that involvement is meaningful. Similar responsibilities may be assigned to board members in other types of centers.

Policy Nature and Scope.   Whether policies are established by a board of directors, a governing agency, group consensus of the staff, or your own decisions as the owner–operator of the center, you must understand the principles on which they are based. Your job is to interpret policies for others as well as to carry them out. Keep in mind two main points. First, policies are established as guidelines to chart a course of action with built-in flexibility. Second, they must be regularly evaluated and modified according to advanced educational theory, changing conditions, or as needed for the growth of the program.

The long-term policies, which must be bylaws if your center is incorporated, deal with the general principles on which the business of your center is based. We will call these governing policies. Short-term policies, or operating policies, define the general procedures of the business and are, in fact, a way of performing the details of the governing policies. The governing policies might include your articles of incorporation, bylaws, or a constitution. They will be changed only by using a prescribed legal procedure. For example, your governing policies might contain a statement that a registration fee must be submitted by the applicant as confirmation of the child's enrollment. No amount would be specified. Your operating policies, however, would contain a procedural statement giving the dollar amount, when it is due, and under what conditions it is refundable. Any decision to eliminate a registration fee would have to be made by a majority vote of the board of directors at a meeting that conformed to that section of your long-term policies dealing with amendments to the bylaws or other governing principles. In contrast, if an increase in insurance rates made it necessary to raise more money, you might easily increase the registration fee for the next year to help cover that increase. This would need to be approved by the board, if your center has one, but would not be a major change. Some centers will want to further define procedures with rules. These are even more specific, such as stating that "Teachers are not to accept any checks from parents" because this bookkeeping function is incompatible with their classroom duties and because the checks might get mislaid and lost.

POLICY WRITING

Remember that administration is made up of three components—planning, operating, and evaluating. Establishing policy is a vital part of planning but these plans are then carried out as part of the operational process and will be evaluated as to their effectiveness. As you write, keep in mind that the governing policies are long-term legal statements and difficult to change. Try to envision how they will be carried out and what problems might arise. Your statements should be clear and understandable, applicable to real situations with assurance of stability. Avoid writing policy statements that are cumbersome or confusing in details. In practice, policies are often drafted by a committee or a board of directors, with an attorney advising them and then making the final translation into legal terminology. You, however, have a crucial role as the professional administrator with knowledge of early childhood program management that will be essential in the establishment of a properly functioning center.

Bylaws or Long-Term Policies

In developing your long-term policies, you will find that there are many possible formats and many alternatives. The following outline and explanations represent the composite experiences of center directors and should be adapted to suit your own program.

Article I.   Name

The corporate name of this center is…

The name is the first thing people find out about your center. It should accurately express your mission statement and goals and may impart additional information that will help in recruiting. Look through the business section of your telephone directory or another listing of preschools and try to picture the listings as parents would if they were looking for a center. What would you expect from Kiddie Korral? Aunty Lulu's Place? Little Red Schoolhouse? Children's Academy? Perhaps you will want to provide a geographic orientation, for example, Downtown Child Care or Fletcher Hills Nursery School. You may identity with a sponsor as Kaiser Children's Services did in the 1940s. An agency, corporate sponsor, college, or religious denomination may require the use of their name. Consider, also, whether the name suggests a logo that will become identified with your program when it is used on brochures, stationery, T-shirts, and other items. It should reproduce well, be original and distinctive, and reinforce your name recognition.

Article II.   Purposes and policies

The purposes of [name of center] are as follows:

Your purposes have been established on Worksheet 4.3, but you may want to add more or rephrase them. List them, stating concisely the reasons why this center is being established.

Article III.   Membership

Who is eligible to attend? Is member income level limited or are there other restrictions based on licensing or sponsors? For example, an employer-sponsored center may only enroll children of employees.

Article IV.   Financial considerations

A fiscal year begins on any calendar date and ends on the previous date twelve months later. A church-sponsored nursery school that is closed during summer vacation months may prefer a fiscal year beginning August 1 and ending July 31 to accommodate the collection of fees and payment of bills. For corporate centers and many other types of centers, tax regulations require a calendar year beginning January 1 and ending December 31.

Section A.   Fees

Designate in general terms your plan for tuition, registration, and other fees. Include dollar amounts with operating policies.

Section B.   Budget

worksheet
8.1
p. 133

You will prepare a budget for your center on Worksheet 8.1. All you need here is a statement telling who is responsible for developing the budget, who approves it, and the general process involved. For example, in a church-sponsored program, the director frequently prepares an annual budget for approval by the advisory board. In a parent-participation school, an elected parent–treasurer may do it. In a private proprietary center, the owner–director would be the sole person responsible. Budgets should be due well before the end of the fiscal year.

Section C.   Auditing

A responsible individual must periodically examine and verify the accounts of the center. This is usually done immediately after the close of a fiscal year. The individual may be a certified public accountant or may be some other trusted individual but cannot be a member of the center staff or board. Federal- and state-funded programs have strict auditing requirements, whereas a private organization may simply have someone such as a tax preparation advisor monitor the accounts.

Article V.   Organization and administration— Policy board or advisory board

If your center is incorporated, your legal and tax status will depend on the establishment of a legitimate functioning board of directors. Many other type of centers voluntarily establish advisory boards. Federal programs usually specify a parent board. Private owner–directors and partners should clarify the following points.

Section A.   Membership of the board (if there is one)

The number of members; method of their selection; and responsibilities, such as selecting staff or approving budget, setting term of office, and so on, should be included.

Section B.   Meetings of the board

Specify a minimum number of meetings per year. Allow for special meetings in addition and include a procedure for how to determine when they will be held. Note that minutes must be kept of the business transacted at all meetings of a corporation. If yours is a small, private center, you might state that all staff will meet periodically to agree by consensus on certain matters. Think about your worksheets to determine how you can best accomplish your goals and express your mission statement.

Section C.   Officers

Article VIII requires a statement of parliamentary procedures. Usually, "Robert's Rules of Order" is considered the standard guide if you have formal meetings. This requires a president, a chairperson, or some other elected or appointed person to preside over the meetings and deal with interim business. Another person, designated to serve as this person's substitute, is called vice president or something similar. A secretary to take minutes and deal with correspondence and a treasurer to handle financial matters may be combined to become the secretary–treasurer. Guides to parliamentary procedures are available. Again, your funding source and program structure will be the determining factors. You should state titles, qualifications, method of election, term of office, and duties for officers.

Section D.   Lines of authority

What is *the* chain of command? What's the role of the director? Lines of authority are particularly important in a program sponsored by an outside group.

Section E.   Committees

Identify the responsibilities of committees that will be necessary to deal with center operations. In a private proprietary center you may not have any committees. With an active parent board, committees might include personnel, fund-raising or finances, community resources, public relations, nominations, and more. Some will be permanent standing committees, whereas others will be special committees or task groups established with designated responsibilities. For each committee you should state how they are formed and what the members' terms of service will be.

Article VI.   Staffing

Section A.   Titles

What titles will be assigned to paid employees, including the person in charge? Note that the NAEYC has initiated standard terminology for staff members, which is determined by education, experience, and responsibilities (more details are in Chapter Five).

Section B.   Necessary clearances

This section usually states that staff members must conform to legal requirements. In some cases, sponsorship or a philosophical model may indicate additional requirements. For example, a Montessori school would probably want to include certification by American or the international training programs.

Article VII.   Amendments

Bylaws may be amended at any regular or special meeting of the advisory board, the board of directors, or of whoever makes policies for your center at which a quorum (half or two-thirds) of the members are present and there is an affirmative vote (half or two-thirds) of those present. Notice of the meeting, with the general character of the proposed amendments, shall be mailed to the membership at least ten days prior to the meeting. This standard phrasing is appropriate for incorporated centers or those with large, formal policy boards; modify it for your own program

Article VIII.   Parliamentary procedures

Robert's Rules of Order shall be followed for the conduct of business meetings of this corporation/center/school.

Your center's structure may not require this formality. The fundamentals of parliamentary law, established approximately one hundred years ago, are to ensure that there is justice and courtesy for all, that the minority be heard but that the majority rules, that each proposal is entitled to a full and free debate, and that the desires of individuals must be merged with those of the organization. During the meeting, any member may, at the appropriate time, bring a motion before the group. If the motion is seconded by another member, it is

CLASS DISCUSSION

What are the advantages of formally structured policies for an early childhood center? What are the disadvantages? How does your own planned center correspond with the bylaws previously suggested? Share and discuss incidents you know about in which written policies were inappropriate or inadequate or where the absence of written policies led to problems.

discussed, amended or otherwise modified by majority vote, and either carried or lost by another vote. Even a friendly staff meeting can benefit by following some parliamentary procedures, such as having a prepared agenda. If it is preferred not to use Robert's Rules of Order, the bylaws should state how business would be conducted, whether decisions are made by several or many people, or indicate that all business would be conducted by the private proprietor center's owner–director.

worksheet
4.4
p. 65

Your specific program may not need to include all of these articles, but they are important to consider. Worksheet 4.4 is designed to help you develop your ideas about your long-term policies. This worksheet provides a beginning stage of the policies that will govern procedures at your program.

OPERATING POLICIES

Operating policies should be established for each area of your center. We will go into more detail about operating policies in Chapter Eleven with the development of the family handbook. You will establish policies, sometimes also called "standing rules" when they are quite specific, for details of the actual business processes, such as purchasing and allocating supplies, budgeting and auditing, or for community relations. At this point, however, we are more concerned with determining your family and child policies. These probably impose more dilemmas than any other aspect of operating a center. Think about both positive and negative outcomes. President Truman had a motto on his desk: "The buck stops here." As an administrator, you will be the ultimate authority in your program. What will you do if the procedure for a birthday celebration is a nutritious snack—and a beaming mother arrives with a gooey chocolate cake, a carton of ice cream, synthetic punch, and some little cups of candy? What will you do if a mother is consistently late in picking up her child, apparently unconcerned that everyone has gone home but you? What will you do if your policy states that children may visit only with prior permission and the chairperson of your advisory board arrives with his grandson just in time for a field trip?

Short-term policies of a school are frequently established or reevaluated in the spring, thus determining standing rules and procedures for the subsequent term. Some of these are included in a contract that parents sign when children are enrolled, and others are included in handbooks or given out as information sheets to staff, parents, and community volunteers. You may want to discuss operating policies during orientation sessions, particularly if there will be emphasis on parent involvement or if there is a problem with language comprehension. In bilingual areas, policies should be provided in the language used in the family homes in addition to English.

WHAT WOULD YOU DO?

It is Friday noontime. An angry mother whose son attends the center only three times a week has come into your office. She has just been told by the teacher that she will have to pay extra because he has attended this morning when he was not scheduled. Her reason for not paying is that he has been absent several times because of illness and she paid for those days. She feels that she deserves some free time in exchange. Your printed policy states that payment must be made for all times that children are present. What would you do?

Typically, operating policies are developed and available in the family handbook. The items to include are discussed in Chapter Eleven.

REFERENCES AND RESOURCES

Bess, G., & Ratekin, C. (2000). Orienting and evaluating your board of directors: Keys to effective board management. *Child Care Information Exchange, 136,* 82–87.

Block, J. (2001). *ABCs of building boards.* Albuquerque, NM: Jean Block Consulting.

Bredekamp, S., & Coppel, C. (Eds.). (1997). *Developmentally appropriate practices in early childhood programs.* Washington, DC: National Association for the Education of Young Children.

Caring for our children—National health and safety performance standards: Guidelines for out-of-home child care programs. (2002). Washington, DC: National Association for the Education of Young Children.

Carver, J. (1997). *Boards that make a difference.* San Francisco, CA: Jossey-Bass.

Child Welfare League of America. (1996). *Board self-assessment checklist.* New York: Author.

Child Welfare League of America. (2002). *Standards of excellence for the management and governance of all child welfare organizations.* New York: Author.

Decker, C., & Decker, J. R. (2001). *Planning and administering early childhood programs.* Upper Saddle River, NJ: Prentice Hall.

Holland, T. P. (1996). *How to build a more effective board.* Washington, DC: National Center for Nonprofit Boards.

Morgan, G. (1996). Licensing and accreditation: How much quality is quality? In S. Bredekamp & B. A. Willer (Eds.), *NAEYC accreditation: A decade of learning and the years ahead* (pp. 129–138). Washington, DC: National Association for the Education of Young Children.

National Academy of Early Childhood Programs. (1991). *Accreditation criteria and procedures of the National Academy of Early Childhood Programs.* Washington, DC: National Association for the Education of Young Children.

Sciarra, D. J., & Dorsey, A. G. (2003). *Developing and administering a child care center.* Albany, NY: Delmar.

Taylor, B. J. (2002). *Early childhood program management: People and procedures.* Upper Saddle River, NJ: Prentice Hall.

Zimmerman, D. P. (1997). *Roberts Rules in plain English.* New York: HarperPerennial.

WEBSITE RESOURCES

Board café for nonprofit boards: www.boardcafe.org

Child care licensing standards: www.nrc.uchsc.edu

Education Law Association: www.educationlaw.org/links.htm

National Association for the Education of Young Children: www.naeyc.org

COMPARING REGULATIONS ACROSS STATES

Name _____ Date _____

Objective: To compare child care regulations between two states.

Directions: Visit the website www.nrc.uchsc.edu and compare the child care regulations for your state and a different state. Complete the following table.

	YOUR STATE	COMPARISON STATE
Teacher qualifications		
Director qualifications		
Teacher-to-child ratio Infants Toddlers Preschool		
Indoor square footage		
Outdoor square footage		
Criminal background check		

WORKSHEET 4.2

SETTING STANDARDS FOR YOUR PROGRAM

Name _____ Date _____

Objectives: To compare legal requirements and professional standards to apply to your program.

Directions: List in parallel columns legal requirements and additional standards that you will try to meet.

LEGAL REQUIREMENTS	MY STANDARDS
Example: State ratio for three-year-olds is one to fifteen	Example: My ratio is one to twelve.

PURPOSES, GOALS, AND MISSION STATEMENT

Name _____ Date _____

Objective: To establish purposes, goals, and a mission statement.

Directions: Write your purposes, goals, and mission statement to guide you as you develop your program.

Purposes (the reasons why)

Goals (the what)

Mission statement (the how)

BYLAWS OR LONG-TERM POLICIES

Name _____ Date _____

Objective: To develop an understanding of the components of governing policies.

Directions: Write your thoughts about the different policy areas of your program.

Article I.   Name

Article II.   Purposes and policies

Article III.   Membership

Article IV.   Financial considerations

    Section A.   Fees

    Section B.   Budget

Section C.   Auditing

Article V.   Organization and administration—Policy board or advisory board

Section A.   Membership of the board (if there is one)

Section B.   Meetings of the board

Section C.   Officers

Section D.   Lines of authority

Section E.   Committees

Article VI.   Staffing

Section A.   Titles

Section B.   Necessary clearances

Article VII.   Amendments

Article VIII.   Parliamentary procedures

Personnel Systems

So important that they deserve a chapter by themselves, personnel systems govern the organization through their influence on the entire staff. Adequate planning in the preliminary stages of a center can help ensure staffing choices that contribute to a positive atmosphere for both children and adults during the operating component. Assignment of duties and schedules, qualifications for employment and advancement, terms of employment, procedures for termination and appeal, and methods of evaluation should be clearly defined and made known to each person involved with the center, paid and unpaid, volunteers and professionals.

The personnel policies should be in a clearly written manual or handbook to help staff members understand their roles and to establish legal conditions of their employment. A loose-leaf binder can be easily updated when policies change. It may include an introductory statement about the history of the center, sponsorship, goals, and the mission statement. This manual or handbook should also include emergency and standard operating procedures established by your center, as well as rules about smoking, the dress code, eating lunch with children, or holiday gift exchanges. If a checklist or other formal performance evaluation will be used, include a copy. Some employers attach a final page that each new employee must sign, date, and return to verify that the material has been read and understood. This page is filed in case there are future problems that begin with the employee saying, "But you never told me that." The employee should be given a copy of the signed form.

WRITING PERSONNEL POLICIES

Personnel policies should be written so that they

- Bring out the best in people, while supporting your mission.
- Can be mutually agreed on by all staff members.
- Provide a reciprocating professional agreement to receive and give the best possible services, with continual improvement based on objective evaluation.

■ Compare favorably with policies for workers in related employment.
■ Conform to union and professional requirements and government-mandated employment policies.

When developing personnel policies, you first need to make an organizational chart that helps you determine how many employees will be needed, where and when the employees will be scheduled, and how each relates to all others in the center. Decide on specific characteristics, both personal and professional, that are desirable for carrying out the purposes of your program. It is increasingly rare to find professional performance without a professional salary, so a balance must be determined at this point. What will you need? What can you afford? Instead of one teacher with minimal qualifications for each class of ten or twelve children, should you consider looking for a more competent and experienced individual at a higher salary to work with fifteen or twenty children, with the assistance of less-costly, entry-level assistants or aides? Can you use team teaching, with two or three teachers sharing space and each one conducting special activities for all the children? Are volunteers available? How about parents? Students? Be realistic, but explore possibilities.

As the second step in developing personnel policies, define the specific tasks and responsibilities of each staff member. Visualize their interrelationships with one another and with groups of children. To avoid monotony, allocation of work should provide for a change of scene. For example, alternate yard supervision with indoor activities. Persons with special skills or interest, such as in science or music, should be encouraged to "switch around" with other staff members so that as many children as possible can benefit from them. Whenever possible, every teacher or paraprofessional should be allowed to carry through with an entire project. One person would be in charge of mixing paints, supervising the easel area, cleaning up, and caring for completed work. This allocation of a complete task helps aides because they know that they are expected to assert themselves and accept definite responsibilities. The chief complaint of assistants is that they always get the dirty work, whereas the teachers get the interesting projects. Each assignment should be as equal as possible, including both desirable and undesirable aspects, with consideration for the training, experience, and capabilities of the persons involved.

The National Association for the Education of Young Children has suggested six levels of professional development as part of the career-ladder/lattice concept. These categories are helpful when developing staff policies.

Early Childhood Professional Level I. Appropriate personal qualities but no specialized training and works under close supervision.

Early Childhood Professional Level II. Child Development Associate (CDA) or community college certificate and may be responsible for care and education of a group of children.

Early Childhood Professional Level III. Associate degree in early childhood education or child development.

Early Childhood Professional Level IV. Bachelor's degree in arts or sciences in early childhood education or child development, including supervised field experience.

Early Childhood Professional Level V. Master's degree in early childhood education or child development.

Early Childhood Professional Level VI. Doctorate of Philosophy or Doctorate of Education in early childhood education or child development (Willer, 1994).

CLASS DISCUSSION

In small groups, share experiences as a volunteer or paid employee regarding personnel policies or handbooks.

Volunteers, unpaid individuals who serve on a regularly scheduled basis under specified supervision, supplement the staff. They may include parents, retired persons, professionals from other fields, college or younger students, or others. Your personnel policies will specify their supervision by paid staff members if you include volunteers in your planning.

You will specify terms of employment as a third step. Components of this part of the policy include compensation, benefits, and standards of conduct, evaluation, grievance, and termination. Some questions to ask as you develop this policy include: Will you pay annual salaries or will you pay hourly wages? Would it be advantageous to have salaried employees if staff meetings and preparation time are paid for by your center? Will you provide "flexible personal time off" instead of calculating sick leave, vacation, and legitimate absences as separate items? How will you deal with overtime? Federal and state regulations have specific requirements concerning immigrant status, Social Security, affirmative action, and other personnel matters. These change frequently, so you need to know what might be required or prohibited. Remember that staff costs and benefits will be your greatest expense. Worksheet 5.1 allows you to consider components of a job description and handbook for your program. Example 5.1 presents a sample job description. Example 5.4 illustrates an example of a staff handbook. You may want to consult these in developing your own policies.

worksheet

5.1

p. 87

SELECTING STAFF

The importance of the center staff in determining the emotional and educational climate of your center was considered when personnel policies were discussed. Your co-workers may include college- and university-trained teachers, Child Development Associates, paraprofessionals and volunteers from a variety of backgrounds, student assistants, office and kitchen staff, custodians, and others who are not hired to work directly with the children. Management research and practical experiences have reinforced the importance of all center adults working together. A grouchy custodian can undo the efforts of a dedicated teacher. Because all members of the staff are directly or indirectly teaching the children, we use the term *staff* in this section to refer to all employees.

Personnel Recruitment

One of the major and continuing responsibilities of the early childhood center director is the recruitment and selection of a well-qualified and congenial staff. Wise selection prevents future problems, but errors are hard to correct. Selecting a teacher involves making a judgment, which requires definite criteria. You have developed goals and a mission statement that are important to your school's success. Suitable candidates

CLASS DISCUSSION

Where do you begin recruitment? How do you locate suitable candidates?

CLASS ACTIVITY

Write an advertisement suitable for the classified section of your local newspaper that would attract applicants for the position you have available.

CLASS ACTIVITY

Once you have some applicants, how do you process them? How valuable would the following sources of information be to you? Why?

Telephone interview

College transcripts

Letters of referral

Personal interview

Resume outlining experience

should have similar beliefs and be able to work within your framework. Personnel policies that list qualifications and job specifications reveal exactly what the job will involve and will help you realize just who you are seeking. You are aware of personalities and work habits of the other teachers or applicants for other positions.

When writing an advertisement to hire personnel, the first word should be *Child* because that is the common terminology. Also include the job title, a brief job description, the qualifications, application process (call for an application or resume and references), contact information, start date, salary range, and other relevant information.

THE INTERVIEW PROCESS

When you actually begin the process of hiring a staff member, you will probably depend on several approaches to find out if this would be the right addition for your center. Regardless of other procedures, the personal interview is a must; no staff member should be hired without a face-to-face meeting with the administrator, a reliable delegate, or a personnel committee. This will permit you to

1. Evaluate the personality of the applicant. Is this a person you can relate to and that you want to have working with children?
2. Gain insight into the applicant's reasons for wanting the position. Will they fit into the framework of your goals and mission statement? (However, this is not the time to discuss your mission statement.)

3. Analyze the applicant's ability to cope with problems.
4. Get an impression of the applicant's future plans and ambitions. Is this job being viewed as just to fill extra time, to earn a few dollars for something special, or because there doesn't seem to be anything else available?

The process of interviewing involves several steps.

1. Receive application forms and support materials.
2. Designate who is involved in the interview process (e.g., board members, the director, teachers, parents), and coordinate activities to conduct the interviews.
3. Review the written applications using a rating scale or a ranking scale. If others are involved in the selection process, meet to discuss the completed scales. Example 5.2 shows a sample candidate rating scale.
4. Prepare a list of interview questions. The categories of interview questions may include educational or previous work experience, planning the environment, guidance areas, curriculum, experience working with parents or families, and long-term professional goals.
   However, you cannot ask about a person's age, marital status, spouse's occupation, whether the candidate has or plans to have children, child care arrangements, religious affiliation, or disabilities. Example 5.3 includes a few suggested interview questions.
5. During the interview, provide a comfortable setting free from distractions. Allow adequate time for the meeting and offer the candidate water or coffee. Take the candidate on a tour of the center to assess how the applicant reacts to children and staff. As a demonstration of the applicant's teaching, ask him or her to do a sample circle time. Plan a second interview if there are several good candidates from whom to choose.

The interview will probably take from thirty minutes to an hour. It should be thoughtfully planned and be conducted without interruptions. Fingerprinting, criminal background checks, and other screening procedures are mandated by different government agencies. It is imperative that you have up-to-date information for your own legal protection as well as for that of the person you are interviewing.

During the entire search process, you should maintain written records that document your compliance with affirmative action regulations. Keep a list of all applicants with notations as to why each was or was not considered. Document the job-related reasons why a person was hired. You must be able to show what your requirements

CLASS ACTIVITY

Divide into groups to study existing methods for evaluating applicants or to develop tools that are appropriate for evaluations. After groups have evaluated methods, they can report their conclusions to the class. Following are suggestions for group topics.

Group 1. Application forms.

Group 2. Testing—Purpose and available types.

Group 3. Form to send to applicant's references, to be filled out and returned to you.

Group 4. Interview questions and techniques.

WHAT WOULD YOU DO?

Your center has an opening for a teacher for the toddler classroom. You have received six applications but two do not meet your requirements (specified in the job announcement). One of these applicants, who has had sixteen years experience teaching kindergarten and first grade in the public schools, calls to inquire of her status for the position. After you review her file, you explain to her that you cannot consider her for the position because she does not have experience teaching children under the age of three years. Two weeks later you receive a letter from her attorney stating that you discriminated against her because of her age. What do you do?

were and how the successful applicant best met them under a fair process that gave everyone an equal chance. These regulations also require you to maintain personnel records, including mutually agreed on evaluations that are the same for everyone at the same job level.

REFERENCES AND RESOURCES

Adler, L. (2002). *Hire with your head: Using power hiring to build great teams.* New York: Wiley.

Azer, S. L., Capraro, L., & Elliot, K. (1997). *Working toward making a career of it: A profile of career development incentives in 1996.* Boston: Wheelock College.

Caruso, J. J., & Fawcett, M. T. (1999). *Supervision in early childhood education* (2nd ed.). New York: Teachers College Press.

Child Care Information Exchange. (2004). *Out of the box training.* Redmond, WA: Child Care Information Exchange.

Falcone, P. (2001). *The hiring and firing question and answer book.* New York: AMACOM.

Hyson, M. (2003). (Ed.). *Preparing early childhood professionals: NAEYC's standards for programs.* Washington, DC: National Association for the Education of Young Children.

Kouzes, J. A., & Posner, B. Z. (2002). *The leadership challenge.* San Francisco, CA: Jossey-Bass.

Lundin, W., & Lundin, K. (1995). *Working with difficult people.* New York: American Management Association.

Mornell, P., & Dunnick, R. (2003). *45 effective ways for hiring smart: How to predict winners and losers in the incredibly expensive people-reading game.* Berkeley, CA: Ten Speed Press.

Willer, B. (Ed.). (1994). A conceptual framework for early childhood professional development: NAEYC position statement, adopted November 1993. In J. Johnson & J. B. McCracken (Eds.), *The early childhood career lattice: Perspectives on professional development* (pp. 4–21). Washington, DC: National Association for the Education of Young Children.

WEBSITE RESOURCES

American Management Association: www.amanet.org/arc_center

Scheig Associates, Inc.:   www.ischeig.com/childcareexchange

Staff Handbook: www.niehs.nih.gov/daycare/staffbook

The Education Job Opportunity Network: www.edjoin.org/jobs/showjobdescription

The Preschool Options Project: www.preschooloptions.org/tools/job_description

EXAMPLE 5.1

SAMPLE JOB DESCRIPTION FOR A MASTER TEACHER

GENERAL REQUIREMENTS

Bachelor's degree in early childhood education or a related field

At least two years experience in group child care

Physician's report of good health

Clearance through the National Child Abuse Index

GENERAL DESCRIPTION

Provide a safe, secure, and nurturing environment for children enrolled in our program.

Plan and initiate developmentally appropriate activities that promote growth and development of the whole child, including activities in the areas of language, social and emotional growth, creativity, science, dramatic play, multicultural issues, gross-motor skills, small-motor skills, and so on.

Train, evaluate, and supervise assistant teachers and volunteers.

Establish positive and productive relationships with the families in our center.

Delegate tasks to parents, volunteers, and other employees.

Help care for equipment and maintain a clean classroom and play yard.

Attend monthly staff meetings.

Articulate program goals and philosophy, and apply them to working with the children and other adults working in the program.

Pay scale: $9.75–$12.00 per hour

RESPONSIBILITIES

Set up classroom and greet children and parents.

Ensure developmentally appropriate activities are planned and implemented by staff daily.

Keep written documentation of individual children in your classroom and complete assessments of children's growth and development.

Assume responsibility for classroom, including maintenance of order and neatness in all classroom and outdoor areas.

Miscellaneous duties as assigned by supervisor.

EXAMPLE 5.2

EXAMPLE OF A CANDIDATE RATING SCALE

Candidate _____   Position _____

Rate each area on a scale from 1 (Unsatisfactory) to 5 (Outstanding) and total the scores at the end of the form.

Unsatisfactory = 1   Fair = 2   Good = 3   Very Good = 4   Outstanding = 5

Add comments for clarification.

_____ Education and training—Relevance (amount and quality)

_____ Job knowledge—Responses (answers to technical questions)

_____ Job-related experience—Relevance (level of responsibility)

_____ Attitude and interest—Job insight (professional orientation, friendliness)

EXAMPLE 5.2 *(continued)*

_____ Alertness and judgment—Adaptability (maturity and logical responses)

_____ Communications skills—Ability (express oneself clearly and concisely)

_____ Overall score

General comments

Recommendation _____

Name _____ Date _____

EXAMPLES OF INTERVIEW QUESTIONS

CANDIDATE WITHOUT A DEGREE

1. Tell me about your past work with young children.
2. If two boys were arguing about a truck, each saying he had it first, what would you do?
3. How would you handle an upset parent who approaches you when the teacher is not in the classroom?
4. What skills and abilities do you believe you can bring to our program?

CANDIDATE WITH A DEGREE

1. Tell us about your previous experiences in this field—both your previous work experience and your practicum placements.
2. What would you do when an irate family member approaches you about an incident (such as children cursing in the classroom)? How would you handle that?
3. Choose an area of the curriculum (e.g., language, math, music, etc.). Tell me how you would prepare the classroom to teach this area.
4. How would you handle problem solving in the classroom? For example, if two children were arguing about blocks, each saying he or she had them first, what would you do?
5. What do you believe are the most important components of a family–teacher relationship?

EXAMPLE 5.4

EXAMPLE FROM A CHILD CARE CENTER STAFF HANDBOOK

PERSONNEL POLICIES

These personnel policies have been adopted by Child Care Center as guidelines for carrying out the personnel administrative functions and for the information of all employees. The policies may be amended by Child Care Center at any time, and employees will be duly notified of any such amendments. All employees will be given a copy of these personnel policies on employment. It is the policy of Child Care Center to provide equal employment opportunity for all persons without discrimination of race, color, creed, religion, national origin, sex, disability, or age.

EMPLOYMENT

Probationary Status

All full-time employees are considered to be in a probationary period for the first ninety days of employment. If an employee should decide to leave during the probationary period, she or he should notify the director in order to process the termination procedure. During the probationary period, the director must decide if an employee is capable of meeting the required standards of performance. If the director decides the employee cannot perform satisfactorily, her or his employment can be terminated without prior notice. Written documentation will be required for the termination of probationary employees. Termination during the probationary period does not reflect on the employee's reference material.

Orientation

Each employee shall receive an employee handbook and shall undergo a required ten-hour orientation period during which the center's policies, benefits, and privileges shall be explained. The center extends certain rights and privileges based on employment status.

TERMINATION AND DISCHARGE

Termination shall mean the separation of an employee from Child Care Center because of reduction in workforce, elimination of position, or other budgetary reasons. Employees who are terminated may be compensated at the discretion of the management up to two weeks pay as severance pay.

Discharge shall mean the separation of an employee because of any form of physical or mental abuse toward the children in the center, unethical conduct, grave personal misconduct reflecting on Child Care Center, insubordination, alcohol use, possession of a controlled substance, fighting, theft, falsification of time records, failure to meet work standards by the employee, incompetence, repeated tardiness or absences, or similar serious charges. A discharged employee may be requested to leave Child Care Center employment immediately.

EXAMPLE 5.4 *(continued)*

OPERATIONAL POLICIES

The center hours of operation are Monday through Friday, 7:00 A.M. to 6:00 P.M.

Hours of Work

The center will maintain work hours that are compatible with the maintenance of an effective and efficient work schedule. The center retains the right to establish, alter, and maintain work schedules. It may be necessary to change individual work schedules as the enrollment fluctuates and load times change. The normal workweek consists of forty hours and the pay period covers one workweek. The normal workday consists of eight hours and is scheduled to provide for an elapsed time of eight and one-half to nine hours from which the scheduled thirty- or sixty-minute break should be deducted in order to result in an eight-hour workday. Overtime will not be permitted under any circumstances without the permission of the director.

Holidays

The following days will be considered as paid holidays for full-time employees at the rate of hours for which the individual has been hired: New Years Day, Good Friday, Independence Day, Labor Day, Thanksgiving Day, and Christmas Day. (These hours are available the first full pay period following the ninety-day probationary period.) Paid time off hours can be used at the discretion of the employee with adequate notice (ten days or more) and satisfactory coverage of the classroom. Vacation time can be scheduled up to six months in advance.

ATTENDANCE AND RECORD KEEPING

In order to maintain an effective working atmosphere and ensure state compliance for staff-to-child ratios, all employees are expected to be at work and on time every day and for the duration of the scheduled duty hours. Consequently, habitual absence or tardiness will have an adverse effect on merit raises and promotional consideration, and, if excessive, will be cause for disciplinary action, including discharge.

Time taken off for any reason, including doctor and dental, will be considered personal time and must be taken as benefit time or time without pay. This time must be approved by the director in advance to be considered as an excused absence.

COMPENSATION

Determination of Compensation and Raises

An employee's compensation is determined at the discretion of the administration, taking account of duties, responsibilities, and qualifications. The employee will be informed of the salary level of the position at the time of hiring. Salaries are set and

EXAMPLE 5.4 *(continued)*

increases are made on the basis of merit and will be approved and reviewed annually. All salaries are of a confidential nature and should be treated as such. Employees should not discuss their salaries with one another.

Payroll Records

A time record is to be maintained on a daily basis by each individual, by clocking in and out using the computer. The actual time you begin and end work will be clearly indicated as well as any time off during the day, which should include meals, appointments, and so on. Holidays and paid time off days should also be indicated when used. The director, on a weekly basis, will print out computerized records of hours worked.

Pay Periods/Paychecks

All employees will be paid every week on Friday for the previous week worked. Please contact the director if you have a question about your work time, salary, or paycheck.

Federal and state income taxes and Social Security taxes will be withheld from your pay and remitted to the Treasury as required by law. The amounts of federal and state tax withheld is determined by your income and number of deductions claimed. On employment, all employees are required to complete a W4 form and to update this information on a yearly basis. Annually, and prior to January 31, you will receive a W-2 statement of your earnings for the previous year. To avoid any delay, please be sure your current address is on file in the office.

On resignation, your last paycheck will be issued the next regular payday. Written notice should be given of where to send your check should you be unable to pick it up.

BENEFITS

Vacation (paid time off)

Child Care Center provides full-time employees paid time off to be used as vacation and sick time. Accrual of paid time off begins on the employee's start date but may not be used until the first pay period after the ninety-day probationary period is complete. Paid time off accumulates as hours that are allocated at a specific rate each three months of employment. These hours may be used after ninety days of employment. The rates of accrual are as follows:

During the first three years of employment, vacation leave will be accrued at the rate of two days per three month period from the date of employment. The entire period must be worked before days are available. Accrual for vacation after three years of employment will be at the rate of one day per month.

Paid time off must be used annually or, with the director's prior consent, employees may receive compensation at their salaried rate per hour for accrued time. If employment is terminated with a proper and written two-weeks notice, the employee will receive pay for the hours accrued. It is the employee's responsibility to

EXAMPLE 5.4 *(continued)*

notify the director when using paid time off and to maintain an accurate record of remaining hours.

Vacations must be scheduled in a manner that is least disruptive to operational requirements. Every reasonable effort will be made to grant vacation requests if proper coverage can be secured for the classroom. Preference for summer vacation requests will be on a seniority basis through May 1 of each calendar year. After May 1, vacations will be scheduled on a first come–first served basis for the remaining openings. Vacation dates, once selected and approved, will be posted and should be traded or changed only by mutual consent and with the approval of the director.

LEAVE OF ABSENCE

There may be times during your employment that, for a variety of reasons, you may need an extended period away from work. Absence without pay up to a maximum of ninety days may be granted

Personal Leave

A personal leave of absence may be requested and granted when an extended period of time away from work is needed. The length of the leave and the timing of the leave must be approved by the director. A thirty-day written notice is required before a leave can be approved and begin. The request will be approved or denied depending on the mutual long-range interests of Child Care Center. After approval of a personal leave, you will be guaranteed the same or a comparable job if you return to work within the approved time or within the ninety days. After ninety days you will be given first consideration for any openings for which you are qualified. Personal leave will be a leave without pay.

Medical Leave (including maternity)

If you become temporarily disabled and cannot perform your regular duties due to illness or injury, you may request a medical leave of absence. A medical leave will begin when your physician certifies that you are no longer able to perform your regular duties. The leave will end when your physician certifies that you are able to return to work and perform you regular duties. The physician must provide a written statement indicating the length of disability. This statement must include the date the disability began and the estimated date the disability will end and you are able to return to work. A medical leave will be a leave without pay. If you wish, you may elect to receive pay for your accrued paid days off.

PROFESSIONAL DEVELOPMENT

Evaluations/Reviews

The center will appraise the job performance of each employee periodically. Performance appraisal is intended to maintain or improve the employee's job satisfaction and performance. Performance appraisal should serve as a systematic guide for the

EXAMPLE 5.4 *(continued)*

director in planning the employee's further training and should indicate the center's interest in the employee's progress and personal development.

Formal reviews are required at least annually. The director will review each employee privately to discuss individual performance and expectations. Should there be areas that require improvements, the specific deficiencies should be clearly stated and discussed. Time frames and goals should be established for improvement. Both the employee and director should document these goals and a copy should be placed in the employee's confidential file.

Seniority

The center rewards employees for length of service. Employment seniority is defined by length of service and is counted from the last date of continuous employment. Hire date is the term for the original date of employment. It is the first date for which the employment begins. A new hire date is established if the employee terminates employment and is subsequently rehired. The first date of full-time employment will be used as the date to consider eligibility for benefits. Job seniority will be considered in layoffs, promotions, salary adjustments, scheduling of vacation or holiday time, and other assignments.

CONDITIONS OF EMPLOYMENT

Medical Statement

All employees are required on employment to have a medical statement and proof of tuberculosis (TB) test completed and on file. Each subsequent year, all employees are required to present an annual medical statement and TB test signed by a licensed health professional. This is at the employee's expense.

Meetings and Conferences

Teachers are expected to be members of appropriate early childhood professional organizations and to attend conferences. Expenses incurred for such meetings and conferences will be subject to approval. You may be reimbursed for up to 50 percent of the expenses, but you must obtain permission from the director before turning in expense reports.

All staff are expected to participate in regular staff development exercises. On-site staff-conducted workshops; local, state, and national workshops; on-site or off-site training from training organizations; and child care courses offered through technical institutes, universities, or other educational institutions are all acceptable methods for meeting this requirement.

Each employee is required by the state to attend at least twenty documented hours of child care training annually. All part-time employees must also attend training hours as required by the state, based on the number of hours worked. The documentation for these hours must be submitted in a timely manner to the director. Employees should attempt to obtain a portion of these hours quarterly in order to keep current. The center may arrange classes to help employees meet this requirement.

EXAMPLE 5.4   *(continued)*

PARENT RELATIONSHIPS

The center director, care givers, or parents may schedule one-to-one conferences either to discuss the progress of the child or to discuss medical, psychological, or behavioral matters that must be kept confidential. It is necessary when working with parents to use generous amounts of personal concern and courtesy. Reasonable requests from parents about their children that do not interfere directly with the center's policies should be honored. Special concern should be given to solving problems. Take care to answer questions parents have about their children in a gentle and truthful way. Always tell the truth about any incident involving the center. Use professionalism in each situation and maintain confidentiality in all matters. Always make management aware of situations that need special attention.

Parents who disagree with the center program or policies should be instructed to contact the director to discuss the matter.

PERSONAL BUSINESS

Personal conduct on and off the job is a concern of the employer. Any of the following offenses on the job will be subject to documentation. These offenses can result in immediate discharge at the discretion of the director. All are subject to warnings and reprimands: theft, verbal or physical assault on another person, falsifying records, destruction of property, insubordination, alcohol use, immorality, leaving work area, solicitation, releasing confidential child information, rumors or gossiping, or gross negligence.

PERSONNEL POLICIES

Name _____ Date _____

Objective: To apply knowledge of staff policies when developing appropriate criteria for selection of personnel and employment issues.

Directions: On this worksheet, you will plan personnel policies that determine how you will recruit, interview, orient, supervise, and evaluate a staff member.

A. Job description

Title of position _____
(State name of position, such as "pre-K teacher")

Nature of work

Function of the job (brief description of work to be performed)

Duties and responsibilities (list of specific tasks to be assumed)

Supervision received from (one individual only)

Supervision given to

Parallel staff relationships

B. Criteria for staff selection

	MINIMUM	ACCEPTABLE	DESIRABLE
Formal education			
Knowledge of child development, art, music, and other skills			
Personal attributes			
Special abilities in communication, planning, and the acceptance of individual differences			
Membership in professional organizations			

C. Terms of employment

Hours/days/other time specifications

Paid vacation

Sick leave/paid time off

Unpaid time off

Maternity leave, paternity leave, or adoption (Paid? Unpaid?)

Employee child care

Procedure when substitute is needed

Insurance coverage provided

Retirement plan (including Social Security)

Professional growth and incentives

Salary and increases

Specific requirements that qualify as income or tax deduction, such as uniforms

Procedures for evaluation

Procedures for grievance

Procedures for termination

Other policies needed for your program

CHAPTER SIX

Staff Orientation and Professional Development

CHAPTER OUTLINE

STAFF ORIENTATION

WORKING WITH STAFF

TEAMS

STAFF MEETINGS

PROFESSIONAL DEVELOPMENT

PARENTS AND OTHER VOLUNTEERS

Now that you have hired your staff, the journey has just begun. The staff is the heart of your program; they can make or break your center. How you implement and support staff development will affect how they work within the center. Therefore, staff should be given opportunities to participate in educational classes, conferences, and workshops.

STAFF ORIENTATION

If your new staff member is to do the best possible work, orientation arrangements must convey the responsibilities and opportunities of your school. The teacher needs to feel an association with friends, knowing that work assignments will be as equitable as possible, that abilities will be recognized and appreciated, and that there is basis for self-respect. The first experience in a new school can determine the future capabilities of a teacher.

Growth and learning are thought to take place best in an orderly sequence. Because an initial step for growth is to prepare an environment in which one can learn, orientation is a logical first step in an ongoing in-service training program. Orientations will vary according to the type of school and your priorities, but certain purposes and characteristics are common to all. Orientation includes an explanation of both short- and long-range goals. It is important to have new staff members settle quickly and easily into the daily routine of the school (a short-range goal). It is equally important that the teacher work as an individual and as a group member to

91

implement the purposes of the school (a long-range goal). Orientation programs may serve several of the following purposes.

1. They establish mutual confidence, set the tone of the relationship of the new staff member with an established group, or establish an easy rapport among staff members with a new member. (This is often best done with a reception or other informal, social event. It may include parents.) In a parent-operated school, this will mean that the original selection committee, which assisted in the choice of the staff member, serves as the introduction committee.

2. They interpret and clarify the school's purposes, goals, and mission statement, and the general principles on which the school functions.

3. They provide written information and oral explanations about the job that is expected. There is no better way of dispelling that feeling of insecurity than this real knowledge. This might include the following:

   a. Information about school ownership, history, organizational breakdown, policies, and physical layout.
   b. A list of staff, parents, directors, and others involved.
   c. Interpretation and clarification of conditions of employment, including job description and purposes, goals, and mission statement of the school.
   d. Specific information as to procedures dealing with supplies and equipment; services and resources of the school, such as audiovisual aids; available community resources, emergency procedures, such as first aid and fire drills; introduction to forms and records system; personal comforts, such as restroom location and lockers; or other storage space.
   e. Information about employee benefits including health, dental, and life insurance; reduced child care fee; vacation time; sick leave; personal time; compensation for overtime (if hourly employee); membership in professional organizations; opportunities for professional development; and others.

4. Supplement the orientation program by

   a. Demonstration teaching.
   b. Providing workshops and seminars with other staff members.
   c. Observation prior to teaching class, perhaps supplemented by videotapes demonstrating approved techniques. For an example of staff policies see Example 5.4 in the previous chapter.

The adequate orientation program treats every new employee as a unique individual with needs and concerns somewhat different from yours or those of others on your staff. A personalized orientation will shorten the adjustment period and aid the

worksheet
6.1
p. 103

new member of your program. It should include a supportive teaching–learning period that is two sided, one in which you are also a recipient. Example 6.1 is a sample of an orientation checklist. Then Worksheet 6.1 encourages you to develop ideas to deal with common orientation issues.

WORKING WITH STAFF

Recent research has confirmed that the mere possession of high intelligence or subject matter knowledge and good college grades do not, in themselves, guarantee that a teacher is competent. Sex and marital status did not affect performance. Socioeconomic status reflected so many other variables that it was not significant. Professional knowledge gained from specific methods courses made teachers more effective than those without these courses. Teaching effectiveness increased rapidly in the first five years, maintained a plateau for fifteen or twenty years, then began to decline (Bellm, Burton, Whitebook, Broatch, & Young 2002). No tests yet devised can adequately predict teaching success, but failure was attributed to two main factors: the inability to maintain discipline and the lack of administrator–teacher cooperation. Some guidelines that foster cooperation include the following:

Acceptance. Accept your staff as they are. Remember that people learn when they are emotionally and intellectually ready and when the relationship is warm and friendly.

Expectation. Foster self-growth in the staff and expect of each member the very best he or she can give.

Support and respect. Help each teacher feel free to express ideas, thoughts, and creative individuality; teachers learn by doing, but they will not experiment without the support and approval of the director.

Authority. Provide the special knowledge and functioning that enables teachers to look to you as a resource person when they need assistance.

Problem Solving

Many of the personnel problems you will be expected to handle as an administrator will need attention immediately. Most of the staff will not even be aware that a problem existed. However, problems need to be handled systematically. Remember that problems are not solved by the exercise of authority but by determining the best thing to do at the moment. This means considering the past, trying to predict the future, listening to all ideas expressed, and considering all alternatives.

Problem solving needs to be approached from two points of view. One focuses on relationships, the other on processes. Both are important and interrelated, but they can be analyzed separately.

RELATIONSHIPS
1. Accept responsibility for a problem. (A director should feel secure and nondefensive, and be able to admit errors in judgment and use them for setting a framework for honesty and continuous evaluation.)
2. Respect staff feelings. (Avoid interrupting any teacher or criticizing in front of children or others.)
3. Let teaching be individualized. (View a mistake only as some violation of the school's basic goals and mission statement, not as a situation that was not handled as you would have liked.)
4. Give positive support and deserved praise, but do not flatter. (The use of names is supportive. Let teachers and other staff members know how they contribute to the program.)
5. Help the teacher personally assess the problem. (I was interested in what you were doing and how you see it moving your children toward our goals for....)

PROCESS
1. State the problem. (Identify the problem, not the symptoms. Be specific. Why is it a problem? What will be gained by the solution?)
2. Gather knowledge. (What is fact? What is feeling? What is your opinion?)
3. Formulate action. (Know your expectations. Then decide on one course and present it.)
4. Follow up. (What results did the action bring?)
5. Evaluate. (Do the results correspond with the expectations?)

As a director, one of the most difficult things you will do is to tell employees that they will no longer be working in your center. Circumstances will determine how this is handled. If you need to reduce staffing because enrollment has dropped with the closing of a nearby major employer, it would be appropriate to have a series of strategy meetings that involved community members in addition to teachers. Remember that you cannot fire an employee without valid reasons. Even if you are certain that this individual has been stealing money from purses or taking the center's property to sell at a swap meet, it is vital to have outside authorities involved. If the cook/matron has not maintained proper cleanliness standards, you might start with suggestions about how to improve the situation, and then progress to warnings and a written statement of expected changes with a two-week probation period. If one teacher has begun yelling at the children and acting negatively with staff, a private conversation might help you understand the problems and help work toward a solution. However, unless the situation improves, termination may be necessary. Remember that employees cannot be discharged on the basis of race, sex, age, or national origin, and that expensive lawsuits may ensue if you cannot document "good cause" reasons. There is no simple way to decide when and how to fire someone. It is usually agreed that closing time on Friday is best for that final interview, with the individual not coming back on Monday. Providing monetary compensation, which can include unused vacation time, helps soften the blow. But, experienced directors warn, be sure to ask for any keys to the center that the terminated employee may have. For whatever reason the employee leaves your program, you should remember the relationship and process point to problem solving.

TEAMS

What makes an organization, such as an early childhood center, cohesive? A successful business is not guaranteed by formal structure and comfortable working conditions, much less by good resolutions. It involves the human factor, the day-to-day, hour-to-hour relationships and attitudes. There is the concept of the organization as a whole, what it stands for, what gives it individuality, its affiliations and its traditions. Is it gleaming new with purposes to match? Has it developed a reputation in the community? Unless members understand what their school stands for, a vital bond to hold them together will be missing. Although we usually do not use slogans like those of large corporations, we can develop a sense that helps each staff member feel that "We simply don't do that sort of thing" or "This is what we believe!"

Each person involved with the program needs to feel that he or she is part of an important program, that there is something that will outlast the present staff and membership. One of the arts of good management is to integrate the needs of the in-

WHAT WOULD YOU DO?

Mary Smith is fifty years old and has been a teacher in your school for ten years. She has always been an excellent teacher, and you have felt yourself fortunate to have her on your staff. Lately, however, you have the feeling that she is not offering as rich a program to the children as she has in the past, and you observe that more and more often she does not have control of a situation. You are beginning to wonder if you see the development expected for the children in her class. As the director, this problem is your responsibility. What procedure will you use to correct it?

dividuals with the common interests of the entire group. An interesting phenomenon is that the feeling becomes stronger when problems arise, such as a financial crisis that threatens the functioning of the program.

However, individuals may sometimes use their work for their own identification as a way of handling personal and family problems. They may involve themselves too closely with the school problems, thereby causing a conflict with the real goals of the school and destroying the delicate balance among the other staff members.

Two major factors appear to affect the happiness of any employee. The first is the desire of everyone to feel important and accomplished. The second is to feel secure and at ease with the job to be done. The director is a key person in helping each staff member gain the sense of being a functioning and contributing member of the group. Three different attitudes can be observed in the employees of an organization: (1) the job may be merely a means of earning money; (2) there may be satisfaction in doing good work and enjoying it on a daily basis because they find pleasure in using their skills; and (3) there is an understanding of why the job is important. On your staff you may have people who fit into each category; the important thing is to find ways they can work together as a team.

Team Building

Every program has a style about how its members interact: They may be one big happy family or one big chaotic family, or something in between. Whether the program has three people or thirty people, they still have to work together as a team to make the program run smoothly. Neugebauer (1997) presents a step-by-step guide for team building as follows: (1) establish goal, (2) clarify roles, (3) build supportive relationships, (4) encourage active participation, and (5) monitor team effectiveness.

All programs have to set achievable goals, that is, goals that are challenging yet attainable and that all can agree on. Once you have the goals in place, then each team member is assigned a role to achieve the goals. Team members need to have clearly defined responsibilities that are connected to the goals. The third aspect of team building deals with creating and developing supportive relationships among team members. Directors can structure activities and events to build support among members. For the team to work well, all members must be encouraged to actively participate. They should want to be a part of the team efforts. Finally, all teams need to be monitored for team effectiveness. Team building is not an easy thing to do, but when people are part of a team, the entire enterprise seems to run more smoothly.

STAFF MEETINGS

Thoughtfully planned staff meetings must be held at regular intervals if the members of your school are to work together with a sense of purpose and harmony and if they are to benefit from continuing professional growth and stimulation. The role of the director is to see that business gets done and that discussions are objective and professional. Someone other than the director may preside at staff meetings or there may be a leaderless group if it is appropriate for the structure of the school. When you plan the staff meeting, consider the following components:

- *Time.* Schedule meetings before, during, or after the workday as accommodates most staff members.
- *Frequency.* Schedule weekly, biweekly, or monthly meetings as needed.
- *Place.* Hold meetings at the center (teacher's lounge, hallway, or empty classroom), at a local restaurant, or at the home of a staff member.

- *Atmosphere.* Maintain a professional yet relaxed atmosphere, with a sense of openness and acceptance; provide refreshments (comfort food and food for energy, such as chocolate).
- *Printed agenda.* Agenda handouts show forethought and respect for the time of staff, and keeps you organized.

Group thinking is richer than individual thinking and the interplay of ideas stimulates creativity. Staff meetings can serve as a means to communicate ideas for planning, community contacts, and work sessions; to work out problems and disagreements; to keep up on current legislation and regulations; to review new research and publications; or to discuss individual children and their needs. The perceptive director will note special abilities and interests of staff members during meetings. These abilities and interests can be encouraged and developed. The discussion of personal problems or those of persons not in attendance is inappropriate and should be avoided.

Presenting Ideas

Another aspect of working with staff involves being able to present ideas in such a way as to develop new modes of operation. First evaluate your idea:

- Does it fill a need or correct a problem?
- Does it have a firm basis? Is it well thought out?
- Can you present it clearly and simply?
- Is it the best solution at this time?
- Will it be a threat if presented in its entirety?

When you have decided to go ahead with the presentation of an idea to your staff (or to the parents or the board), you might follow a procedure such as this:

1. Get the attention of the group or the key individuals.
2. Explain the idea or need and the potential benefits. Present the idea so that it will be as easy as possible for others to agree to. Remember that it is your idea; you have lived with it and mulled it over but others have not. Be prepared to present the whole picture with pertinent facts, but be concise.
3. Listen for understanding, for feelings, and for arguments. You have hit a block when you hear that nobody does it that way or that your staff has never done it that way. Why change?
4. State the agreed-on idea. It may help to request changes that facilitate the new idea for a trial period or with a small group first.
5. Implement the idea. Be sure everyone knows his or her responsibilities and any adjustments to be made.
6. Follow through. Do not drift back into old ways of doing things.
7. Evaluate. Assess the implementation of the idea after a stated period of time and in light of your expectations.
8. Modify if necessary. On the basis of evaluation, make a further decision concerning the permanence of the new procedure.

Facilitating Discussions

Presenting ideas is important at staff meetings but so is facilitating discussion. Most of us have attended meetings that involved simply a reading of facts or events to remember; however, staff meetings should be a forum for discussing and sharing ideas

■ ■ ■ ■ ■ ▬▬▬▬▬▬▬▬▬▬▬▬▬▬▬▬▬▬▬▬▬▬▬

CLASS DISCUSSION

List some possible subjects you would include on your agenda for a staff meeting. What are appropriate ideas to present at a staff meeting?

about how to better educate and care for the children and families in the program. Neugebauer (1997) offers suggestions for facilitating discussions during staff meetings. The first suggestion is to "plant proper expectations." If the staff members expect to be engaged and to participate in the discussion, they will attend the meetings with ideas and believe it is a worthwhile endeavor. The second suggestion is that you as the director keep your energy level high. If you present information or lead a discussion with enthusiasm, your excitement will be contagious, and the meetings will be more productive. To start and keep discussions progressing, ask open-ended questions. "How should we address the concern of...?" is more of a facilitator than "Do you think we should address...? More importantly, when suggestions are made, avoid excessive negativism. People are more willing to offer suggestions if their previous ideas have been given the entire group's attention and consideration. Encouraging good listening among the participants can facilitate attentiveness, and all options should be explored before an idea is rejected. These are only a few suggestions to help keep meetings flowing and open for all to feel a part of the solution to the concerns presented.

PROFESSIONAL DEVELOPMENT

In order for your staff to grow as professionals, they need to have opportunities to enhance and increase their skills and knowledge. There are many types of professional development activities. You should select the development events that are right for your program. Your staff may choose the national, state, or local conferences of the Association for the Education of Young Children (AEYC) or other early care and education professional organizations. If your program is part of a corporation, there may be regionwide training or workshops for staff to attend. If your program is a faith-based program, you may want your staff to attend the denomination workshops or training. Whatever the type of professional development you select for your staff, it should build on their strengths and provide information where it is lacking. There is not one right way to gain professional development. There are many methods and a few are suggested here.

1. A teacher resource room or area can be set up with books, journals, videotapes, and Internet access. You should allow time for the teachers to read and explore the available resources.

2. Mentoring or coaching of individual staff members is important in all programs. This can be done by the director or by an experienced teacher. The one-on-one attention is specific to a person and their class needs. There are several resources on coaching and mentoring available through professional organizations and a few are included in the references listed at the end of the chapter.

3. As mentioned earlier, part of staff meetings can be used for professional development. Staff members can read and discuss articles at the meeting, watch videotape segments then discuss them, and share "what works" in their classrooms.

4. The NAEYC Accreditation process is another way to improve the quality of care and education provided by your staff. There are self-study materials (the first step in the Accreditation process) available for you and your staff to observe and evaluate your program. This self-study process is a good way to measure your program's strengths and to determine areas that continue to need improvement.

5. Center workshops led by outside speakers are another way to enhance skills. One good use of resources involves planning a workshop with another center and splitting the cost. This lets your teachers hear about other programs as well. A joint workshop also promotes collaboration within the community, which is a positive feature for your program.

6. Workshops and conferences sponsored by professional organizations are productive for some. If they are members of the organization, your staff may receive cost reductions to attend conferences. These conferences are a great way to "recharge your batteries" and to motivate staff, especially if the center can afford to help pay for the conference.

7. Enrolling in a community college or university to complete a degree is a big step for many teachers. Directors should find ways to support and work with staff who are trying to finish degree programs. The center, children, families, and the staff member all benefit from the knowledge and training obtained through education courses.

No matter what type of professional development your staff is involved in, it should be specific to your program goals and mission statement, and it should serve to assist your staff in improving the care and education that they provide to the children in your center.

PARENTS AND OTHER VOLUNTEERS

When recruiting volunteers, you will want to look for physical and mental health. Volunteers must respect children and approach them in a positive manner. They should be able to take directions from you and the teachers and then use their own initiative within your guidelines. They must be willing to take whatever in-service training you provide, and they need to be reliable. It will be your responsibility to make these support people feel comfortable and secure in what they are doing. The staff orientation program, with appropriate modifications, will help them realize that they are making a real contribution and will give them enough information to be effective.

As we learn more about effective teaching methods and develop concern about the complicated society children must deal with, we find ourselves relying on parents and community volunteers to increase the quality of education. Because many children live in homes without male role models, fathers and other men are particularly valuable. These support persons can be an essential addition to the teaching team if careful planning is done.

First, establish the purpose for the volunteer program. How can bringing additional adults into your school increase the scope of services for children who need the guidance and stability of the same trained teachers every day? The volunteer cannot be a substitute for the teacher but can provide regularly scheduled supplementary services. What are the volunteer's duties? Consider your children and your program for answers. You may find that they can assist in these areas:

- Nonprofessional clerical work, preparation of materials, and housekeeping chores to help you and your staff spend more time with the children.

GROUP DISCUSSION

Consider the specific activities in which volunteers could participate at your center. Who would probably be most interested in each of the following categories?

Classrooms (sharing a talent, gardening)

Office duties (word processing, answering phone)

Materials preparation (flannel boards, classification games)

Housekeeping (laundering dress-up clothes, cleaning art supply area)

Supplies (scrounging materials, repairing equipment)

Setting up and maintaining a website

- Helping with field trips, or sharing talents, hobbies, and cultures to extend the experiences of the children or in working with other parents.
- Satisfying special needs of specific children, giving physical help to those with disabilities, providing one-to-one activities to correct deficiencies, or simply reading to or comforting a child.

Second, during the process of recruitment and orientation, assess the motivations and potential contributions of each volunteer and decide what responsibilities can be assigned. Even though it is not required in all states, you should incorporate a background check as a routine procedure for volunteers not associated with the center. Expect a firm commitment of time and a professional attitude toward the children, the families, and the school, with all behavior and information treated as confidential.

Because salaries are low and for other reasons, there are few men who teach in preschools. Volunteers, fathers, and others who are interested can add a valuable dimension to your program. However, one of the reasons men often are reluctant to become involved is the lack of respect they get. For example, one father with a degree in child development and an executive position with a major publishing company was particularly interested in reading some of their new books to his daughter's class. But whenever he arrived at the school, the director handed him a broom and asked him to sweep the patio, clean out the rabbit cage, or do a similar menial task. Other fathers have been appreciated because they share their professional skills with the children. For Halloween, an x-ray technician not only showed the children how skeletons looked but let them see the bones in their own hands when they held strong flashlights in their palms. And a custodial grandfather from Mexico who did

WHAT WOULD YOU DO?

A seventy-year-old volunteer from Volunteer America has been in the infant room for three months. She has done a good job and really enjoys interacting with the babies. This morning she picked up a bottle of regular formula to feed a baby that can only tolerate soy formula. The teacher noticed the mistake in time and stopped her before she gave the baby the wrong bottle. Afterward, the teacher came and talked to you and asked that you remove her from the infant room. What would you do?

not speak English became a minor celebrity after a Spanish-speaking teacher discovered that he had played in a mariachi band for many years. He took his guitar to the center every week and played while the children (and teachers) danced to his music. As one result, his three-year-old grandson, formerly somewhat of an outsider, became a special friend to his classmates.

Many examples can be cited of the positive effects on children when the men in their families are involved. They do not always have time to be available during school hours. There was great pride displayed by the son of a pediatrician and the son of a milk carrier when they told the other children that their dads had been the ones who had assembled the new climbing structure the previous weekend. In return for the volunteer services, you and your staff will reciprocate by expressing your appreciation for the work done, by accepting parents and volunteers as co-workers, and through some sort of public recognition or awards.

REFERENCES AND RESOURCES

Albecht, K. (2000). *The right fit: Recruiting, selecting, and orientating staff.* Washington, DC: National Association for the Education of Young Children.

Beaty, J. J. (2000). *Skills for preschool teachers.* Upper Saddle River: NJ: Merrill.

Bellm, D., Burton, A., Whitebook, M., Broatch, L., & Young, M. (2002). *Inside the pre-K classroom: A study of staffing and stability in state-funded prekindergarten programs.* Washington, DC: Center for Child Care Workforce.

Berl, P. S. (2004). Insights into teacher development—Part 1: The emergent teacher. *Child Care Information Exchange 155,* 8–12.

Howes, C., & Ritchie, S. (2002). *A matter of trust: Connecting teachers and learners in the early childhood classroom.* New York: Teachers College Press.

Hyson, M. (Ed.). (2003). *Preparing early childhood professionals: NAEYC's standards for programs.* Washington, DC: National Association for the Education of Young Children.

Neugebauer, R. (1997). *Does your team work? Ideas for bringing staff together.* Redmond, WA: Child Care Information Exchange.

Seligson, M., & MacPhee, M. (2001). *The relevance of self at work: Emotional intelligence and staff training.* Boston: Wellesley Centers for Women.

Struck, D., & Stratton, J. (1998). *Build a better staff: Hiring, evaluating and staff.* New York: Aspen.

Tertell, E. A., Klein, S. M., & Jewett, J. L. (1998). *When teachers reflect.* Washington, DC: National Association for the Education of Young Children.

Whitebook, M., & Bellm, D. (1996). Mentoring for early childhood teachers and providers: Building upon and extending tradition. *Young Children, 52*(1), 59–64.

Whitebook, M., & Bellm, D. (1999). *An action guide for child care center teachers and directors.* Washington, DC: Center for Child Care Workforce.

WEBSITE RESOURCES

National Association for Family Child Care: www.nafcc.org/accred
NAEYC Professional Development: www.naeyc.org/profdev
U.S. Department of Labor Child Care Workers: www.bls.gov/oco

EXAMPLE 6.1

EXAMPLE OF AN ORIENTATION CHECKLIST

Staff member name/position _____

Start date_____

Orientation dates_____

_____

Forms and documentation needed before employment

_____ Fingerprinting

_____ Child Abuse Index

_____ Medical forms/TB test results

_____ Transcripts

_____ Other

Staff member receives handbook

Discuss:

_____ School's purposes, goals, and mission statement

_____ Information about school ownership, history

_____ Organizational breakdown, policies

_____ List of staff, parents, directors

Job description

Procedural aspects

_____ Dealing with supplies and equipment

_____ Services and resources of the school, such as audiovisual aids

_____ Available community resources

_____ Emer7gency procedures, such as first aid and fire drills

_____ Introduction to forms and records system

_____ Restroom location, storage space, and personal break space

EXAMPLE 6.1 *(continued)*

Benefits explained to the employee and appropriate forms signed

_____ Health, dental, and life insurance

_____ Reduced child care fee

_____ Vacation time, sick leave, and personal time

_____ Compensation for overtime (if hourly employee)

_____ Membership in professional organizations

_____ Opportunities for professional development

I have received orientation on the information identified above.

Employee Signature _____   Date _____

I verify that the above employee has completed orientation for Child Care Center.

Director Signature _____   Date _____

STAFF ORIENTATION ISSUES

Name _____ Date _____

Objective: To use text knowledge to address staff orientation issues.

Directions: Consider these issues of new employees and write suggestions for how you could help them through the adjustments to their positions.

Learning center routines, such as snack and lunch for the children, opening or closing procedures

Learning about the children and families in their rooms

Getting to know the other staff

Learning supplies and materials inventory and how to make appropriate requisitions

CHAPTER SEVEN

Operating Systems

KEEPING RECORDS

As previously noted, certain records and forms are required by state and local regulatory agencies. Others may be expected by a sponsoring organization. Programs for research purposes have specialized requirements written into the original proposals. However, all types of centers keep records to justify tax and personnel benefit payments. These frequently change and it is a responsibility of the director to be aware of requirements and to make certain that they are adhered to.

The trend in business is to simplify or to eliminate record keeping as a cost-reducing measure because both time and space represent money. How will you organize the information flow before it drowns you? Records should be limited to those that can be kept up-to-date. The responsibility for maintaining them should be specified as part of the job description for a member of the support staff or an outside accounting service, if the director does not assume it. This includes eliminating obsolete material but retaining essential documents. Be sure that you have duplicate backup files for those on your computer. Keep the backup files in a secure location and make sure that designated individuals have access to them.

A filing classification system should be designed for quick retrieval. Long-term storage can be in a less convenient place but the time required for finding a paper or computer file should be three minutes or less. Organize your forms, correspondence, and other materials into categories that are appropriate for your center. As director, you may want some information close enough to reach while you are talking on the telephone. Some forms, such as those that tell who is authorized to pick up a child from the center, would probably be in the classroom for quick access by the teacher.

Originals of the center's lease or mortgage, fire insurance, and other documents with legal importance should be off the premises in a lockbox or vault. Copies should be in the office with information about the location of the originals.

Most of the records, forms, correspondence, and information materials should be in well-designed, heavy-duty file cabinets with easy rolling drawers. Sturdy file folders can be arranged alphabetically according to content, using broad generic headings. For example, you would put *taxes, property,* right behind *taxes, personnel.* Label folders with nouns, the names of things or topics, using familiar, simple, common words. Some categories will expand to require additional folders; *families, current forms,* for example, might have a folder for each family arranged alphabetically from Adams to Zelberg. You might even have folders in calendar sequence, for example, the newsletter. The important thing is to have your record keeping system efficient for your own use and logical enough that others can locate things. Much frustration can be avoided if your system is accurate and accessible.

worksheet

7.1

p. 119

Worksheet 7.1 encourages class members to bring in examples of records and forms, and to evaluate them as to their usefulness, clarity, strengths, and weaknesses. Examples 7.1 and 7.2 may also be used for this worksheet.

CENTER MANAGEMENT SYSTEMS

Will a computer be necessary to manage records and accounts? Many directors with complicated enrollment schedules and accounting systems, particularly those with public or agency funding, insist that they could not function without computerized record keeping. Other directors who use computer programs, either commercially produced or developed in their own centers, find that they are less efficient than traditional systems.

Directors not already familiar with computers can find information about them at professional conferences, from dealers who advertise in early childhood publications, or from their local computer stores. Like any other purchase made for the center, the acquisition of a computer system should be thought through carefully. What type of computer do you really need? Be realistic in identifying tasks that you want it to do. Who will set up the programs? Who will enter data to keep it current? Will you actually save money by finding a good dealer who will support you with service, training, and technical assistance? The price of the original hardware is minor compared with the cost in time and effort spent learning how to operate the computer, in converting paper records into electronic files, and in buying state-of-the-art software. Experts in the computer field warn that choosing the right computer from hundreds of major brands and the right software from an endless variety of packages and add-ons is a tough job that requires careful study. Each purchaser has different needs and desires, and there is no one right choice.

Child care management computer software should provide a data base system that allows flexibility in the variety of ways to print and access information. Each system has different options, from child and family information to bookkeeping to personnel information. Most management programs will perform the following functions: managing family and child data including medical and emergency contact information, accounts receivable, attendance tracking, food program monitoring, employee data monitoring, payroll, accounts payable and general ledgers, schedule planning, managing waiting lists, time clock monitoring, electronic fee collection, generating year-end tax statements for parents, and immunization tracking.

CLASS ACTIVITY

You will need to organize the records and other information materials essential to the operation of your center. List the headings and subheadings that would be used for appropriate files for your own program.

Benefits of software management programs include saving time and providing enhanced security, heightened accuracy, and increased efficiency. Many companies provide a demonstration version to try at your center. When you choose to purchase a computer, most companies will provide technical support and training on how to use the system. One way to access the potential software programs is by accessing company websites. Simply go to any search engine and type in "child care center software." You then can choose those that you want to investigate further. Another method is to visit commercial exhibits at professional conferences and talk to the company representatives.

FINANCIAL SYSTEMS

The whole field of financial systems is characterized by lack of agreement. It is too specialized for detailed treatment in this guidebook. Before directing an early childhood program, you should take a basic accounting class as part of a college degree program, through local adult education classes, as a seminar given by the small business administration or your sponsor, or even by correspondence or as a computer class. As part of the operating component of your center, you will continue to discover new ideas about financial systems and will continually seek to make yours more efficient and more accurate while reducing energy costs and stress.

Accounting

As the language of commerce, accounting is the way you keep track of how much money you take in, where it comes from, how much money you spend, and where it goes. Through the accounting procedures of your center, you have access to its business history, a summary of its operations, a statement of its financial condition, and a measurement of profits or losses.

There is a story that Sir Walter Raleigh, in attempting to compute the weight of smoke from a pipeful of tobacco, weighed the tobacco and then weighed the ashes after he had smoked it. The difference, he assumed, was the weight of the smoke. Some businesses do little more than this. They know how much they earned during a period of time, subtract the amount left, and presume that the operating expenses were the unaccounted for difference…gone up in smoke.

Systems vary widely—as widely as the types of programs and the preferences of their directors. Some centers employ experienced accountants with elaborate bookkeeping methodologies, some use computers with spreadsheets and other software designed for child care programs, and others have functioned for years with simple procedures that are easily mastered. Some directors do their own accounting,

■ ■ ■ ■ ■

CLASS DISCUSSION

Cite examples of good and bad procedures that you have heard about or have experienced concerning financial systems in early childhood centers.

---

some have full- or part-time office help, some depend on a parent or community volunteer, and others rely on accounting services that handle finances for many small businesses in the community. Centers affiliated with educational institutions or large agencies frequently have access to a central computerized accounting office. Franchised networks provide their own training and support services. Cooperative preschools have an elected treasurer, for example, one of the parents who handles tuition records and keeps the accounts. As a director, regardless of the system your center uses, you should be able to understand the language of accounting and make sure that you are businesslike in handling its financial affairs.

Years ago, one director who did her own bookkeeping for a large private preschool invested in an impressive maroon leatherette ledger. She asserts that when she kept the same records in an inexpensive notebook, parents often insisted that she was wrong. In the first two years of using the tremendous book, not one disagreed with her accounts. Similarly, another director believes that since she switched from handwritten to computer printout tuition statements, payments have been faster and delinquencies fewer. The appearance of professionalism is an important factor in the management of any business.

Accounting Terminology.   Following are some of the keywords used in bookkeeping. Familiarity with their meaning provides an essential introduction to accounting.

Accounts receivable. File of individual customer accounts (tuition or fees for your center) showing charges (debits) and payments (credits) with balance owed by each customer (family).

Accounts receivable schedule. End-of-the-month listing by customer of total amount owed, amount overdue, and amount currently due. It has two important functions: to show accounts to which attention should be given and to provide reconciliation between individual accounts receivable sheets and the ledger account.

Assets. Things of value owned, including cash, accounts receivable, land, buildings, equipment; the total worth of your center.

Balance sheet. Listing of all assets and all liabilities of your school or center on the date for which it is prepared.

Double entry bookkeeping. Traditional bookkeeping system in which each transaction requires two equal entries, one a debit and one a credit. At all times, the total debits equal the total credits—the "ins" and the "outs" must balance. The debits are on the left side of the account form and the credits are on the right side.

Journal. Book of original entry for each transaction; a daily and detailed account of each transaction. Includes cash received and its source, payments and their purpose, all salaries and wages with deductions, and similar transactions.

Liabilities. Debts, accounts, notes and mortgages payable, unpaid taxes, and wages. Your obligations to pay.

Net worth. Assets minus liabilities. The actual value of your center.

Petty cash fund. The sum of money kept on hand to take care of small payments.

Reconciliation of bank account. Procedure by which a bank balance in a given month is checked against the ledger account for cash in the bank. Deposits and checks drawn are listed and totaled if they do not yet appear on the bank statement, with the ledger balance adjusted to reconcile the two.

Trial balance. Procedure for totaling debit and credit balances of all ledger accounts to make sure they balance (equal each other). Taken at the end of the month, it serves as a check on the accuracy of the posting (writing down) in the ledger.

DESIGNING THE SYSTEM

For directors starting a new center, or considering modifications for the accounting practices of one already in operation, it is helpful to review the center's mission statement, goals, purposes, and funding sources. Is the center a private proprietary designed to be profitable? Is it a community agency with its main function the service provided to families and its operation designed as not-for-profit? Following are some issues to consider when designing a new center or modifying operations in an existing center: From where will the funds come? What method of payment will you accept (check, credit cards, automatic payroll deductions)? How will the funds be spent? Who will be responsible for the bookkeeping or computer programming? What support services will be provided? How large and complicated are the business aspects of the center? Whether your program is for ten children or two hundred, you must develop an accounting system formal enough to satisfy the Internal Revenue Service, licensing agencies, and sponsoring organizations. The accounting system should be kept current, with such clearly defined procedures and classifications that a new or substitute person could take it over.

One indication of a satisfactory accounting system comes with the auditing of your center's financial records at the end of the fiscal year. The simplest type of audit is a mere verification of the accounts, by a responsible person not financially connected with the center, that on the basis of banking and other records, on a certain date there was a specific balance in the account. At the other extreme is an audit that involves the engagement of a certified public accountant to check every transaction from the past twelve months to state that records are accurate with no evidence of fraud or misappropriation, and that the operating statement is accurate. Usually, the audit is somewhere in the middle range. It should be viewed as an evaluation process that may lead to suggestions that certain adjustments be made in the center's procedures, or it may contain evaluative comments.

Internal Controls

As a director, you are responsible for internal systems that safeguard receipts and disbursements. If several persons are responsible for handling money, perhaps by collecting tuition and purchasing supplies, large amounts can slip away without being recorded. You will be held accountable. Numbered duplicate (or triplicate) receipt books can be used with voided pages noted. Purchase orders can be required, with documentation that items requested were received. A petty cash fund to take care of small purchases can be used by individual teachers for classroom needs and should be handled by one person. The teachers might be given advance petty cash for making small purchases. They would present receipts to have the fund replenished. This method saves time and gives teachers a feeling of autonomy. It saves money because they can pick up "good buys" when they see them.

Different procedures are used in various types of centers. For example, checks for nonprofit incorporated programs usually require two signatures. Owner-directors of private proprietary programs would probably be the only ones to write checks or use credit cards but they should carefully document all personal money invested or withdrawn. Large centers will want a type of insurance called bonding to protect the treasurer or accountant and to safeguard the center's funds.

FUNDING SOURCES

Before you can spend money, you need to get it! How will your center be supported? Funding sources were a major variant for the programs investigated for Worksheet 2.1. Yours will probably depend on one or more of the following:

- Parent fees and tuition, which may include direct deposit, payment vouchers, or scholarships
- Public funds, such as federal, state, county, or city funds; school district taxes; other tax monies; or revenue bonds
- Philanthropic organizations, such as the United Way, the Jewish Federated Council, and others
- Foundations, including national, regional, or local organizations
- Corporations giving directly or creating foundations or employee groups
- Social, civic, or professional associations, for example, the Junior League, the Rotary club, the Association of American University Women, sororities, fraternities, and union or employee associations
- Individuals giving bequests and gifts

In addition to actual dollar amounts, you may have *in-kind* contributions. These include free use of classrooms, donated goods and supplies, professional services by attorneys, and similar noncash resources. Campus, church, corporate, and agency programs depend heavily on these contributions, and public sponsorship may require in-kind contributions from the community as a condition of funding.

As you determine funding sources for your program, particularly if it will be private proprietary, think about such factors as maximum use of your building. Will it be empty over the weekends? If so, would it be possible to sponsor a gym or dance class? Will you close at five or six or would there be an opportunity for evening care so that longer hours would serve the needs of parents. Creative innovations might increase income without a large increase in expenditures. Consider, however, whether these other sources of funding will be cost-effective and whether there will be misuse of the facilities or excess cleanup.

Fund-Raising

Fund-raising through traditional bake sales, rummage sales, theater parties, walk-a-thons, and similar group endeavors has a long history. A poster popular since its inception in 1979 has expressed the sentiment: "It'll be a great day when our child care centers have all the money they need and the Navy has to hold a bake sale to buy battleships." However, we should recognize that these fund-raising events become a goal-directed activity for the participants and have value for your program because parents and others benefit from working together. In the article "Keys to Success in Raising Funds," Neugebauer (2003b) presents suggestions to help with fund-raising. The first issue involves defining the purpose. Is the money for playground equipment, scholarships, field trips? Then you should set an attainable goal based on the number of families in your center and the event.

The fund-raising event should be fun and something to which all can contribute. Once you have decided on the event, publicize aggressively so all concerned and all who can help are aware of it. The biggest follow-up to fund-raising involves thanking the people who participated and those who contributed, either through letters of appreciation or in other ways to show that their support is needed and that you will hope to count on them in the future. Fund-raising can be fun and prosperous, but it does take hard work and commitment from many people. Think about the benefits of fund-raising.

Proposal or Grant Writing

For most sponsored centers, and to receive additional support for private programs, it is usually necessary to write a proposal to a funding source. Your first task is to search for an appropriate source for the assistance you need. Your community may have a funding resource center just for that purpose. Public libraries have current lists of foundations and agencies that can be screened for potential donors and also may have the Catalog of Federal Domestic Assistance Programs. If a center is affiliated with a large institution, someone at the institution will be designated to assist with finding sources for funding. Religious denominations and public service agencies also provide assistance. Federal and other agencies maintain lists for the mailing of Requests for Proposal (RFP) announcements. You may also consider asking local business, religious, and fraternal associations for regular sponsorship or intermittent donations of money or services, a letter of request would be informal but cover the points made in a major proposal.

■ ■ ■ ■ ■

CLASS DISCUSSION

List possible ways to raise funds through the activities of parents or support groups. How much money might they be expected to make? In terms of effort and energy, would this be cost-effective? In terms of fostering group spirit or public awareness, would the center benefit?

■ ■ ■ ■ ■

WHAT WOULD YOU DO?

As a fund-raiser, your program has a dinner and silent auction of donated items. The items are on display at the center the week before the auction, so all of the parents can participate even if they cannot come to the dinner. A local artist donated a rather obscure sculpture, which no one has bid on as of the final bid time. The local artist attends the fund-raiser dinner and notices that there are no bids on her donated art. How would you handle this?

As we keep repeating in this guidebook, there is no uniform way to do things in early childhood programs. Proposal writing is no exception. However, here are some suggestions from experienced proposal writers:

1. Know your mission statement and goals. Be able to express the unique aspects of your center. Establish a specific program need that you want to get funded. What are current local and national interests? What is the funding source particularly concerned with? Why should they give money to you?

2. Be able to estimate your budget and do not be modest. Include adequate staff salaries, including your own. Who will administer the funds? If you have an ongoing program, have you recently been given a satisfactory audit report? Show that you are responsible. Also show that you have supporters and backers. Include donated facilities and in-kind or other cash equivalent contributions.

3. Provide requested information. A proposal outline will often be sent to you in response to a letter or phone call for information. It usually includes a title page, agency forms, an abstract or abbreviated version of the proposal, and other items that require you to merely fill in the blanks. This is followed by a "what and why" section where you will include your statement of need, your purpose, your objectives, and the significance of what you plan to do. This problem statement is the essential rationale for your proposal. The practical portion will cover the "how" of your proposed project procedures, activities, collection and analysis of data if you include research, use of equipment and facilities, project management (Is this you?), evaluation and dissemination. This last item is important. After you have spent their money, how do you intend to let the world know about what you have done? Be prepared to tell "who" with a short resume of key personnel; do not be hesitant about asking persons with prestige value but do not forget to include those day-to-day workers. An organizational capability statement establishes your credibility, showing significant accomplishments and community support.

4. Be sure to have input from parents and others in the community. As you work out your proposal, specify roles and responsibilities of parents and other volunteers in policy making, planning, budgeting, program administration, and staff recruitment.

5. If appropriate, attach a sample menu and tell how federal and community food programs will be used. What facilities do you have for food service? How do you get professional nutritional advice?

6. What social services will be provided? How do they fit into your goals and objectives? What is the cost? Know your community resources!

7. Before you send the proposal off, ask yourself what impression it gives. Do you appear businesslike but frugal? A too-slick layout may turn off potential funding sources but the format should be attractive. Check and then check again to make sure that you have included everything that is asked for. Be sure you have followed directions. Include all signatures in the proper places. Finally, make the number of copies that were requested, including at least one to keep. Then mail or deliver it before the deadline.

8. Follow up to find out why the proposal was not accepted, if that occurs. This is an important evaluation mechanism to help with the next proposal you prepare, whether for this funding source or another. Analyze both the process and the rejected proposal and try again. If funding was granted, determine why you were successful and plan to maintain that level of accomplishment.

worksheet

7.2
p. 121

Worksheet 7.2 allows you to develop your ideas about writing grants.

REFERENCES AND RESOURCES

Block, J. (2000). *Fast fundraising facts for fame and fortune.* Albuquerque, NM: Jean Block Consulting.

Donohue, C. (2003). Transforming your computer from paperweight to management tool. *The Art of Leadership: Managing Early Childhood Organizations.* Redmond, WA: Child Care Information Exchange.

Herzer, L. (2004). Getting grant money: How to connect. *Child Care Information Exchange, 155,* 50–55.

Kalinowski, M. (2002). The special nature of management software. *Child Care Information Exchange, 140,* 79–84.

Levenson, S. (2002). *How to get grants and gifts for public schools.* Boston: Allyn & Bacon.

Neugebauer, R. (2003a). Getting organized: Fifty ideas for more effective use of your time. In B. Neugebauer & R. Neugebauer (Eds.), *The art of leadership: Managing early childhood organizations* (pp. 66–71). Redmond, WA: Child Care Information Exchange.

Neugebauer, R. (2003b). Keys to success in raising funds. In B. Neugebauer & R. Neugebauer (Eds.), *The art of leadership: Managing early childhood organizations* (pp. 156–158). Redmond, WA: Child Care Information Exchange.

Stephens, K. (2003). Where the bucks are: Sources for funds to grow your child care business. *The Art of Leadership: Managing Early Childhood Organizations.* Redmond, WA: Child Care Information Exchange.

WEBSITE RESOURCES

Fund-raising for child care centers
  Regal Greetings: www.regalgreeting.com
  Fund Raising Zone: www.fundraisingzone.com
Lake Shore: www.lakeshorelearning.com/links.grants

EXAMPLE 7.1

CHILD CARE CENTER ENROLLMENT
LICENSE NUMBER 123456789

CHILD'S NAME	BIRTH DATE	HOME ADDRESS	PARENT/ GUARDIAN NAME(S)	DAYTIME CONTACT INFORMATION	DATE ENROLLED

EXAMPLE 7.2

APPLICATION FOR CHILD CARE CENTER

Name (Last) First MI	Telephone
Address	Are you at least 18 years of age?
Social Security Number	Do you have a state driver's license?
Position Applying For	If hired, date you can start.

Education

Circle highest year completed: 10 11 12	Diploma?	Year of completion	City, state

Name and address of college or university	Major/subject	Diploma degree or certificate	Date completed

Previous Employment

Job title and duties	Name and address of employer	Telephone number	Dates employed

References

Name	Address	Telephone number	Relationship to you

I certify that the above information is correct and I give permission for any necessary verification.

Signature_____ Date_____

KEEPING RECORDS

Name _____ Date _____

Objective: To critique existing forms for usefulness in your program.

Directions: If they are available to you, bring examples of forms for record keeping (employment applications and contracts, physical examination forms, time sheets and personal information sheets, admission applications, health histories, physical examination reports, medical emergency consent forms, excursion permits, daily attendance reports, accident report forms) to class to discuss their usefulness or use the two examples (Examples 7.1 and 7.2) provided. Evaluate them by answering the following questions.

1. **How useful do you believe the form is?**

2. **Is the form clear as to the information requested?**

3. **List the strengths of the form.**

4. **List weaknesses of the form. How would you improve the form?**

PROPOSAL OR GRANT WRITING

Name _____ Date _____

Objective: To gain an understanding of the proposal writing process.

Directions: Write information for a grant.

Statement of need that includes your purpose

Objectives and the significance of what you plan to do

The "how" includes your proposed project procedures

Activities

Collection and analysis of data (if you include research)

Use of equipment and facilities

Project management

Evaluation and dissemination

CHAPTER EIGHT

Budget Considerations

A *budget* is an itemized estimate of anticipated income and expenditures to cover a definite period of time. Although it would actually be set up as part of the planning phase of the management process, the need to maintain constant surveillance over income and expenses comes during the operating phase. Previous worksheets provide information necessary for you to prepare the budget for your center.

Budgets cannot be adopted at the beginning of the year and ignored until the end. The concept of a continuous budget means that you will evaluate it at staff and board meetings, will maintain a file to remind yourself during the next year of items to consider or change, and will schedule its preparation to allow ample review time. At regular intervals, perhaps monthly, you will prepare a budget review analysis to show how well your center is keeping within its planned expenditures or whether there is overspending on any items.

The budget pulls together all of the systems involved in the center and serves as the culmination of them. You will find that a dynamic, continuing budget will

1. Focus attention on past activities in relation to those you plan.
2. Necessitate foreseeing expenditures and anticipating revenues.
3. Coordinate staff efforts in planning and in using supplies and for making purchases.
4. Establish a system of management controls.
5. Serve as an information system for those involved in the program.

ESTIMATING EXPENDITURES

The following items are usually included in center budgets. Note that almost all items would be included in the start-up budget for a new center and also for the annual budget of an ongoing program, but the amounts to be allocated would differ and should be indicated in reports.

1. Personnel

   Salaries of regular personnel (administrative, office, teaching, custodial, other)

   Raises and bonus pay (percentages or set amounts)

   Substitutes (for sick leave, jury duty, training, personal time off, compensatory time replacement)

   Special teachers for swimming, dance, language, and so on

   Benefits (Social Security/FICA, Workers' Compensation, unemployment insurance, medical/dental/vision insurance, disability insurance, dependent care)

   Reimbursed expenses (conference attendance, pre- or in-service training)

2. Consultant and Contract Services

   Visiting nurse, other medical or mental health advisers

   Specialists for pre- or in-service training

   Bookkeeping or tax preparation services, auditor

   Computer software management/website

   Other regular supplements to center staff

3. Physical Facilities

   Rent or mortgage payments

   Maintenance, renovation, repair, general upkeep

   Telephone, Internet, electricity, gas, fuel oil, water, garbage

4. Children's Program Supplies and Equipment

   Outdoor equipment (climbing structure, wheel toys, sand, etc.)

   Classroom equipment and furnishings (tables, chairs, blocks, etc.)

   Consumable supplies (paper, crayons, etc.)

   Animals (feed, cages, replacements)

5. Equipment and Supplies for Other Areas

   Office equipment (desks, files, computers, etc.; may buy or lease)

   Office consumable supplies (paper, business cards, record forms)

   Isolation areas for sick children (include adult chair, special toys)

   Family and staff lounge (might include curriculum preparation space, teacher resources)

   Food preparation and service facilities

   Security systems (alarms, sign in and out)

6. Taxes, License, Accreditation Fees

   Business license, charitable organization permit, similar costs

   Tax on profits if not exempt

   Accreditation fees and renewals to NAEYC or other professional organizations

   Zoning variance, building inspections, other start-up expenses

   (Note that some taxes are included under personnel benefits.)

7. Insurance

   Owners or tenants fire insurance with riders for vandalism and other risks

   Vehicle insurance

   Accident and liability insurance to cover enrolled children, staff, and visitors to the premises

   Malpractice insurance

   Fidelity bonding insurance to protect custodians of funds against loss, theft, or mismanagement

8. Family and Community Relations

   Advertising, brochures, website, e-mail maintenance, other media expenditures or promotional materials

   Newsletters, published reports and similar printed items

   Video/Internet subscription for parents to view the program

9. Transportation

   Purchase, lease, or contract for transporting children

   Field trips, medical emergencies, child transportation (state regulations met)

   Reimbursement of staff for mileage and insurance riders on private vehicles

10. Miscellaneous Expenses

    Personnel items (birthday cards, certificates of appreciation, etc.)

    Medical (first aid) supplies and equipment

    Diapering supplies for infant–toddler classes

    Membership dues for professional associations (center and staff)

    Journals, books, magazines, videotapes to be used by adults in center

    Bank charges, lockbox or vault, post office box, answering service

What other expenses would you anticipate for the center?

BREAK-EVEN ANALYSIS

Many concepts from the field of administration emphasize complicated financial control through programs bearing names such as cost utility or "benefit-cost" or Planned Programming Budgeting System (PPBS). These involve a determination of goals and objectives, consideration of various ways goals and objectives can be met, a highly technical and expensive analysis of various alternatives, and a selection of the most appropriate ways to allocate funds to reach these objectives. If yours will be a publicly funded program, you may be expected to follow such a system and you will be given professional help with it.

Decision theories from business management also deal with the budget process. Using information you have gathered about funding sources and probable expenditures, your ongoing control over finances in your center might adapt one of these, called the *break-even analysis.* It is based on three assumptions.

1. Some costs (your rent or mortgage payment, for example) are fixed regardless of the number of income units (enrolled fee-paying children).
2. Other costs increase linearly with increasing volume (more teachers need to be hired if you have larger enrollment).
3. Income per unit is constant regardless of volume (the fee paid for each child does not change whether your center is full or has vacancies).

The problem dealt with under a break-even analysis, therefore, is to find out how many income units (children) should be enrolled to maximize the fixed costs so that your center takes in as much money as it spends. What costs might be cut? Distinguish between wants and needs, keeping your standards appropriate to your goals. Just as you determined both minimally acceptable and desirable qualifications on the worksheet for personnel policies, so will you distinguish between wants and needs for all facets of the program. Would it be possible to raise tuition or would added fees simply cause a loss of income units and make the situation worse? This is a complicated process, one that is easier if your computer software program enables you to work out a variety of scenarios, but it deserves consideration as you begin budgeting for your individual center. This approach will involve weighing priorities and finding alternative methods of accomplishing your objectives so that the budget becomes not simply an instrument of planning but a valuable method of control during the operating phase of administration.

worksheet **8.1** *p. 133*

Summary of the Budget Process

As you begin setting up a budget for your own real or simulated center on Worksheet 8.1, these are the steps that need to be taken. Remember, if yours is a computerized office, a program designed for your specific style of operation simplifies this process.

1. Review previous worksheets and other materials to clarify what services your center will offer, its funding sources, and its purposes and goals.

2. If yours is an operating facility, estimate replacement costs for supplies and equipment. For a new program, remember to include renovation or construction needed to bring the building up to requirements, utility deposits and hook-ups, legal assistance, public relations activities, and preopening operating expenses that include salaries for a specified period of time.

3. Determine your anticipated income. For tuition calculations, will you charge by the week or the month? Will it be an expected expense of the parents to pay or be faced with a late fee penalty? A new center will probably have much less than full-capacity enrollment, perhaps only 60 to 70 percent for the first year; an operating center should be budgeted at 90 to 95 percent to allow for unfilled vacancies, unpaid tuition,

■ ■ ■ ■ ■ ▬

WHAT WOULD YOU DO?

In calculating your break-even budget you have $750 profit. However, your program is non-profit. Where would you put the $750 to be the most beneficial for the center? Some possibilities are classroom supplies and materials, professional development for staff, or a one-time bonus. How do you decide? Who do you include in the decision-making process?

discounts for additional children from the same family, and other factors beyond your control.

4. Using a variety of sources and following either the list of estimated expenses or a budget outline required by your licensing or sponsoring agency, summarize the projected amount each item will cost. (For example, under consumable supplies for classroom use, you will estimate how much construction paper, glue, and crayons will be needed. Only the total will be written on the budget. However, it is usually wise to include these calculations with the budget statement or to have them available if the amounts are questioned.) If you are not using a computer program, one way to present the budget is to list expenditure items on the left side of the page. The right side will then have three columns, the first for an item by item total (such as the amount for consumables) and the second for a total of all items under that category (which would include children's program supplies and equipment under our listing). The third column would be used for the total of all major categories, the sum of all estimated expenses. Matching columns would have been used for income if there were several sources.

5. To find out if your program will operate at a profit or at a loss, subtract the smaller total from the larger one. If income is larger than the estimated expenditures, you have a profit or positive balance. If your estimated costs are going to be higher than your anticipated income, you are operating at a loss. Consider factors in the break-even analysis and try to bring the budget into balance.

For Worksheet 8.1, consider a start-up or operating budget. You can use the template provided or complete one specific to your type of program. Example 8.1 may be of assistance in planning your budget.

INTERPRETING YOUR CENTER TO THE PUBLIC

There will be many occasions when you will want to present information about your school in a professional way. You will want to explain your program's mission statement, goals, and purposes and you will want to anticipate questions and provide answers. As you think about this aspect of operating your center, determine what you want to accomplish. Are you trying to build enrollment? Are you maintaining your image as an excellent community resource, not necessarily directing your efforts toward new applicants at this time but simply maintaining your visibility? Have you changed direction or location or sponsorship and want to tell the public?

As we consider interpreting the center to the public, we must also recognize that there is such a thing as negative publicity. How would you handle something that potentially could harm your center? Informational systems developed in the corporate world, often called issues management, provide strategies for regular public relations as well as procedures for potential problem events. Develop some type of press kit, with up-to-date information about your center, for anyone inquiring about it. Determine who will meet media people or write press releases. That individual should know both your center and basic media techniques. Keep the public aware of the good job you are doing as part of an ongoing system. Do not wait for a crisis. You can use a wide variety of methods to market your program, including these:

- Paid advertisements in newspapers, telephone directories, local parenting publications
- Postcards or brochures
- Posters in shopping centers and libraries
- Participation in the NAEYC Week of the Young Child activities
- Participation in professional organizations
- Volunteering the building as a site for community meetings
- Flyers in pediatricians' offices, the Chamber of Commerce, and so on.
- News stories in community papers; announcements of events
- Director or staff participation in community affairs
- Public access television or community service spot announcements
- Word-of-mouth through satisfied parents and contented staff talking with others about how great you are.
- Website information about your program

What will work in your community? What will it cost? Will the publicity for your program enhance the image of education and care of young children?

Brochures

One widely used method of communication is the brochure. Its effectiveness will depend on the thought and care put into composing it. Perhaps you will be able to use the talents of a clever staff member or parent. Consider using children's artwork or photographs with written permission. Investigate computer software programs designed for desktop publishing. Considerations when designing a brochure include these:

- The format must be appealing enough to make people want to read it. It should be interesting and have a pleasant tone.
- The type should be varied for interest and there should be a large amount of empty space and a minimum number of words.
- The spacing should be arranged to lead the eye from one point to another.
- The size should be convenient for mailing and for picking up to take home.
- The paper should be heavy enough to have a good "feel" and to take the print, strong enough not to tear or bend readily but light enough to take minimum postage.
- Consider legal size (8-½ × 14 inches) heavy paper folded into fourths, printed on both sides with one end panel for addressing to avoid envelope costs.

The cost of preparation will involve paper, folding, cutting of irregular shapes, color choice, illustrations, and distribution. Expenses will also depend on whether it is done commercially or at your school with the photocopier. Your price per copy will almost always be less if a large number are run off at one time but a large stock that becomes outdated is not economical.

The content of a brochure should include the following:

- Name of school, address, phone numbers, e-mail, contact person
- Type of school, sponsorship or other identification (some states require license numbers on all publications)
- Hours and days in session, including vacation and holidays
- Ages of children served, a nondiscrimination clause and any restrictions
- Tuition and other fees
- Briefly stated purpose, mission statement, and goals (an indication of the value to parents and children)
- Professional affiliations

Websites

A method of marketing that is growing in popularity is a program website. The website journey should start with your Internet service provider to set up a domain name and website storage. In order to build websites you can attend workshops sponsored by community agencies or from your Internet provider. Also, some computer software programs provide templates for web page design. There are websites available to help you build your site and advertise your center. Websites available in the references and resources section at the end of this chapter might serve as examples to get you started. You can also check those advertising in the phone book or computer magazines.

To develop your website you would use the same basic information needed for a brochure, but you can add color, pictures, and animation to liven up the information. Some tips for website design include the following.

1. On the home page place the basic contact information.
2. Make the page sizes regular at 8-½ × 11 inches, to limit the amount of scrolling up and down on the page.
3. Drop-down boxes or a table of contents may include the following:

   a. Mission
   b. Maps or directions (link to Mapquest or other map site)
   c. Services (ages and programs)
   d. Hours and calendar
   e. Links to other sites, (e.g., licensing regulations in your state, local resource and referral, NAEYC and your local affiliate)
4. Make the background printable without colors or detailed graphics to encourage the users to print out the information.

worksheet
8.2
p. 133

Worksheet 8.2 and Alternate Worksheet 8.2 will assist you in developing your ideas about how to design a brochure or website for your program.

REFERENCES AND RESOURCES

A to Z: The early childhood educator's guide to the internet. (1997). Washington, DC: ERIC Publications. www.eric.ed.gov

Brower, M. R., & Sull, T. M. (2003). Five fundamentals of financial health—Guidelines for building financial strength. *Child Care Information Exchange, 149,* 7–10.

Dugan, A. (Ed.). (1998). *Franchising 101: The complete guide to evaluating, buying and growing your franchise business.* Chicago: Upstart.

Edwards, P., & Edwards, S. (1998). *Getting business to come to you.* New York: Penguin Putnam.

Gross, M., & Warshauer, W. (1995). *Financial and accounting guide for nonprofit organizations.* New York: Wiley.

Hewes, D. W. (2003). When shaming fingers point. In B. Neugebauer & R. Neugebauer (Eds.), *The art of leadership: Managing early childhood organizations* (pp. 355–357). Redmond, WA: Child Care Information Exchange.

Neugebauer, R. (1996). *On target marketing: Promotion strategies for child care centers.* Redmond, WA: Child Care Information Exchange.

Neugebauer, R. (2003). Guidelines for fine tuning your salary schedule. In B. Neugebauer & R. Neugebauer (Eds.), *The art of leadership: Managing early childhood organizations* (pp. 132–138). Redmond, WA: Child Care Information Exchange.

Penkert, K. S. (1998). *Marketing to managed care organizations.* Washington, DC: Child Welfare League of America.

Popcorn, F., & Marigold, L. (2000). *EVEolution: The eight truths of marketing to women.* New York: Hyperion.

Potts, S., & Kopak M. (2003). *Teach yourself web service in 24 hours.* Indianapolis, IN: SAMS.

Sklar, H., Mykyta, L., & Wefald, S. (2002). *Raise the floor: Wages and policies that work for all of us.* New York: South End Press.

Smith, B., & Rebak, A. (2002). *Creating web pages for dummies.* New York: Wiley.

Tiger, F. (1995). The art of the brochure. *Child Care Information Exchange, 102,* 24–29.

U.S. Small Business Administration. (2001). *The small business resource guide: What you need to know about taxes and other topics.* Washington, DC: Department of the Treasury, Internal Revenue Service.

Zeece, P. D. (2003). And away we grow! A five phase model for growing a child care business. In B. Neugebauer & R. Neugebauer (Eds.), *The art of leadership: Managing early childhood organizations* (pp. 72–75). Redmond, WA: Child Care Information Exchange.

WEBSITE RESOURCES

Budget: www.wccip.org/group_budget
Child Welfare League of America: www.cwla.org
Child Care Resource Center: www.ccrcinc.org
Insurance Forest T. Jones & Co., Inc., Website: www.ftj.com
Marketing Ideas
   www.uri.edu/ce/faceit/hdc2
   www.co.dakota.mn.us/child_care/marketing_ideas
   http://childcarefriends.com/marketing
U.S. Postal Service "Simple Formulas":   www.usps.com/directmail
U.S. Small Business Administration: www.smallbusiness.com

EXAMPLE 8.1

CHILD CARE CENTER BUDGET

Income	
Tuition	
Infants (6 × $185 × 51)	$ 56,610
Toddlers (10 × $160 × 51)	81,600
Preschoolers (50 × $150 × 51)	382,500
Total Gross Tuition	**$520,710**
Discounts	
Vacancy (3%)	
Sibling discounts	
Total Discounts	*<$15,621>*
Other Income	
Application fees (24 × $25)	$600
Total Income	**$505,689**
Expenses	
Personnel	
Director	$ 31,000
Master teachers (5)	140,000
Teachers (5)	101,000
Assistants (8 part time)	46,800
Substitutes	2,000
Cook	8,500
Custodian (1/4 time)	6,000
Secretary	9,000
FICA, unemployment, Workers'	62,589
Compensation, and insurance	
Total Personnel	**$406,889**
Other Expenses	
Rent	$ 30,000
Utilities, telephone, Internet	17,500
Food	36,000
Professional development	1,750
Teacher's petty cash	550
Class equipment/supplies	5,300
Office supplies	1,200
Custodial supplies	500
Marketing	900
Consultant fees	1,000
Insurance	3,600
License	500
Total Nonpersonnel	**$ 98,800**
Total Expenses	**$505,689**

CENTER BUDGET

Name _____ Date _____

Objective: To gain experience in producing a budget for your program.

Directions: In a format of your choice (or the example provided), develop the budget for your center. Use these pages for preliminary notes. You can choose to do A or B.

A. Start-Up Budget. There will be no tuition income. Funds will come from a grant, from sponsors, through a loan, or from some other source. If yours is a program already in operation, assume that you are setting up its duplicate or research the actual start-up process of its origin.

B. Operating Budget. Develop an annual budget for your center. Indicate the number of children to be served, their age categories (e.g., fifteen infants), and both the hours per day you will be open and the portion of the year. Specify the number of teachers and assistants.

Some suggested estimates to help in the budget process (alter to fit your own location)

70% personnel
10% facility/utilities
5% equipment
2–3% supplies
2–3% food
9–10% miscellaneous

Salary Ranges
Directors $25,000–$40,000
Teachers $7–$11 per hour
Assistant teachers $6–$7 per hour

Income
Tuition
Infants
Toddlers
Preschoolers
Total Gross Tuition

Discounts
Vacancy (3%)
Sibling discounts
Total Discounts

Other Income

Application Fees

Other

Total Other Income

Total Income

Expenses

Personnel

Director

Master teachers

Teachers

Assistants

Substitutes

Cook

Custodian

Secretary

FICA, Workers' Compensation, unemployment and insurance (~18%)

Total Personnel

Other Expenses

Rent

Utilities, telephone, Internet

Maintenance

Food

Office supplies

Custodial supplies

Classroom equipment and supplies

Professional development

Advertising

Consultant fees

Insurance

Licenses

Teachers' petty cash

Miscellaneous

Total Nonpersonnel

Total Expenses

THE BROCHURE

Name _____ Date _____

Objective: To develop skills to produce a brochure to market your program.

Directions: Develop a sample brochure. Use this worksheet to develop ideas for the brochure.

Contact information (name, address, phone numbers, website/URL)

Directions to center

Description of program

Sponsorship of program

Children served and enrollment procedures

Licensing number/accreditation

Operating hours/days/and so on

Benefits/specials of the program

Consider color/graphics/space usage

THE WEBSITE

Name _____ Date _____

Objective: To develop skills to produce a website to market your program.

Directions: Design the web page for your program and turn it in on a disk. This can be done using computer software programs or by using the Power-Point program, with each slide representing a page of your website. Use this worksheet to develop ideas for the website.

Contact information (name, address, phone numbers, website/URL)

Map to center (create link to map)

Description of program

Sponsorship of program

Children served and enrollment procedures

Licensing number/accreditation

Operating hours/days/holidays

Benefits/specials of the program

Consider color/graphics/space usage/layout

CHAPTER NINE

The Physical Environment

CHAPTER OUTLINE

FACILITY CONSIDERATIONS

CURRICULUM CONSIDERATIONS

PLAYGROUND

MAINTENANCE

In order to carry out the aims of your program, it is necessary to consider the impact of the physical environment. Although the educational value of the center is affected by the capabilities of the staff, nothing can fully compensate for a dearth of equipment and materials or for poorly planned buildings. An inefficient plan makes supervision difficult and more expensive. The work/play curriculum of the children will depend on their surroundings, and the utilization of staff functions are often determined by the arrangements of indoor and outdoor areas.

What does an adequate facility consist of? Some parent participation nursery schools have operated for years in public parks with no real classroom space. Since 1856, when the Schurz home was used for America's first kindergarten class, the number of schools in converted or improvised residences has been beyond estimating. Small store buildings or office courts, church school rooms or new condominium complexes, community recreation buildings or any other spaces with adequate room indoors and out are worth investigating.

For children who spend a great portion of their lives in centers, it is becoming imperative that their surroundings provide a developmental environment. If you can help make the choice, try to visualize its possibilities and then call in professional guidance to estimate the costs of bringing the site up to legal standards. How is the wiring? What will plumbing cost? Will it pass fire inspection? And, of course, will it really satisfy your needs and those of the children and their families?

Perhaps you will build a new facility. This will mean a substantial investment even if you are creative in your use of materials, but considered over the life of the building it will amortize to a more reasonable amount. A well-designed and effective early childhood center is a joint undertaking with an understanding architect. The developmental perspective will need to be established by those who work with groups of young children and can visualize traffic patterns, supervision requirements, and other considerations.

Whether your facility is new or old, your planning will be determined by your mission statement, goals, and purpose. Yours may be a building that is essentially formal and directive, a no-nonsense sort of place, or it may promote a feeling of casual freedom. The spacial arrangement will control such important factors as the adequacy of supervision for individuals and groups, the number and types of activities that can be provided, the accessibility of various areas, and the traffic patterns. The arrangement will also determine the comfort and efficiency of the staff.

FACILITY CONSIDERATIONS

Following is a discussion of some areas to consider in planning your early childhood center. However, not all of the areas mentioned will be needed or will fit into your budget allowances.

The entire facility should meet the current Americans with Disabilities Act codes in all areas of the center. The entrance should be easy to operate and appropriate in width for someone in a wheelchair or with a walker. The restrooms need to be accessible to all with special needs. The playground should have material that allows a child or adult in a wheelchair or using a walker to access it and some of the equipment should be low enough to facilitate participation by these individuals. Classrooms need to be on one level to allow for special equipment, and there needs to be enough space between pieces of furniture for mobility.

Parking needs to be accessible to the building and ample enough to facilitate staff parking as well as drop offs and pick ups. The number of spaces depends on your enrollment and staff, but you should be able to park five family cars in the lot at any one time. The parking spaces need to be in a safe location so your staff feels comfortable in the lot in early mornings or late afternoons.

Your entrance should be warm, friendly, and inviting. There should be a space for a parent bulletin board for licensing information and other important material for families. The entrance should be large enough for parents, children, and supervising staff members to accommodate arrival and departure routines.

The administration area should have adequate office space with comfortable desks and chairs. It should provide privacy for conferences with parents or staff. The staff lounge should be conducive to staff relaxation, with things such as adult-size chairs, a refrigerator, and a microwave for staff use, as well as adequate provision for storage of personal belongings. You will want an area for preparation of educational materials with a copier, a paper cutter, and other supplies. Another consideration is space for meeting with groups of teachers or parents.

In your kitchen the first concern should be sanitation. The floors should be able to be easily cleaned and the preparation and cooking surfaces durable and easily sanitized. There needs to be adequate storage, refrigeration, cooking, and cleaning spaces. Most states have requirements for kitchen equipment and regulations for the type of services offered from a full kitchen to a receiving kitchen. If children bring their lunches, there must to be an appropriate storage facility, either refrigeration or clean surfaces.

If your center conducts a full-day program, the children will need accommodations for sleeping and resting. Provisions include a quiet, restful atmosphere with adequate ventilation and adequate space between children's mats for health and safety reasons.

Another area of concern in all child care programs involves storage. You are required to have storage areas for cots or mats as well as for children's personal belongings (cubbies). There should be adequate storage for maintenance and cleaning supplies. You might want to consider where you will store holiday decorations, curriculum/program materials, and equipment. All of these items need clean, safe, uncluttered storage that does not take away space from the children.

Toilets are a necessary part of any program. There are several things to consider when designing or redesigning the toileting area. Restrooms must be easily accessible from the classrooms and the playground. The facilities need to be the appropriate size and height for young children, and there needs to be enough toilets and sinks for the number of children enrolled. Most states have requirements, for example, one toilet and one sink for every fifteen children. Don't forget the adult restrooms, they should be of appropriate size and facilitate privacy.

Classrooms need to be large enough for the number of children enrolled but not so big that the children feel lost. The classrooms should be painted with a calming background color. Neutrals or pastels are best. They need to contain both soft (carpets and pillows) and hard (linoleum floors) areas for a variety of activities, and the arrangements should provide interest centers. We provide additional suggestions for materials in the interest centers a little later in the chapter.

The playground must be safe and include an adequate fence with a childproof gate latch. It should be designed to facilitate easy supervision. All states have requirements for outside space and use. The general rule is seventy-five square feet of space per child. There also should be a sheltered area for rainy days with enough space for both sun and shade events. The playground should have a variety of surfaces to allow for different activities to take place at the same time. Another thing that is often forgotten on a playground is access to a drinking fountain. Children get hot and need water when they are on the playground, so you should have drinking fountains or find alternative ways to provide the children with water. Can you think of other areas to include in your program and what issues need to be considered with those?

The next issue to consider is selection and arrangement of equipment and materials. Remember that your budget must cover equipment for administration, food preparation, sleeping accommodations for full-day programs, a library and adult lounge, as well as equipment for the children's program. There should be a close relationship between equipment and curriculum objectives. The absence of adequate equipment or materials will inhibit the effectiveness of the learning experience. However, resourcefulness and imagination are more important than money. You can show ecological awareness by recycling otherwise discarded items.

As you review equipment lists and catalogs, ask yourself what each piece of equipment has to offer. Does it duplicate other items? If you decide that an item will be a valuable asset, ask yourself if you can afford to buy it? Is it possible or worthwhile to make it? Is it designed to satisfy the needs of children or to appeal to adults? What are you willing to pay for high quality? What may be the hidden costs of low quality? Where can you reduce costs?

Remember that the value of the play space depends on its organization as well as its content. While you are considering traffic patterns, remember that a free-flow program or zone control, with staff stationed in different areas and children going from one to another, will be the most efficient. Children can spend more time *doing* and less time *waiting.* It will also reduce problem behaviors and make your staff time more effective.

Some children will be active and noisy, whereas others will be passive and quiet. Everybody requires time for quiet contemplation, and small children are especially appreciative of isolated spaces, such as large concrete pipes and cardboard cartons. It is easy to ignore these unobtrusive children when planning for the group.

CURRICULUM CONSIDERATIONS

Now that you have ideas concerning your own needs, here is a list of questions to help you evaluate the possibilities of the indoor and outdoor environment:

- Does the environment allow freedom yet achieve self-discipline?
- Is the space versatile and flexible, allowing for easy and frequent innovation and improvement?
- Are learning materials easily available and displayed to invite use?
- Is there a variety of activities available, for example, running, climbing, crawling, riding wheel toys, digging, water play, painting, block building?
- Is much of the equipment abstract or open to facilitate self-initiated play?
- Have you included varied textures and spaces made of sturdy materials so that children can use them without concern of breakage?
- If carpet is used, are there adequate areas elsewhere for messy or wet play?
- Are facilities child oriented and child size to foster independence and initiative?
- Does the facility enable the teachers to really teach and not police?
- Does the facility inspire, please, and satisfy its occupants?
- Is there provision for out-of-sight storage of materials children are not supposed to use?
- Is it possible to have adult observation space that does not disturb the children's activities?

NAEYC Accreditation Guidelines

The NAEYC *Accreditation Criteria and Procedures* manual (1998) presents elements of high-quality programs for young children that should be considered in designing your program. The components include interactions, modifications for children with special needs, schedule, and developmentally appropriate material for all ages.

The first element addressed involves interactions among staff and children. This includes staff and children interacting frequently during the day, staff being available and responsive to children, and staff treating all children with respect. The second criterion involves curriculum modifications for children with special needs. The indoor and outdoor environments should be accessible to all children. The schedule and the curriculum materials need to be modified for each child. There should also be individualized education plans for all children three years old and older who need special services and accommodations, and those services need to be offered in the regular classroom as appropriate for each child. The schedule needs to include a balance of quiet time and activity throughout the day. There should also be opportunities for small-group, large-group, and individualized play each day, and a balance of teacher-directed and child-initiated activities.

CHECKLIST FOR CENTERS/AREAS IN PRESCHOOL CLASSROOMS

ART AREA

Paper (construction paper, recycled computer/photocopying paper, newsprint, finger-paint paper, butcher paper, tissue paper, foil, cardboard)

Paper plates, paper grocery bags

Catalogs and magazines (with pictures reflecting the children and families in your program)

Painting and printing materials (tempera paints, watercolor paints, finger paints)

Paintbrushes and easels, smocks or paint shirts

Modeling materials (moist clay, play-dough, plaster of paris)

Modeling accessories (rolling pins, cookie cutters, plastic knives)

Collage materials (cardboard tubes, wood pieces, cloth, felt, scraps)

Drawing and cutting materials (crayons, colored pencils, markers, chalk, scissors)

BLOCK AREA

Large hollow blocks, ramps, boards

Unit blocks (as many shapes and sizes as possible)

Small blocks (multicolored or plain)

Sheets, blankets, tarps, tents

Rope and pulleys

Interlocking blocks and boards

Toy dump trucks, pickup trucks, cars

Boxes, cartons, baskets, cans, buckets, crates, picnic baskets

Small vehicles, people, animals

Multiracial dollhouse people, dollhouse furniture

Wooden, rubber, or plastic animals

BOOK/LANGUAGE AREA

Books written in children's home languages

Books depicting a variety of racial, ethnic, and cultural groups

Books showing children and adults with various disabilities

Magazines (for example, *Cricket, Ranger Rick, National Geographic World*)

Storytelling props and puppets

Flannel board and felt pieces

HOUSE/DRAMATIC PLAY AREA

Dress-up clothing reflective of the community, including occupations of the children's parents

Child-size sink, stove, refrigerator

Cooking containers (dishes, plates, bowls, cups, saucers)

Things to cook and serve (seeds, beans, nuts, shells, plastic food)

(continued)

CHECKLIST FOR CENTERS/AREAS IN PRESCHOOL CLASSROOMS *(continued)*

Empty food containers (boxes, cans, cartons, jars, and bags, with original labels)

Dolls (female and male, doll beds, blankets, stroller, etc.)

Mirror

Two telephones

MUSIC AND MOVEMENT AREA

Record or CD player

Instruments reflective of children's cultures.

Drums, triangles, maracas, bells, kazoos, whistles

Music tapes, tape recorder

Movement games characteristic of the children's culture

Scarves, ribbons, hoops, limbo sticks

MANIPULATIVE AREA

Puzzles reflective of the community atmosphere (for example, rural or urban)

Puzzles representing occupations of parents and others in the community

Toy figures, puzzles, and so forth, depicting multiracial people and avoiding sex-role stereotyping

Beads and strings (large and small)

Nesting cups, boxes, rings

Pegs and Peg-Boards (large and small)

Interlocking blocks/shapes

Connecting straws

Shape sorters and shapes

Sewing boards

Counting bears

Games (memory card games, dominos, picture lotto games, Candyland)

SCIENCE/SAND AND WATER AREA

Scales, balances

Magnets, gear sets

Buckets, measuring cups

Strainers, colanders, funnels, shovels, trowels, scoops, spoons

Floating materials (corks, sponges, stones, shells, Styrofoam pieces)

Toy boats, cars, trucks, and construction vehicles

Waterproof smocks

WOODWORKING AREA

Claw hammers, saws, hand drill, pliers, clamps

Sandpaper

Safety goggles

Nails, golf tees, screws

Wood scraps, Styrofoam packing pieces

Source: Adapted from Hohmann, M., & Weikart, D. P. (1995). *Educating young children.* Ypsilanti, MI: High/Scope Press.

Developmentally appropriate material for infants include manipulable and easily washable toys. Rattles, squeak toys, cuddle toys, and pictures of real objects are all acceptable. In the infant room there should also be sturdy, stable furniture for the children to begin to pull up on and begin to walk. In the toddler room there should be push–pull toys, picture books, music, simple puzzles, dramatic play toys, large paper and crayons, and sand and water toys. In the preschool room, materials include equipment for climbing and balancing, blocks and accessories, puzzles and manipulatives, picture books, music and musical instrument, art materials, dramatic play materials, and sand and water toys. In the school-age room appropriate materials would allow for art or hobby projects, organized games, construction projects, dramatics, cooking, science, books, music, and board and card games.

PLAYGROUND

Outside regular physical activity should be part of every curriculum. You do not have to have a great amount of commercial equipment for your playground to be developmentally appropriate, but you do need to allow for a variety of activities to occur at the same time; equipment to encourage climbing, sliding and jumping; opportunities for dramatic play; and places for organized games, especially if your program has preschool and school-age children. The space for infants and toddlers should be separated from the space for older children to allow all involved to be safe. The Consumer Product Safety Commission (www.cpsc.gov) provides guidelines for playgrounds and safety tips.

PLAYGROUND CHECKLIST
1. Make sure surfaces around playground equipment are surrounded by at least twelve inches of wood chips, mulch, sand, or pea gravel and that mats are made of safety-tested rubber or rubberlike materials.
2. Check that protective surfacing extends at least six feet in all directions from play equipment. For swings, be sure surfacing extends in back and front equal to twice the height of the suspending bar.
3. Make sure play structures more than thirty inches high are spaced at least nine feet apart.
4. Check for dangerous hardware, such as open S hooks or protruding bolt ends.
5. Make sure spaces that could trap children, such as openings in guardrails or between ladder rungs, measure less than three-and-a-half inches or more than nine inches.
6. Check for sharp points or edges on equipment.
7. Eliminate tripping hazards, such as exposed concrete footings, tree stumps, and rocks.
8. Make sure elevated surfaces, such as platforms and ramps, have guardrails to prevent falls.

MAINTENANCE

Maintenance, the preservation, repair, and upkeep of the learning environment, is usually the responsibility of the director. As you plan facilities and equipment, be

■ ■ ■ ■ ■ ■

CLASS ACTIVITY

Consider early childhood programs that you have observed. Evaluate their environments using the checklists and guidelines in this chapter. What cues about the environment do the children and adults provide? Are there other questions that should be asked or materials that should be added?

■ ■ ■ ■ ■ ■

WHAT WOULD YOU DO?

A church-sponsored, low-budget preschool had a high board fence separating it from the adjoining parking lot. Its tan paint was looking shoddy, so the director was pleased when two fathers volunteered to paint it over a weekend. They would even provide the paint. Imagine her surprise when she arrived on Monday morning to find that the boards were now a dazzling red, orange, green, yellow, and purple. Her philosophy was that the environment should be a background for the children's activities, but now the fence shouted for attention. What should she do? What should she have done? How would you deal with these proud dads and the admiring parents?

aware of their costs, both financial and in the energy required for their upkeep. Effectiveness in maintenance is often taken for granted, but it is a major determinant of staff morale and will affect the educational program if the system breaks down. Your concerns will be with costs, safety, and serviceability. Your choices among various alternatives will involve balancing these factors. It will be your job to determine which routine work should be done by the regular staff and which by contract or outside labor. You may determine, for example, that each classroom floor is cleaned daily by the teacher using the room or an aide. The cook/matron/housekeeper mops the kitchen and restrooms daily after the children are gone, using a specified disinfectant solution. A commercial cleaning service uses heavy-duty equipment to mop and buff floors on the first Saturday of every month. All of these types of maintenance and cleaning will need to be specific to your program.

Two other types of maintenance should be recognized. *Corrective* or *emergency* work is done *after* trouble occurs and may be costly, dangerous, or simply inconvenient. It would cover such things as replacement of a broken furnace fan belt, adjustment of malfunctioning toilet valves, or repair of wind-damaged trees. Some problems can be prevented but not all, and budget reserves must include reasonable amounts for these contingencies. *Preventive* or *periodic* maintenance is performed *before* trouble occurs; it is preplanned on a regular schedule. It includes routine inspections of swings and wheel toys, furnaces and air conditioners, fire extinguishers and alarm systems, or cleaning debris from roof gutters. Repainting walls or replacing floor tiles would fall under this category. This preventive periodic maintenance is also included in your budget.

Proper tools are an investment and should be cherished as such. When they are needed, they are usually needed immediately. A basic kit should include a sturdy claw hammer, regular and Phillips screwdrivers of various sizes, pliers that also cut wire, a crescent wrench that fits wheel toy bolts, a crosscut saw, a toilet plunger, and an assortment of nails, screws, and extra belts to fit the equipment. If there is a competent person to use them, a plumber's snake and pipe wrenches can be added. The local tool rental store can provide specialized equipment.

All operating manuals and warranty contracts should be filed in an orderly way for quick reference as soon as equipment is purchased. Itemized duplicate order forms for small equipment should also be kept on file. Make certain they have legible dates. Your office computer and backup files should include the following readily accessible "vital statistics" for equipment:

- Name (for example, tape player) and identifying number if more than a single unit (tricycles may have enamel numerals painted under the frame)
- Location, if there is more than one in the school or per classroom
- Manufacturer (where purchased, when, and price paid)
- Equipment numbers and descriptions (for example, chair height and material, wheel diameter of tricycles, serial and model number of the refrigerator)
- Maintenance schedule (when oiled, cleaned, repainted, etc.), coordinated with master schedule for all equipment
- Services performed (dates and annotations as to service facility or repair shop used, fees, new parts)

An annual inventory of all equipment should be taken, preferably at the end of each fiscal year, and information about all equipment should be duly noted with the initials of the person responsible for the assessment and the date completed.

Some Suggestions from Experienced Directors

Maintenance should not be delegated to the person least able to refuse or to an eager volunteer who may or may not be qualified.

- Have names of reliable services (plumber, electrician, carpenter) posted so that they may be called quickly even in your absence. Know when to call them. Labor unions strictly limit the types of work their members may do so do not expect the plumber to do electrical work or carpentry.
- Recognize the limits of amateur repairs, but also recognize that some female teachers are more skillful at them than some males who might be available.
- Certain outside services are required, such as maintaining fire extinguishers.
- Remember that "time is money" when service workers are called. Extra trips for materials or parts are expensive. Be sure you have information about the model or type of equipment needing service and a tentative diagnosis when you call. Sometimes preventive service can be performed during a service call, for example, when the plumber unstops the sink or does other emergency repairs, preventive service like putting in new faucet washers can be added at no extra charge. Find out how service call fees are computed.
- Consider a timer clock for such routines as activating night-lights and lawn sprinklers. This not only ensures that these activities are done on time but also vandalism may be discouraged because the building looks occupied.
- Watching the work of adults is an educational treat for small children. If possible, allow the children to see what is going on and allow them to play and talk out their impressions.
- Preplanning will allow the administrator to project the use of both time and money over the years. Low-cost/high-success maintenance can best be achieved through choice of materials, selection of equipment, and purchase of supplies.

Can you add to this list?

CLASS ACTIVITY

worksheet

9.1
p. 149

In small groups, compare and contrast the environmental features described by classmates for Worksheet 9.1. What elements do they have in common? How do individual mission statements, standards, funding sources, and locations affect the features that are suggested?

REFERENCES AND RESOURCES

Arce, E. M. (2002). *Curriculum for young children: An introduction.* Albany, NY: Delmar.

Banks, J. A. (2001). *Cultural diversity and education: Foundations, curriculum, and teaching.* Boston: Allyn & Bacon.

Bronson, M. B. (1995). *The right stuff for children birth to eight: Selecting play materials to support development.* Washington, DC: National Association for the Education of Young Children.

Greenman, J. (1998). *Caring spaces, learning places: Children's environments that work.* Redmond, WA: Exchange Press.

Haughland, S. W., & Wright, J. L. (1997). *Young children and technology: A world of discovery,* Boston: Allyn & Bacon.

Hohmann, M., & Weikart, D. P. (1995). *Educating young children.* Ypsilanti, MI: High/Scope Press.

National Association for the Education of Young Children. (1998). *Accreditation criteria and procedures of the national academy of early childhood programs.* Washington, DC: Author.

Neugebauer, R. (Ed.). (2004). Beginnings workshop on space. *Child Care Information Exchange, 155,* 33–48.

Sandall, S., & Ostrosky, M. (2000). *Natural environments and inclusion.* Washington, DC: National Association for the Education of Young Children.

Stine, S. (1997). *Landscapes for learning: Creating outdoor environments for children and youth.* New York: Wiley.

Wardle, F. (2003). *Introduction to early childhood education: A multidimensional approach to child-centered care and learning.* Boston: Allyn & Bacon.

WEBSITE RESOURCES

Consumer Product Safety Commission: www.cpsc.gov

National Association for the Education of Young Children Accreditation
   Criteria: www.naeyc.org/accreditation

National Program for Playground Safety: www.uni.edu/playground

THE LEARNING ENVIRONMENT

Name _____ Date _____

Objective: To consider children and staff needs in planning the environment.

Directions: Based on the program that you are planning, what are some of the features you will design into your child care center? Do not include features already mandated by regulations, such as room size.

Classroom for infants and toddlers

Classroom for preschoolers

Outside environment for infants and toddlers

Outside environment for preschoolers

To satisfy staff needs in my program, I plan to include

Meeting spaces

Adult-only spaces

Conference area

Other considerations

CHAPTER TEN

Health, Safety, and Nutrition

CHAPTER OUTLINE

HEALTH RECORDS/IMMUNIZATIONS

RECOMMENDED PRACTICES

SICK/EXCLUSION POLICIES

EMERGENCY PROCEDURES AND POLICIES

SECURITY SYSTEMS

CHILD ABUSE

NUTRITION

HEALTH RECORDS/IMMUNIZATIONS

Most parents are concerned about the health of their children, so your center needs to work with families to provide a favorable environment. One way to do that is to make sure that children have all necessary medical/health forms completed before they enter the program. Most state licensing authorities have forms that can be used to obtain the necessary information. Each center can request additional information about the child as needed for your program. The basic information needed is as follows:

- Child's name (preferred "calling" name)
- Names, home addresses, places of employment, and other contact information for all persons responsible for the child.
- Record of physical exam for the child (usually performed within one year of enrollment) stating general health of the child and whether the child needs a special diet or other modifications to function in group care
- Emergency contact information (insurance provider, hospital preference, doctor, dentist, etc.)
- Names of people who are authorized to pick up the child from the program

Another component of health records is up-to-date immunization information on the child. All states require immunizations of children. The federal guidelines can be found at the Centers for Disease Control (www.cdc.gov) or at the American Academy of Pediatrics (www.aap.org). The universally recommended vaccines are diphtheria, tetanus, pertussis, poliomyelitis, measles, mumps, rubella, Haemophilus influenzae (Hib), varicella (chicken pox), pneumococuss, and influenza (Aronson, 2002). It is the responsibility of parents to keep their child's immunizations current. Additionally, all states require child care programs to have documentation of current immunizations.

RECOMMENDED PRACTICES

Group child care is notorious for spreading germs, and hand washing is very important to reduce the spread of germs. According to Aronson (2002), all staff who work with children should wash their hands often and especially at these times:

- On arrival at work
- Before preparing or serving food
- Before giving medication
- After diapering, toileting, wiping noses (or any exposure to body fluids)
- After the staff member visits the restroom
- After handling pets
- When returning from outside

Similarly, children should be encouraged to wash their hands

- On arrival at school
- Before and after eating food
- After visiting the toilet or wiping noses (or any exposure to body fluids)
- After playing in the sand or at the water table
- After handling pets
- When returning from outside

Hand washing is the first line of defense against spreading germs in group situations. Some other suggestions include the following:

- Allow fresh air into the classroom daily and take children outside at least once daily (weather permitting).
- Clean and sanitize toys, tables, chairs, and areas at least once a day (a recommended sanitizing solution is one-quarter cup bleach to one gallon of water).
- Teach children to sneeze and cough away from others and, whenever possible, to use a tissue and then discard the tissue and wash their hands. If a tissue is not available, they should cover the mouth and nose with the upper arm, bent elbow, or shirt sleeve.
- Do not allow sharing of personal items, such as combs, hats, and so on.
- Toileting facilities should be cleaned and sanitized at least once a day.

SICK/EXCLUSION POLICIES

No matter how often you wear gloves or wash your hands, children and staff will become sick. So you need to have policies in place to deal with sick children and for contacting their parents. Sick/exclusion policies should be part of your operating policies and be included in your family handbook. They should be discussed with the family at the orientation.

Most programs are not designed to care for sick children, so policies should state expected compliance. When a child runs a temperature of one hundred degrees

Fahrenheit or higher, vomits or has persistent diarrhea, or exhibits other signs of illness, typically a parent will be called and expected to come for the child. The general expectations are that the child will need to be picked up within one hour from the time of the call.

General guidelines state that a child will be excluded from attendance if any of the following illnesses or conditions exist:

Fever. A fever includes a temperature of greater than or equal to 100 degrees Fahrenheit axillary (under arm), 101 degrees Fahrenheit aurally (in the ear), or 101 degrees Fahrenheit orally (in the mouth). The child will be restricted from the center until he or she is without fever for twenty-four hours *without* the use of fever-reducing medication. A child with a fever will only be permitted to attend if there is a note from the child's physician stating that the fever is due to a noncontagious condition. The physician must *specifically* document that the fever is due to a noncontagious condition.

Diarrhea. Diarrhea includes two or three loose (watery) stools within a two-hour period or an increase from normal stool frequency and consistency (i.e., increased number of stools and a change from formed to loose). The child will be restricted until at least one normal stool has occurred or until free of diarrhea for twenty-four hours.

Vomiting. Vomiting is the inability to hold stomach contents. This does not include "spitting up" that might occur when formula fed babies are "burped." The child has to be free of vomiting for twenty-four hours without the aid of antinausea medicine before he or she can return to the center.

Rashes. Rashes are skin eruptions, excluding diaper rash. The child will be permitted to attend the center when the condition resolves, is adequately treated, or the child's physician provides a note *specifically* stating that the rash is due to a noncontagious disease.

Eye drainage. A child may have yellow, white, or green drainage from the eyes along with redness of the lids or skin surrounding eye (pink eye appearance). Often there is matting of the eyelids after sleep and there may be pain and burning of the eyes. The child will need to be on appropriate medication for twenty-four hours before he or she can return to the center.

Hand, foot, or mouth disease. A child with a hand, foot, or mouth disease may not attend the center until the condition resolves or until a physician writes a note to say that the child may return.

Lice. Children with lice may not return to the center until at least twenty-four hours after effective treatment.

■ ■ ■ ■ ■ ▬▬▬▬▬▬▬▬▬▬▬▬▬▬▬▬▬▬▬▬▬▬▬▬▬▬▬▬▬▬▬▬▬▬

WHAT WOULD YOU DO?

Laura, a twenty-two-month-old, was sent home Tuesday with an aural fever of 101 degrees, with a yellow discharge from her nose, and complaining of an earache. When her mother picked Laura up at 11:30 A.M., Sandy, the teacher, reminded the mother of the policy that Laura should not return to the center until she had been free of fever for twenty-four hours without the aid of fever-reducing medicine (as stated in the policy). Wednesday morning Laura's father brought her to school and said she has an ear infection and has not had a fever since they took her home yesterday. Do you tell him he cannot bring her in (following the center policy), or do you let her stay because an ear infection is not supposed to be contagious?

Strep throat. Children with strep throat may not return to the center until after at least twenty-four hours of effective treatment and the fever is gone.

EMERGENCY PROCEDURES AND POLICIES

In addition to the daily management of safety, a director must have the ability to cope in times of crisis. When emergency situations are under consideration, it is natural to assume that they will never actually happen—that you will only be involved with the planning phase and never need the operating and evaluating components. However, planning and rehearsing for potential emergencies must be integrated into the preparations for operating your center. Your emergency policies should address the following areas:

- Emergency numbers and locations
- Emergency systems (e.g., fire alarm)
- Evacuation areas and paths for different events (fire, flood)
- Lock-down situations (emergency rations and methods of communication)
- Fires (exits and locations of fire extinguishers)
- Medical emergencies (staff with CPR and first aid training, location of first aid kit)
- Natural disasters/weather-related emergencies depending on your location (snow and ice storms, tornadoes, hurricanes, floods, earthquakes)
- Utility disruption or emergency (water, gas, electricity)
- Hazardous materials (chemicals, bombs, suspicious articles)
- Disgruntled employee, parent, or other
- Hostage situation
- Missing child
- Other information relevant to your program

worksheet

10.1
p. 163

After the policies are in place, each staff member should be aware of the expectations. The policies should be reviewed periodically to ensure that the information is current and accurate. Your local Red Cross and public safety offices have important information, and there are national programs that may be of assistance. For examples, Disaster Child Care, sponsored by the Church of the Brethren, provides care in case of traumatic events. Their website is www.brethren.org. Worksheet 10.1 encourages you to develop your ideas of what would be appropriate emergency procedures and policies for your specific program.

First Aid and CPR

All staff should be trained in first aid and infant/child CPR and should be able to handle minor emergencies. A first aid kit should be available in the center. Following are the basic components of a standard first aid kit.

- A current edition of a first aid manual
- Sterile first aid dressings
- Bandages or roller bandages
- Adhesive tape
- Scissors
- Tweezers
- Thermometer

- Antiseptic solution
- Saline solution (for eye injuries)

SECURITY SYSTEMS

Safety is one of the most important components of a child care program operation. Your program has to be a safe place for everyone involved. Some facilities are turning to technology for assistance in providing security for the children, parents, and staff. Security systems can take on a variety of forms from coded entry into the building to videocameras in all rooms and at access points. For the coded entry to the building, family members and staff are given a numeric code to be entered into a touch keypad system by the front door. This is the only way to gain access to the building unless someone inside the building admits you.

Another security feature many centers use is an electronic sign-in procedure. Most centers throughout the United States require parents or other caregivers to sign their children in and out for safety reasons. This program uses cards similar to credit cards but with the child's name and contact information encrypted on the card. The parent swipes the card to enter or exit the center. Information such as date and time are recorded and can be used for lunch counts, tuition charges, and attendance records.

A more elaborate security system comes in the form of video monitors. The system consists of cameras, a television or computer monitor, and a computer program. The cameras are installed in the classrooms and wired through a computer-monitoring program. The center director or others with authorization can view each classroom and the playground. Parents can access their children's classroom from their office or home computers via the Internet. This system uses protected password access, and only members or those who have the user name and password can actually view the classrooms. These security programs have installation and Internet fees, but some centers offset the charges by requiring parents to pay monthly charges for access.

There are many benefits to this type of security system. It allows for better communication between families and centers. Center enrollment is increased because parents believe their children are safe and they can view their children whenever they have access to the Internet. The security system could also be a marketing tool, being advertised as an added measure of safety for the children. Additionally, it may lower insurance rates because the classrooms are under visual supervision at all times of the day.

Whatever security system you choose for your program, make sure it meets your needs and budget. You can contact local surveillance companies or check out the latest systems at professional conferences.

CHILD ABUSE

When there is suspicion of child abuse or neglect, communication with parents is difficult and needs special consideration by the teacher and director. Parents should be aware of the policies your center will follow if members of your staff come into contact with children they believe are physically or emotionally neglected or have been physically or sexually abused. Those who work with children on a daily basis often detect developmental lags in physical, social, emotional, and cognitive areas. Although stress from family problems, such as prolonged unemployment or marital discord, can also result in developmental problems, these children usually act out their concerns through normal play. Drawings, dramatic activities, lunch table conversations, and

■ ■ ■ ■ ■ ▬▬▬▬▬▬▬▬▬▬▬▬▬▬▬▬▬▬▬▬▬▬▬▬▬▬▬▬▬▬▬▬▬

CLASS DISCUSSION

What resources are available in your community to train early childhood program personnel in recognizing and reporting physical and emotional abuse and neglect? What is the status of local, state, and federal abuse legislation?

other parts of daily life in the center will reveal much of what troubles children. Abused children, however, tend to be seclusive or violently aggressive, or they may alternate between these behaviors. They may display precocious or inappropriate sexual knowledge in their play. Because it is only through repeated patterns of behavior that some types of abuse will be revealed, there should be established procedures for staff to follow in documenting activities that cause concern and for determining evidence of physical abuse, such as bruises. In addition to documentation, there should be policies about the point at which you report the case to authorities. Because there are legal procedures required in all states and communities, you and your staff need to be aware of what to look for and what to do when there is evidence of child abuse.

Another consideration of child abuse is when personnel are accused of child abuse in the program. The utmost responsibility is for the safety of the child and the staff member. Unfortunately, there have been many accusations of abuse by personnel in programs, and you should have policies in place to address this type of occurrence. Following are some questions to address before abuse happens in your program:

1. What procedures for handling accusations of abuse are provided in the staff and parent handbooks?
2. Do your procedures adequately address how you would notify parents and other staff of the allegations?
3. What legal services are available for the personnel to effectively deal with the allegations? What program assistance is available?
4. What personnel policies are in place to handle dismissal or work codes for an accused staff member?
5. What type of counseling service is included in the benefits for the staff involved in a case of accusations or suspicion? Are there services for the other staff members or children?

No one thinks this can happen in their center, but a good manager has a plan in place to address issues of abuse and neglect.

NUTRITION

Your system for providing food for children and staff will be as individualized as any other and can be worked out by the same process. Food service is an expensive but important part of your center. However, this is one area in which the mission statement and goals of a program are often ignored.

Certain aspects of a food service system need to be considered. The goals include introducing children to a variety of foods and processes, developing a sense of pleasure at mealtimes, fostering social skills in conversation and routine good manners, establishing independence, and developing cognitive skills. Another aspect involves financial decisions, such as who will pay for your food program. Parents may send brown bag lunches or take turns supplying snacks, food costs may be included in the tuition or be billed as an additional fee, federal programs may subsidize part or all of the expense, a local agency may provide meals, or they may be provided as part of a corporate service to employee parents.

Other aspects of the food service system involve menu making, including knowing what a balanced meal is, issues of purchasing and delivery of food, the mechanics of serving the food, the amount of storage needed, the size and type of available equipment, and limitations and time available of a cook. The serving, eating, and clearing procedures should be set up after determining how far apart and where the tables are set, what the toileting and hand washing routine will be, what help the children will provide, the time allowance for meals, and transitions to the next activity.

Unlike most of the systems that you will use, those of menu making and nutrition have a long-established scientific basis. If yours will be a program in which you will plan and supervise feeding large numbers of children or if your objectives are beyond your present skills in this field, you may want to take classes or workshops in child nutrition or hire a person with education and experience in the food service area. Our goal, whether we are feeding children who are indulged with expensive "empty calories" or children whose parents cannot afford to buy enough food of any type, must be to provide foods that feed, not merely fill.

Sanitation and Safety

Procedures for preparation and service of food for your center should minimize the possibility of illness or injury. Children should have access to the food preparation area only under vigilant supervision and for designated purposes, such as observing the cookies being placed in an oven after they have been mixed and put onto baking sheets in the classroom. Utensils and equipment should be developmentally appropriate. For example, younger children would cut with serrated plastic knives and the older ones would be taught how to properly handle sharp-blade instruments for snack preparation. Both adults and children should thoroughly wash their hands with soap and water before beginning work or after handling nonfood items, using the bathroom, or blowing their noses.

The kitchen and its contents should have a designated cleaning schedule, with food preparation surfaces sanitized by a solution designed for that purpose. Storage areas should have no food fragments to attract insects, and susceptible foods must be stored in containers that protect them from infestation. Bacteria can also cause foodborne illnesses, either by microorganisms or by the toxins they produce. Perishable goods should be kept cold until eaten and hot foods should be kept hot. Protein foods (meat, poultry, eggs, or products containing eggs) may appear to be safe but can cause illness if left at room temperature for several hours.

Meal Planning and Nutrition

As the director of a large early childhood program, you may find yourself supervising a licensed dietician and a kitchen staff. However, you also may plan, purchase, prepare, and do dishwashing yourself. Most centers fall somewhere in between, perhaps with a matron doing both food preparation and cleaning of the building. You will want to explore the possibilities of frozen prepared foods that can be quickly microwaved on serving plates or the availability of food brought in from a sponsor's

CLASS DISCUSSION

What regulations are there in your community regarding sanitation and safety in food preparation at your center? Is a food handler's permit required? Who enforces regulations?

cafeteria. Yours may be a morning program with only a light snack or it may be extended-day child care program stretching from breakfast through supper. Federal, state, and local programs are available to provide supplementary foods or funds. Child care resource and information agencies or your state agricultural extension service may help you find them and may also give assistance in the purchase of equipment and the planning of service. Additionally, there are computer software programs that may help in menu planning and food cost calculations. The references and resources section at the end of the chapter provides additional information.

Food Guide Pyramid

The most common guide to menu planning, the Food Guide Pyramid, is updated periodically by the USDA. This guide needs to be followed in centers that receive public funds for food service. Daily food needs are broken into these groupings to show that they have similar nutrients:

> Grains (six servings). Includes all breads and cereals, rice, and pasta
>
> Vegetables (three servings). Cooked vegetables or raw leafy vegetables
>
> Fruits (two servings). Fresh, canned, dried fruit
>
> Meats (two servings). Beef, veal, pork, lamb, poultry, fish and eggs; also dry beans, peanut butter, nuts
>
> Milk (two servings). All forms, including whole milk, powdered milk used in cooking, cheese, ice cream, and yogurt
>
> Fats and sweets. Limited amount daily

Use of the Food Pyramid standards will help ensure against extremes. The Food Guide Pyramid is included in Appendix B. To download information about the Food Guide Pyramid go to www.usda.gov/cnpp/KidsPyra/KIDPYRbw.pdf. Another resource to consult is the U.S. Department of Agriculture child care meal patterns for infants and children available in Appendix C and online at www.fns.usda.gov/cnd/care/ProgramBasics/Meals.

Other Considerations with Menu Planning

5 a Day: The Color Way.   It is important to eat a variety of fruits and vegetables every day. Colorful fruits and vegetables provide essential vitamins, minerals, and fiber for our bodies to stay healthy. It is important to offer children a variety of foods so they will develop beneficial habits and interests in different foods. The Produce for Better Health Foundation suggests that we eat a fruit or vegetable from each of the five colors daily: blue or purple, green, white, yellow or orange, and red. Considering "5 a day the color way" involves children in their own food choices. For more information go to www.5aday.com.

Parental Choices for Their Children.   You need to meet the dietary needs of children but also to respect and implement the wishes of the parents. For example, some families are vegan and eat no eggs, meats, or dairy products, no products from living creatures. Vegetarian families may eat fish and poultry but not red meat. Still others may have faith-based dietary restrictions, and you should respect their choices as well. In order to meet the needs of all, you have to obtain the appropriate information from the parents (preferably during orientation which is discussed in Chapter Eleven).

Protein–Calorie Balance.   Many nutritional scientists, rather than following the Food Guide Pyramid, tend to think in terms of protein intake or protein–calorie balance. Americans are aware of vegetable proteins, particularly those that are on the grocery shelves as "helpers" for hamburger and chicken, or tofu and other staples of Asian cultures. If we are to accept ecological predictions, today's preschoolers will be dependent on such foods when they are adults so perhaps we should orient them toward soya casserole instead of barbecued steak. Many food service administrators are finding that these protein supplements are important in keeping food costs under control while maintaining high standards of food value and pleasurable eating.

The importance of the protein–calorie balance lies in the need of growing children to have enough protein intake. The human body is almost half protein. The skin, muscles, hair, eyes, and even brain are protein tissues. Undernourished children given protein supplementation not only show increased intellectual performance but also an increased ability to interact socially. Even if malnutrition is not severe, children can only develop their genetic potential when they have enough of these "building blocks" for their bodies to use.

In choosing protein foods, it is important to remember that they are composed of many amino acids. Those that have about the same amino acid combinations as the human body are termed *complete* and include animal meat, eggs, and milk. There are many amino acids in plant foods but some are missing in each source. These are termed *incomplete* because they must be combined with one another or supplemented by animal sources. There are varying amounts of such completeness, with soybeans, brewers or torula yeasts, peanuts, garbanzos, and some other vegetable proteins ranking close to the animal foods in their value. Bread, dry beans, cereal, macaroni, and other grain products also have some proteins.

If the intake of any of the essential amino acids is too small to meet the body needs, some of the other essential acids will be deaminized and treated as waste products. It is as though many jigsaw puzzles were being assembled, with those having missing pieces thrown away. We need to make sure that the supply of protein is not only generous but also that it comes from a mix of foods. Many traditional combinations fit together particularly well in their amino acid content—bread and cheese, rice and fish, beans and corn tortillas, cereal and milk, and almost any traditional casserole.

In addition to their value as protein sources, foods with high amino acid content also contain B vitamins, minerals, and other nutrients—most of the forty or more substances known to be essential for health and development. These are "synergistic" in the human body, which means that they all work together to accomplish more than would be expected. It is a case of 2 + 2 = 5. Too much of any one may be harmful but such excess is avoided by providing a wide variety of simple but well-prepared and colorful foods.

Nutrient Density.   Closely related to the concept of protein–calorie balance is nutrient density or index of nutritional quality (INQ). Instead of being limited to amino acids, nutritionists use the INQ to compute the ratio of various nutrients to the caloric or energy value of a food. It is an attempt to look positively at the most nutritive foods rather than emphasizing the negative aspects of so-called junk foods. Because children need highly nutritious food but consume small amounts, a consideration of the INQ can help you plan optimal meals. Foods that supply a high proportion of nutrients in relation to their energy calories are said to have high-nutrient density. Examples might be eggs and broccoli. However, low-density foods, such as boxed gelatin desserts and lemonade, may provide virtually no nutrients except sugar calories. Even without using INQ formulas, which are beyond the scope of this guidebook, awareness of nutrient density provides a tool for evaluating possible menu choices.

Tips from Directors

Following are some suggestions that have been expressed by school directors and other persons involved in feeding young children. Do you agree with some of them? Do you disagree with some? Can you contribute others?

■ In addition to providing proper food, nutrition service for young children includes the education of their parents, the training of teachers to support each child's progress toward both physical and emotional control, and the involvement of staff.

■ Food service, whether a snack or a full meal, is part of the curriculum, integrated with stories, vocabulary development, excursions, and all elements of cognitive development.

■ The playground is not only a place for children to let off steam but it is also an integral part of the process of nutrition. During playtime, the child uses food rapidly, eliminates waste material through perspiration, breathes deeply to assimilate more oxygen, and generally "tones up" the body processes.

■ The physical needs of the child must be met. During snacks and meals, each child should sit comfortably with feet on the floor and back supported. Dishes should be heavy enough to stay in place, with rims to hold runaway foods. Glasses should be small enough to be encircled by children's hands and have firm bases. Utensils should be scaled to the child, with short, wide forks and shallow bowl spoons.

■ Mealtime is important for emotional growth, habit formation, and maturation. Children thrive on regularity and the rhythm of routines; regular meals provide a sense of security. Mealtimes should be scheduled so that the children are hungry but not so hungry that they are irritable and have lost their appetites. Midmorning and midafternoon snacks are important. Children will enjoy eating if they are allowed to regard food as good because it eases the pangs of hunger.

■ Complete self-choice for children is virtually impossible and probably not desirable but some choice is important, if only fresh fruits from an assortment, the preferred color of apples, or how much of a food each child will eat at a certain meal; small servings initially allow for success and the chance to take more of favorite items.

CLASS DISCUSSION

What creative ideas can you think of to help children become more interested in choosing nutritious foods?

■ ■ ■ ■ ■

WHAT WOULD YOU DO?

A family with very strong beliefs about food consumption (mainly preferring organically grown food) has their daughter, Jamie, enrolled in your toddler class. At your program, two snacks and a lunch are served as part of the tuition. The parents insist on providing the snacks and lunch for their daughter. Recently, Jamie has refused to eat "her food" and keeps requesting the food that is provided by the center. The teachers have talked to you and are very concerned about Jamie's lack of food consumption during the day. What would you do?

■ Table manners are best taught by the example of adults, not by scolding or nagging. An adult should sit at each table, eating the same foods as the children.

■ Recognize what the labels really are telling you. When "cheese" is combined with "spread" or "orange" with "drink," you are not really getting cheese or orange juice benefits for your money. Combinations of ingredients are listed with the largest percentage first, so beware if the label on the can lists "water" ahead of "apples." The same is true of "beef stew" with potatoes, water, and other ingredients listed before the meat.

■ Children have a keener sense of smell than adults; cabbage and other odorous vegetables may be more acceptable if they are cooked in milk. For example, chopped broccoli in a quiche may be accepted when steamed broccoli is pushed aside.

■ Consistency is important; you should serve mashed potatoes that are fluffy, not dry or gummy. Texture can be disturbing so tough strings should be removed from celery and gristle from meat.

■ Crisp raw vegetables are preferable to cooked vegetables. Pieces of raw carrots, cauliflower, celery, and lettuce and cabbage leaves make good snacks; young children cannot consume enough of these vegetables to fill nutritional needs, but the chewing is important and children will begin to form lifelong preferences.

■ Fruit combinations are popular, especially mild and sweet mixed with tart, such as cooked peaches and raw oranges. Mixtures of vegetables are usually not enjoyed, and many children will patiently separate the peas from the carrots before eating them.

■ The combination of two disliked vegetables may be overwhelming. A tiny portion of the unpopular vegetable, served with a favorite one, may be eaten willingly.

Questions to Consider in Menu Planning

■ Are sweet foods viewed as rewards for eating the unpleasant essentials?
■ Are the children learning to make choices, to take responsibility for themselves, to develop their self-esteem and ability to cope? Do they find mealtime a pleasant event, a time to enjoy one another and the adults?
■ Do you include a variety of foods, with foods sometimes served in a different style or in a different place, such as a picnic of finger foods eaten under the trees?
■ Have you made an effort to avoid "junk foods" that are high in cost and low in food value?
■ Have you been able to avoid duplicating items common in the fast-food franchise market, which many children may have for their evening meals?

worksheet
10.2
p. 165

Worksheet 10.2 provides opportunities to put menu-planning skills to use. The information in this chapter as well as Appendixes B and C may be helpful to plan meals for a week for your program.

REFERENCES AND RESOURCES

Aronson, S. S. (Ed.). (2002). *Healthy young children: A manual for programs.* Washington, DC: National Association for the Education of Young Children.

American Dietetic Association. (1999). Nutrition standards for child care programs—Position of ADA. *Journal of American Dietetic Association, 99,* 981–988.

Marin Child Care Council. (2004). *Childhood emergencies: What to do.* St. Paul, MN: Red Leaf Press.

Moratz, L. R., Rush, J. M., & Cross, M. Z. (1993). *Health, safety, and nutrition.* Albany, NY: Delmar.

National Association for the Education of Young Children. (2004). *Preventing child abuse and neglect: The early childhood educator's role.* Washington, DC: Author.

Robertson, C. (1998). *Safety, nutrition, and health in early education.* Albany, NY: Delmar.

Sayre, N., & Gallagher, J. (2001). *Young child and the environment: The issues related to health, nutrition, safety, and physical activity.* Boston: Allyn & Bacon.

Warash, B. G., Fitch, C., & Bodnovich, K. (2003). Snack choices: Helping young children make decisions. *Journal of Family and Consumer Sciences, 95*(2), 60–64.

WEBSITE RESOURCES

American Dietetic Association: www.eatright.org.

Centers for Disease Control and Prevention: www.cdc.gov

Food Guide Pyramid: Tips for using the Food Guide Pyramid for young children two to six years: www.nutrition.gov.

Hand Washing: www.nrc.uchsc.edu/hwash

Health in Schools: www.healthinschools.org

Immunizations: www.cdc.gov/nip/acip

International Food Information Council Foundation: http://ific.org

Keep Kids Healthy: www.keepkidshealthy.com

ProCare Childcare Management Software: www.procaresoftware.com

Security Systems

    Parent Watch: www.parentwatch.com

    Kinder Cam: www.kindercam.com

    Little Lamb Cam: www.littlelambcam.com

    Secure Cam Kids: www.securecamkids.com

    Child Care TV: www.childcaretv.com

The American Professional Society on the Abuse of Children: www.apsac.org

U.S. Department of Agriculture: www.usda.gov.cnpp/KidsPyra

U.S. Department of Health and Human Services, Administration for Children and Families, National Clearinghouse on Child Abuse and Neglect Information: http://nccanch.acf.hhs.gov

Waste Free Lunches: www.wastefreelunches.org

EMERGENCY PROCEDURES

Name _____ Date _____

Objective: To gain an understanding of the components of emergency procedures.

Directions: Use the areas listed to write down a few ideas for your emergency policies.

Emergency numbers and locations

Emergency systems (e.g., fire alarm)

Evacuation areas and paths for different events (fire, flood)

Lock-down situations (emergency rations and methods of communication)

Fires (exits and locations of fire extinguishers)

Medical emergencies (staff with CPR and first aid training, location of first aid kit)

Natural disasters/weather-related emergencies depending on your location (snow and ice storms, tornadoes, hurricanes, floods, earthquakes)

Utility disruption or emergency (water, gas, electricity)

Hazardous materials (chemicals, bombs, suspicious articles)

Disgruntled employee, parent, or other

Hostage situation

Missing child

WEEKLY MENU CHART

Name _____ Date _____

Objective: To consider a variety of issues when planning a menu for your center.

Directions: Using the menu chart provided, plan meals for a five-day school week. Assume that you are going to operate a full-day program, without breakfast or an evening meal, for children ages two to five. Appendixes B and C may be of assistance in completing this worksheet.

As you complete the menu, check it against these questions:

Are new foods used in combination with those that are popular?

Is a bun or sandwich-type lunch limited to once a week?

Are foods of different ethnic origins included?

Does the menu include a good balance of

Color in the foods themselves or in their garnishes?

Texture with soft, crisp, firm, starchy?

Shape with different sizes and forms?

High- and low-calorie foods? Varied vitamin C sources?

Warm and cool temperatures, avoiding icy cold or very hot?

Flavor combinations with bland and tart, mild and strong?

Finger foods with those needing utensils?

Would both children and adults enjoy eating these meals?

WORKSHEET 10.2 *(continued)*

Name _____

Date _____

Weekly Menu

	MONDAY	TUESDAY	WEDNESDAY	THURSDAY	FRIDAY
Morning Snack					

Lunch
  Meat
 	
  Vegetables
 	
  Fruit
 	
  Grains
 	
  Milk					

Afternoon Snack					

CHAPTER ELEVEN

Working with Families

CHAPTER OUTLINE

Although lengthy volumes have been written about family involvement, the primary focus for this guidebook is the mission statement of your own center and the policies established for it. Do you expect a parent advisory board to actually tell you what should be done? Or will you own the center and assume that parents conform to its rules? Are you prepared to deal with criticism? Who has final authority for curriculum? Can you develop a sense of ease and mutual trust or will yours be a no-nonsense place in which you maintain your distance and an authoritarian stance? If there is a local resource and information agency, what guidelines do they provide to parents who are seeking a preschool or child care center?

Your attitudes and their implications will be reflected throughout the center and have been dealt with in several previous worksheets. What sort of welcome have you prepared in the entry? How do your teacher in-service or staff meetings incorporate training or sensitivity sessions to help them deal with family problems? Experienced observers quickly pick up underlying feelings about school–family relationships, even when visiting an empty building, through the bulletin board and general layout, just as they detect attitudes toward children by noting whether the walls are decorated with teacher-made art or by that produced by children. Does your center say, "Look at me, the director. Aren't I great?" or does it tell the observer, "We are all involved here in producing a creative environment for growth and development of staff, families, and children."

FAMILY HANDBOOK

No matter what the size or type of program, you need a parent handbook to communicate your program's mission statement, policies, and procedures. Handbooks come in a variety of types and styles from several pages stapled together to a printed multipage book. How the handbook is presented to parents will depend on your program type and budget. In all cases there are certain things that must be included in your program's handbook. Some of these items you already may have addressed in your policies, and others may be specific to the parent handbook. Following are the main topics to include:

- History of the program
- Mission statement (purpose, goals, objectives)
- Program description (full, part, combination)
- Organizational chart/directory of staff
- Class schedules (specifics for each age group, e.g., infants)
- Application and admission process (forms, fees, wait time, withdrawal)
- Schedule (hours of operation, holidays)
- Tuition (billing, acceptable payment, late fees, emergency fee waivers)
- Arrival and departure information (security systems, safety procedures, sign-in/out procedures)
- Health and safety (illness exclusion policy, medication, immunization requirements)
- Meal/snack information (what is provided, flexibility of menus, provisions for special diets)
- Celebrations at the center (birthdays, holidays)
- Field trips and special guests to the center (transportation, allowances, finances, safety procedures)
- Child abuse and neglect (requirement to report, center procedures)
- Emergency information (where to call, how to contact staff)
- Parent participation and communication (volunteer, fund-raising, communication, newsletter)
- Guidance/discipline (state licensing requirements, center philosophy)
- References to other agencies
- Other policies as deemed necessary to present your program and its strengths to the parents and the community

worksheet

 **11.1**
p. 181

Make sure that the handbook looks professional, including clear copies, correct grammar, quality paper, and so on. The image that you present in writing is just as important as the image you present in person. Worksheet 11.1 provides space for you to write down a few ideas to develop the family handbook for your program. Also Example 11.1 offers some suggestions for items to include in your handbook.

FAMILY DIVERSITY

Families with Special Needs

According to the Americans with Disabilities Act and P.L. 99-457, children with special needs cannot be discriminated against. Therefore, you will have children with disabilities in your program. Depending on the child, the family, and the special need, you will make adaptations to include the child and family in your program. If the child has a physical disability, you may want to make space accommodations within the classroom. For example, the dramatic play area would need to be large enough for a child in a wheelchair to participate with at least two other children. If the child has feeding differences or requires a special diet, you may have to consider resources to help with planning or preparation of the special foods. The child may have medical needs that require administration of certain medicines, for example, an asthma inhaler. You will want to make sure your staff is comfortable and knowledgeable with the medicine and procedures that are required. The two most common adaptations include variations with the curriculum and staffing arrangements.

Curriculum adaptations are usually the easiest modifications to make. The teachers should consider each child's individual developmental level and plan accordingly. Many early care and education teachers do not believe they have the education or the experience to properly care for and educate a child with a diagnosed disability. You, as the director, set the tone and the atmosphere for accepting all children's differences and making the curriculum fit the child instead of making the child fit the curriculum. The other significant adaptation deals with staffing. Some children with special needs require a special teacher or therapists to assist them in the classroom. If a child has an Individualized Family Service Plan (IFSP) for ages birth to three years or has an Individualized Education Plan (IEP) for ages three to twenty-one years, then there will be other staff (paid for by public agencies) who are available to help with the accommodations for the child. You should invite this teacher or therapist to the program and work together for the child's benefit.

Another consideration may involve a family member with a special need, and your center would want to accommodate that member as well. If the parent has a physical disability, do all the entrances meet the specifications? If your program has a keyed entry system, is the keypad located so that a parent in a wheelchair can reach the keypad without assistance? A parent who is deaf may need an interpreter for parent conferences. A parent with vision problems may require the handbook in a format that he or she can read, perhaps in large print or on a specific color of paper. You must consider different forms of communication with parents depending on the special need. As you are preparing your family handbook, orientation procedures, meeting events, and other methods of working with parents, consider each family's individual needs and how your program can best meet those differing needs.

Diverse Family Structures

An important aspect of the relationships of the staff with family members is the nonjudgmental understanding of those individuals who are responsible for each child. In the 1940s, when preschool programs first became popular, it was assumed that the typical American family was similar to that of Dick and Jane in the first-grade primer. Those blue-eyed, brown-haired children matched their homemaker mommy and businessman daddy. This complacent acceptance of a stereotype is outdated. Directors now have enrollments with increasingly diverse family configurations. Variations may include single parents, stay-at-home fathers, foster families, grandparents rearing their grandchildren, or even older siblings who have taken on the parenting role. Sailor (2004) has described positive parenting practices of same-sex couples. Not only are there lesbians with children but also increasing numbers of gay males are becoming recognized by society as forming households in which children have two fathers.

Another change since the 1940s has been the racial integration of neighborhoods and businesses, with people from many different ethnic backgrounds living and working together. Large cities report that combined students speak seventy-five or more different home languages. However, many of the immigrant families who arrived in the United States following World War II have descendants who are thoroughly Americanized. In many centers, ancestral roots are honored by programs

---

WHAT WOULD YOU DO?

Trevor is an African American three-year-old in your program. Two Caucasian women have adopted him and he calls both of them "mother." In Trevor's class the teacher has had lots of questions about why Trevor does not look like his parents and why he has two mothers and no father. The children seem to understand about adoption but still ask about "two mothers." A few of the other parents in Trevor's class have asked questions about his family structure. One mother tells you that she does not want her daughter taught about homosexuality and that we should not acknowledge that he has two mothers. What would you do?

---

that involve parents and grandparents who provide ethnic music, handicrafts, and stories. Teachers should be aware of different religious traditions. A decorated Christmas tree might be seen as an appropriate feature of a classroom, but children whose families practice other religions would feel left out.

One example of differing American families involves two mothers. Mrs. Yamashita and Mrs. Nokamora volunteered to bring everything needed for the pre-K children to prepare a special snack. They laughed about what it would be and said it was a surprise. On the scheduled day, they arrived with two electric skillets and a bag of ingredients. It really was a surprise when they showed the children how to make English muffins. Well, did you expect something Japanese?

To further complicate the situation for early childhood staff, Caucasian parents are adopting children with different ethnicities, perhaps Mexican Americans from their own communities, baby girls from China, Romanian orphans, or others. They do not "match" and may create unique problems. Wardle and Cruz-Janzen (2004) have pointed out that children begin to explore individual differences between the ages of three and seven. Preschool directors should recognize that multiethnic and multiracial children, those who do not "look" like their parents and those whose parents do not "match" one another should not be stereotyped. Classroom books, dolls, and other materials should reflect diversity. These are readily available, and the NAEYC accreditation criteria require them.

COMMUNICATION SKILLS

Operation of an early childhood center depends on interaction. Communication has been discussed as a key element in the preceding pages; it is important in determining goals, in translating goals into terms that are meaningful to others, and in coordinating efforts of all members toward mutual objectives.

WHAT WOULD YOU DO?

Two three-year-old girls were assembling a large puzzle when one exclaimed, "Look, our hands are different colors!" When the teacher led them to the bathroom mirror, they were able to see that their faces were also different colors. They looked at other children in the diverse classroom and recognized that there were many variations in skin and hair coloring. Then they went back to finishing their puzzle, but the teacher was reminded that this had to be an important element in the classroom. Simply acknowledging differences is not enough. How would you deal with this situation?

Verbal Communication Skills

Communication is an exchange or sharing of ideas, verbally or nonverbally. When we truly communicate, we extend something of ourselves to others and take back a part of them. Effective communication makes growth and change possible. This involves two risks: We may expose what we really are inside and we may change into something different.

Communication takes place on three levels:

1. Intrapersonal, or with one's self, for weighing ideas, values, and actions; for making decisions; and for developing a way of life.
2. Interpersonal, or with one other person.
3. Group interaction, which relies on interaction among several individuals.

The process of communication can be visualized as having a sender who decides on a code (way) to send a message and a receiver who decodes (interprets) it. Feedback is then sent from the receiver to the sender; it is a process similar to a game of toss. It is the responsibility of the sender to gain the attention of the receiver through such devices as using understandable words, speaking loudly enough, using color or size, or appealing to certain psychological or physical needs. We must know the field of experience of the receiver so that we can select the right code. For example, we do not use the same way of speaking to parents as we do with small children.

Communication can be a complex system. When two people talk to each other, six voices are heard:

1. What you THINK you say.
2. What you DO say.
3. What the other person THINKS you say.
4. What the other person THINKS he or she says.
5. What the other person DOES say.
6. What you THINK the other person says.

It is important when communicating with parents to be clear in your words and actions to avoid misunderstandings.

Active Listening.   "Active listening" involves repeating the feeling of the statements back to the person with whom you are communicating. It is necessary to put yourself into the position of the other person, to be able to feel as he or she does and see the world as he or she is now seeing it. Very briefly, it might be stated that you are accepting the feeling of the parent without judging whether the parent is right or wrong and are reflecting these feelings back to the parent in a way that lets him or her know that you understand the issue. Frequently, the parent is able to solve the problem or work through the issue independently. You part friends and the usual conclusion to a well-handled conference of this sort, if you have listened well, is that THEY thank YOU for working things out.

Written Communication Skills

Program Newsletter.   The newsletter has been accepted for many years as the best way to communicate with parents and friends of the center. Even with increased reliance on websites and e-mail communication, an attractive newsletter is worth the time and effort entailed. There are sources that provide newsletters ready for you to duplicate, but these lack the personal touch of one unique to your program. You may be the editor, but perhaps your center can use the editorial talents of a teacher or volunteer.

The first page has a masthead at the top with the name of your center, the date of publication, perhaps your phone number or website address, and brief motto or slogan that identifies your program. A paragraph or two from the director can highlight special events or even the way problems are being dealt with. A representative of each room, usually the head teacher, has a similar brief statement about what is happening there. Other items that are frequently included are a listing of important dates, policy reminders, children's favorite snack recipes, requests for special volunteers or donations, welcome notes to new families, or expressions of sympathy to those who have experienced unfortunate events.

One critical element is proofreading the final copy. Words that are not spelled correctly or sentences that are improperly phrased will project an image that reflects poorly on your center's abilities as an educational program. Also do not simply rely on the spell check on your computer because inappropriate words can be spelled correctly but not convey the message you intended.

After the content is ready then you can add formatting. Children's line drawings add a bit of spice and can be done best with fine black felt pen on white paper. You may choose to add clip art from your computer software programs or from the Internet. The newsletter can be duplicated on site or at an office supply store. The result should look professional and unique to your center and its mission. You may want to use the same color paper for all the newsletters. Parents can associate the "blue" paper in the child's backpack as the newsletter and not a child's drawing.

Parent Bulletin Boards.   Most programs have a parent bulletin board. This should be located at the entrance to the center and should show the program license or registration information from the appropriate state agencies. This is also a good place to display items such as the menu, policies, notices, photographs, reminders, and printed items of interest. Be sure to keep the bulletin board updated to be a good form of communication. If you have the notice that October 15 is picture day and it is now December 3, your board will loose credibility as a place to obtain current information.

FAMILY ORIENTATION

Orientation is important for board members and teachers, but it also is necessary to have a carefully planned welcome and introduction for families. Remember that a family today may be quite different from the traditional one of a mother and a father. Family and work obligations need to be respected in order to meet with the family. Years ago, parent orientation often meant an afternoon tea for mothers, but that is as obsolete in most programs as dainty hats and white gloves. Certain procedures will need to be worked out that will be appropriate for your center. Will you operate year round, admitting children when openings occur, or will you follow a public school schedule? Will each child visit the empty classroom with a parent? Will a "hold-over" group of children assimilate newcomers? Will there be a staggered opening schedule so that some children arrive on the first day, more on the second and so on? Will teachers make preliminary home visits? Your child orientation program will depend on decisions you make.

If all children do begin at the same time, it is tempting to have everything out on display. Most authorities agree that this is too difficult for adults to supervise and for children to cope with. Stop to think about what these children probably have at home. Crayons? LEGO sets? Have a basic layout of easily supervised materials with a wide variation of appeal, including some that the children are accustomed to and some that are new to them. Perhaps they have never used play dough but they have undoubtedly messed with mud or helped their mothers in the kitchen. This may be their first creative material and the alert teacher will be able to diagnose the strengths and weaknesses of individual children as they manipulate and explore it.

Each teacher should know in advance which procedures and rules are to be explained and enforced from the beginning. For instance, four-year-olds may appreciate a straightforward announcement such as, "You may play with anything you want in this room until ten o'clock. I will tell you when that is. We will have snacks at this table and some games and then it will be time to go outside. Our most important rule is this: I cannot let you hurt the other children or spoil their play but I will help keep other children from spoiling your play." How will you deal with rules and limits during child orientation at your school? Evaluate them to see if they are necessary for the smooth functioning of the program. Can you project yourself into the minds of small children to get a feeling for your center from their viewpoint?

When we consider the orientation of parents to the school or center, it is necessary to combine parts of the child orientation approach with that of the staff orientation. A parent handbook mentioned earlier should be provided for permanent reference. Again, is it possible for you to visualize how these adults view your center? Are they well-educated, middle-class professional people accustomed to filling out forms and following routines, perhaps laughing about the reminders of college registration? Are they confused, possibly baffled by language barriers and hindered by an inability to read well but too proud to ask for help? Are they intimidated by an aura of sleek professionalism, or do they feel comfortable in these surroundings? One director never has parents come into her office but takes them to a corner of the kitchen where the coffee pot is handy and where they can watch the children on the playground. What message is she sending by this gesture?

Families need to gain an understanding of what the program will do for their child and be helped to understand how they can respond to the child's work so that maximum growth will be attained. They must also have an understanding of the operating policies of the school and the rationale behind them. Each school will base its parent orientation program on the needs of the parents. The indicated interests of these associates of yours who share your concerns for the children will determine a good parent education program.

Research studies confirm the belief that parents seek programs where their children will be safe, valued, and cared for. Orientation is a time for the director and teachers to listen to the concerns and expectations of the parents and children and to initiate an ongoing communication process. Parents gain an understanding of the operating policies of the school and the rationale behind them.

During orientation you will need to gather information about the child and family. Most state licensing facilities provide forms for the necessary information, but you may want to design your own forms to fit your program. The basic information needed from families is as follows:

- Contact information, such as address, phone numbers, parent/guardian work information

- Emergency information, such as authorized pickup and so on
- Child's health and medical information, including vaccinations, and allergies
- Parental permissions for field trips, photographs, and so on
- You may also want information about how issues such as discipline, routines, playmates, toileting issues, and bedtimes are handled at home

You should use the orientation time as an opportunity to get to know the families and for them to get to know you. The more information you can obtain in writing the better able you will be to meet the needs of the child and family. Your program will be based on the wants of the parents and children it serves and on the goals, purposes, and mission statement that you have determined. Worksheet 11.2 encourages you to consider components of orientation. List ideas that you will consider when new children enroll in the program.

worksheet

11.2
p. 183

FAMILY CONFERENCES

A family conference can be a sharing process that will reveal new thoughts and ideas. It has possibilities for both help and harm and there is truth in the old saying, "Fools rush in where angels fear to tread." Know your own capabilities and keep a current file of resources so that you can refer parents with serious problems to the proper agency. Remember that your long-term goal is to develop a satisfactory home–school program for the healthy adjustment of each child. There are no firm rules for being a good parent; what seems "wrong" to you may have no real basis. Recognize and accept cultural and individual differences.

During the conference, your short-term objectives are (1) to establish rapport and clarify any questions as to school procedures; (2) to exchange information; (3) to give parents an opportunity to talk; (4) to discuss, report, and evaluate progress; and (5) to consider a behavior problem. Realize that many parents are uncomfortable, or even threatened, in any sort of school situation; try to make them feel welcome. Also recognize that the parent feels on display when the child is part of a group. Accept the fact that there are parents you cannot help at this particular time.

Family Program Conference Guidelines

    I. Planning
        A. Keep records or notes over time to develop patterns and note progress, and to recognize specific skills attained and areas needing attention.
        B. Be prepared with art samples, assessment forms, notes, and other materials.

CLASS ACTIVITY

In small groups, role play a director, a teacher, a parent, and a child, with each person expressing expectations of what the early childhood center should do and be. How are they similar? How do they differ?

C. Arrange to meet in a comfortable place that ensures privacy and will be free of interruptions. Do not sit behind a desk because this may suggest that you are the one in power.

II. Conference
   A. Open and close the conference on a positive note.
   B. Listen carefully and sympathetically to the parent.
   C. Allow parent to express concerns and explanations to situations or problems before offering your interpretation.
   D. If the parent offers a plan of action, accept it if it is at all possible. You can try your idea later if that one does not work.
   E. Focus on solutions arrived at jointly.
   F. Recognize problems that are beyond your scope of expertise and be prepared to make referrals.

III. Closing the conference
   A. Determine how the center and home will work together.
   B. Make plans for follow-up on recommendations that have resulted from the conference.
   C. Possible questions to ask the parents include the following:
      1. What are his or her special interests at home?
      2. How is after-school time spent?
      3. Does he or she have home responsibilities?
      4. What does he or she share with you about school?

IV. Cautions
   A. Focus on discussion of the child and his or her home life as it relates to school.
   B. Keep the conference to a reasonable length of time.
   C. Avoid educational jargon; keep it simple.
   D. Concentrate on one or two major problems or concerns; do not overwhelm parents with every little detail.
   E. Do not assume the parents want help or advice.
   F. Do not make comparisons with or otherwise discuss other children or their families.

Remember: Family conferences should serve as a means to enhance the life of the child at home and at school. You are partners for the child, not enemies against the child.

Questions and Issues to Consider after a Conference.

- Did you let the parents talk about whatever they chose?
- Did you remain an acceptant listener?
- Did you remember that you need not ask questions to get at the important issues?
- When you made comments, did you talk in terms of parent feelings, rather than about what they are doing?
- Were you able to restrain yourself from giving advice?
- Did you remember that suggestions are usually nothing more than advice under a different guise?
- If you did offer suggestions, did you provide more than one so the parents had options?
- Did the parents do most of the talking?

- Were you able to restate to the parent the feelings just expressed?
- Did you listen? Furthermore, did you listen because you really cared?
- It is a natural tendency to put faith in objective information. Be aware of any emotional barriers!

REFERENCES AND RESOURCES

American Red Cross Staff. (2001). *Choosing quality child care: The American Red Cross guide.* Washington, DC: American Red Cross.

Davis, M. D., Kilgo, J. L., & Gamel-McCormick, M. (1998). *Young children with special needs: A developmentally appropriate approach.* Boston: Allyn & Bacon.

Diffily, D. (2004). *Teachers and families working together.* Boston: Allyn & Bacon.

Diffily, D., & Morrison, K. (1996). *Family-friendly communication for early childhood programs.* Washington DC: National Association for the Education of Young Children.

DiNatale, L. (2002). Developing high quality family involvement programs in early childhood settings. *Young Children, 57*(5), 90–95.

Epstein, A. S., Larner, M., & Halpern, R. (1995). *A guide to developing community-based family support programs.* Ypsilanti, MI: High/Scope Press.

Feeney, S., & Moravcik, E. (1995). *Discovering my world and me: A teacher's resource guide.* Circle Pines, MN: American Guidance Service, Inc.

Gennarelli, C. (2004). Communicating with families: Children lead the way. *Young Children, 59*(1), 98–99.

Goldberg, S. (1997). *Parent involvement begins at birth: Collaboration between parents and teachers in the early years.* Boston: Allyn & Bacon.

Gordon, A., & Browne, K. W. (1996). *Guiding young children in a diverse society.* Boston: Allyn & Bacon

Hamner, T. & Turner, P. (2000). *Parenting in contemporary society.* Boston: Allyn & Bacon.

Howes, C., & Smith, E. W. (1995). Relations among child care quality, teacher behavior, children's play activities, emotional security, and cognitive ability in child care. *Early Childhood Research Quarterly, 10,* 381–404.

Isenberg, J. P., & Jalongo, M. R. (2004). *Major trends and issues in early childhood education.* New York: Teachers College Press.

Jaffe, M. (1997). *Understanding parenting.* Boston: Allyn & Bacon.

Koplow, L. (1996). *Unsmiling faces: How preschools can heal.* New York: Teachers College Press.

Lerner, J. W. (2003). *Preschool children with special needs: Children at risk, children with disabilities.* Boston: Allyn & Bacon.

Lynch, E. (1998). *Developing cross-cultural competencies: A guide to working with children and their families.* Baltimore, MD: Paul H. Brookes.

Murphy, J. C. (2003). Case studies in African American school success and parenting behaviors. *Young Children, 58*(6), 85–89.

Olsen, G., & Fuller, M. L. (2003). *Home-school relations: Working successfully with parents and families.* Boston: Allyn & Bacon.

Sailor, D. H. (2004). *Supporting children in their home, school, and community.* Boston: Allyn & Bacon.

Shore, R. (2002). *What kids need: Today's best ideas for nurturing, teaching, and protecting young children.* Boston: Beacon Press.

Spinetti, C. (2002). Home–school collaboration at the early childhood level: Making it work. *Young Exceptional Children, 2*(2), 20–26.

Stonehouse, A., & Gonzale-Mena, J. (2001). Building trust and respect through communication. *Child Care Information Exchange, 142,* 57–59.

York, S. (2004). *Roots and wings: Affirming cultures in early childhood programs.* St. Paul, MN: Red Leaf Press.

Wardle, F., & Cruz-Janzen, M. (2004). *Meeting the needs of multiethnic and multiracial children in schools.* Boston: Allyn & Bacon.

WEBSITE RESOURCES

Biracial Kids: www.biracialkids.org

National Parenting Network: www.npn.org

Work and Family News Brief: www.info@workfamily.com

EXAMPLE 11.1

EXAMPLES FROM A FAMILY HANDBOOK

THE PROGRAM

The Child Care Center serves approximately one hundred children between the ages of twelve weeks and twelve years. The center is licensed by the Department of Human Resources. It is inspected annually by the fire and health departments and by the Community Child Care Licensing Department. The Child Care Center is accredited by the National Academy of Early Childhood Programs of the National Association for the Education of Young Children.

The Child Care Center strives

- To provide developmentally appropriate activities that stimulate the children's growth in the following areas: physical and motor skills, cognitive and problem-solving skills, communication skills, social/emotional skills, self-help skills, and self-discipline.
- To offer children the opportunity to develop positive relationships with adults and other children.

APPLICATION AND ADMISSION

Application

- Applications may be obtained from the office of the Child Care Center or downloaded from the website at www.childcarecenter.com.
- Any parent or legal guardian may make an application for a child regardless of race, color, creed, or socioeconomic status.
- The children's names are placed on a waiting list. As vacancies occur, the parent of the next child on the waiting list will be contacted. Placement also depends on the age of the child needed to fill the vacancy that occurs. Priority is given to siblings of children already enrolled at the center.

Admission

Children between the ages of twelve weeks and five years are accepted for care in the full-day program. Children enrolled in kindergarten to age twelve years are accepted into the after-school program. The Child Care Center provides transportation to the center from three area schools: Brookview, Colfax, and Hamilton.

Prior to enrollment, the center schedules an interview with a family member to discuss policies and procedures, obtain information about the child, and become familiar with the center. The registration form, physical record, immunization records, and consent form must be completed and required fees paid before the child is officially enrolled.

After acceptance, arrangements will be made for the child to visit the center for short periods of time for several days prior to entering the full-day program.

EXAMPLE 11.1 *(continued)*

Withdrawal

A one-week written notice is required when a child is leaving the center. The official withdrawal form is available from the office. All tuition payments must be made before leaving.

SCHEDULE

The center operates year round, Monday through Friday, from 7:00 A.M. to 6:00 P.M. except for the following holidays: New Year's Day, third Monday in January (Martin Luther King, Jr., Day), Good Friday, Independence Day, Labor Day, Thanksgiving Thursday and Friday, and four days at Christmas. The center will close for two professional development days. The families will be notified in advance.

TUITION: RATES/PAYMENT

Infants:	$200 per week
Toddlers:	$180 per week
Two-year-olds:	$165 per week
Preschoolers:	$150 per week
After-school care:	$100 per week (includes transportation from the school)

Payment Policies

A nonrefundable $25 application fee is due at the time of enrollment. Tuition is due the first day of each period covered by that payment. Monthly payments are preferred; however, payments may also be made on a weekly or biweekly basis.

All tuition payments shall be made directly to the office. Checks may be made payable to Child Care Center. A $25 fee will be charged for any returned checks; a cash-only policy will be required if more than one check has been returned. No refunds will be given for absences.

ARRIVAL AND DEPARTURE

- The center opens at 7:00 A.M. No child may be left at the center before it opens.
- The center should be notified when a child will be absent or when there will be variations in his or her schedule.
- Please hold your child's hand when arriving and leaving the classroom and the building. Sign in your child and be certain that the teacher has acknowledged your child's arrival before you leave.
- The center closes at 6:00 P.M. Parents, or other approved adults, must tell the teacher when picking up a child and must sign the child out.
- Only adults previously specified in writing by the parents will be allowed to pick a child up from the center unless the parent has notified the center in advance.

EXAMPLE 11.1 *(continued)*

- Parents who do not arrive for their children by 6:00 P.M. will be charged a late fee and emergency contact persons may be called to pick up the child. The fees for late pickup are

1–10 minutes: $10
11–20 minutes: $20
21–30 minutes: $30

HEALTH, SAFETY, AND NUTRITION

Each child must have a current immunization record and a physical examination record on file at the center within thirty days of enrollment. Parents are responsible for providing the center with updates of immunizations as they are received. A child who is not immunized according to the schedule will not be permitted to attend the center until the appropriate immunizations are received.

Prescription medication (in a bottle with a prescription label from the pharmacist) will be administered at the center. Over-the-counter medication will *not* be given by the staff to children. Medications will only be administered after the parent has completed the medication form available from the staff.

If the child sustains a minor injury, a center staff member trained in first aid will provide care. In case of illness or injury, the family will be contacted as soon as possible. In the event of a life-threatening emergency, an ambulance will be called and a parent notified immediately.

Meals

The children are provided daily with breakfast, lunch, and afternoon snack in the classroom. Menus are designed to emphasize nutrition as prescribed by the Food Guide Pyramid and to minimize sugar, salt, and fat intake. Menus are available and posted in each classroom monthly.

Parents should notify the center in writing and also discuss with the child's teacher any special diets, allergies, or food needs.

Parents of children under sixteen months of age shall give the teacher a written statement concerning the child's food requirements. All formulas will be provided by the parent in labeled and dated bottles and fed to their child only.

Emergency Information

The center will maintain on file the names and telephone numbers of persons to call for each child in case of an emergency when the parents cannot be located.

Authorization of persons who may pick up the children must be recorded. This information must be kept up-to-date. If changes occur, such as home address, telephone numbers, or contact people, please notify the staff immediately. Children will not be permitted to leave with persons not listed on the registration form unless notification, in writing, has been given to the center staff.

EXAMPLE 11.1 *(continued)*

Child Abuse and Neglect

State law requires that anyone suspecting that a child has been abused or neglected must report available evidence to the Department of Social Services, Protective Services Division. The Child Care Center staff will comply with the law in reporting such suspicions and simultaneously contact the child's parents or guardians.

Referral to Other Agencies

A conference will be held with the parents when it is believed that a child needs a special program or community resource. Then an appropriate referral will be made to the resources of Greenville and Hampton County.

FAMILY PARTICIPATION

Family participation is a welcome and vital aspect of the center program. Family members are welcome at any time and are encouraged to join their children throughout the day. Family programs are scheduled at various times during the year and you are encouraged to participate in these programs.

Monthly newsletters and classroom calendars will provide information about activities occurring at the center. Ideas and suggestions for the newsletter are welcome.

Family members are encouraged to request appointments for conferences to discuss their children with the teachers or director in addition to the informal communication at arrival and departure. The teachers will schedule two conferences per year to share with the family the progress the child has shown and to receive any information that may help them provide high-quality care and education to the child.

FAMILY HANDBOOK

Name _____ Date _____

Objective: To develop the family handbook.

Directions: For each of the following areas, write down ideas that would be necessary to include in a family handbook for your program. Review previous worksheets because some of the components have already been addressed.

Mission statement

Program description

Application and admission process

Schedule

Tuition

Arrival and departure information

Health and safety

Meal/snack information

Celebrations at the center

Field trips and special guests to the center

Child abuse and neglect

Emergency information

Parent participation and communication

Guidance/discipline (state licensing requirements)

Other policies

FAMILY ORIENTATION

Name _____ Date _____

Objective: To use knowledge to plan a family orientation program.

Directions: Considering information discussed previously, describe the components of a family orientation program.

Written information provided to parents

Written information obtained from parents

Center tour/visit
       Opportunities for parents

       Opportunities for child

Other ideas

CHAPTER TWELVE

Evaluating the Program

CHAPTER OUTLINE

ONGOING EVALUATION

CHILD EVALUATIONS

STAFF EVALUATIONS

ENVIRONMENT OR PROGRAM EVALUATION

ALTERNATIVE EVALUATIONS

SELF EVALUATION

Evaluation of progress and effectiveness is an integral part of the learning–teaching–administering process. You will recall that at the beginning of this guidebook a diagram with arrows was used to show the triangular nature of the management components of planning, operating, and evaluating. Evaluation can be viewed as a clear picture of a program or some portion of a program at a specific point in time. In managing a center, you establish goals and purposes. You then make plans and act on them in operating your center so that you will reach those goals and purposes. After that, through a deliberate process, you select and interpret information to make an informed judgment as to how well you have accomplished what you have set out to do. This final step is the evaluation process. Its purpose is to make some sort of decision. You may conclude that you are doing well and should simply continue doing what you have been doing. As the old saying goes, "If it ain't broke, don't fix it." However, the evaluation may indicate that you need to rethink and reassess your goals or your systems for reaching them (refer back to Chapter Three, "The Administrative Process"). This may not be negative. In fact, you may be doing so well that you decide to enlarge your scope or set higher targets. If the evaluation pinpoints problems with which you need to deal, this should be seen as a growth process for an individual or an institution. The evaluation should consider what has been done, should show what changes have taken place, and should pinpoint areas of difficulty.

ONGOING EVALUATION

Evaluative elements have been included in many topics throughout this guidebook, for example, in the evaluation of your personnel policies. You will evaluate your

185

record keeping and financial systems, perhaps revising forms when a reprinting is necessary, changing a computer software program to more clearly indicate areas in which costs exceed income, or pointing out the need for restructuring certain management functions. Like all other aspects of early childhood center management, your evaluation process will depend on the mission statement and structure of your center. Funding sources often define the need for specific evaluation and assessment procedures. Head Start is one example of a heavily evaluated program. This and other federally subsidized programs have academic requirements for the children. Parent education might be the primary function of a preschool funded by a high school for student parents and your position as its director would actually be that of a child development instructor. This would entail quite a different type of evaluation than that of the owner–proprietor of a private child care center or of an employer-sponsored on-site center. Some generalized characteristics of evaluation include the following:

1. Evaluation must address goals and objectives. Meaningful evaluation must always begin with the setting up of points to be reached. If you do not know where you are going, how do you know if you have gotten there?

2. Evaluation cannot be left for specific calendar dates or for the end of the term, although some portion of it might be assigned to those times. Some evaluation is ongoing and should be recognized as such. Allow time for it.

3. Evaluation must be both comprehensive and specific. It must be concerned with the total teaching experience of early care and education but must also define specific variables of your program and tell how they should be measured.

4. Evaluation should include self-analysis and a cooperative process for all of those involved if it is to be most valuable. There should be concern for the personal equation.

5. Evaluation should be viewed as a system in itself, with the establishment of definite lines of authority and the assignment of duties and responsibilities. Although a lengthy discussion of evaluation methodology is not possible in this guidebook, you as the director will hold management authority and will be responsible for the implementation of policies. You will be expected to make professional recommendations to the advisory board, if your center has one, or to comprehend directives from a sponsoring agency, if your center has that funding source.

Behavioral Objectives

As previously mentioned, to evaluate your program is to consider objectives. In contrast to the sometimes-vague goals that began with phrases such as "to understand" and "to enjoy" that were used in the past, there was a trend in the 1960s toward specification of instructional goals. To justify the use of tax money or foundation funding, some early childhood programs developed behavioral objectives to evaluate their curriculum activities. The following elements are specified:

1. *Who* is expected to accomplish the learning behavior? The three-year-old class? A teacher? The pre-K boys? An infant?

2. *What specific behavior* is required to demonstrate accomplishment of the objective? Use a statement that tells what the teacher or children will be doing while demonstrating this achievement.

3. *What learning outcome or product* will serve as the evidence of accomplishment of the objective to be evaluated? This may be the ability of four-year-olds to walk the entire length of a balance beam.

4. The *conditions* under which terminal behavior will occur should also be detailed. This identifies curriculum materials used, the limits to be placed on the task, the area in which it takes place, and other data.

5. The *criterion* or *standard* used to evaluate the accomplishments of the performance should answer questions as to how well the adults or children perform, at what level they are competent. This is also stated precisely in terms of a predetermined level, such as four out of five or 100 percent correct within ten minutes.

CHILD EVALUATIONS

The gathering of qualitative and quantitative materials and their organization into some sort of record of children or others is often called *assessment.* This may be an appraisal of kindergarten readiness on the basis of art products and anecdotal records or it may be a ranking of children in a class on the basis of height and weight to find those who are below norms for their age. It may involve testing by a psychologist from a central office who brings standardized intelligence tests, or children may be informally questioned about their mastery of concepts such as colors and numbers. A wide range of assessment techniques can be found in early childhood programs. These can be generally categorized as *formative evaluation,* to give you ongoing information as to how well you are meeting your objectives as you go along, and *summative evaluation,* to study the effectiveness of a program after you have reached your designated completion date.

A city school system trying to improve its performance ratings decided to have psychologists screen the kindergarten applicants to assess the students for readiness for first grade the following fall. On the day after her class had taken these tests, one mother was concerned because she had been told that her daughter had serious problems and should see a therapist. This was based on the "Draw a Man" test, for which she had made a tiny figure down in a corner of the page. That morning at school, she had painted a large picture of two little girls with ruffled dresses and bows in their hair. Between them they held an Easter basket, and behind a bunny was peeking out of a bush. Later that morning, the teacher heard this child asking others if "that psychologist" had asked them to draw a man, and they said that he had. "Well," said the girl in question, "I didn't even know him. I wasn't going to draw a penis for him to look at so I made it very tiny so he couldn't see it." Yes, she did well in kindergarten and entered advanced-placement first grade.

Administrators have some concerns about assessment of children in their programs. Standardized tests often are not relevant to the objectives of the curriculum. For comparison, researchers might show a crop failure because there are no oranges but the test is being done in an apple orchard. A second concern is that outsiders coming in to test children often are seen as disruptive or threatening by the teachers and other classroom staff. Additionally, administrators may believe that too much time is spent on testing and recording, and not enough time is spent on the things that are seen as most important. Another issue with standardized assessment is that children have widely variable responses. Assessment at one time may be completely different in its results from that done on the same child at a different time by a different individual or in a different environment The results, however, may go on a permanent record that affects future schooling.

If they are properly used, evaluation programs will incorporate a combination of informal methods (teacher observations, examples of children's work, parent conference notes) with staff-constructed or standardized tests that will give a true picture of the "whole child" development. An example of a checklist for children one to seventy-two months is available in Appendix D, "Developmental Skills Checklist." Evaluations should help everyone concerned with the children and the curriculum determine how individual children are progressing as well as how well the program is serving the objectives of the center. Results of assessment can also be used in your reports, perhaps to show how well your program is functioning and perhaps in an appeal for additional staff or more money.

Formal assessment should be taken as one aspect of the total picture when assessing children. Another important component of the evaluation involves written documents. You will need to make sure not to be overly positive or negative when writing about children's developmental skills. Also do not assure or guarantee any developmental skills or abilities in writing. One prekindergarten teacher learned this lesson the hard way. On the year-end evaluation for a child going to kindergarten she wrote, "Tim is a wonderfully creative child and will do great in kindergarten." As it turned out, Tim did not do so well in kindergarten. His new teacher did not have a curriculum for "creative" children and Tim had a hard time the first three months in class. The parents were very upset with the teacher in this program for making this prediction in writing. They confronted the teacher and director and asked for an explanation. The director had to explain that in their environment Tim did well, but the teacher did not account for the kindergarten being very different from her classroom. You should be careful what you put in writing, or it may come back to haunt you.

STAFF EVALUATIONS

There will not be a day in your center in which there is not staff evaluation, by the children and their families as well as by other employees. It is informal and nonstructured but ever present and can result in a climate of mutual help or one of friction. Formal staff evaluations are easier if the director has established a pattern of ongoing support. Some programs have established peer committees to conduct annual reviews, whereas others prefer to have outside evaluators who come in with their own rating lists of traits, activities, and performances. Whatever method of staff evaluation is done in your center, your function as an administrator should be to make certain that it follows these guidelines:

1. It should be something the teachers appreciate and look forward to because it helps them realize their strengths and growth needs, *not* something they dread as a threat to their self-esteem or their jobs.
2. It should be a process the staff has helped to develop or select, so that they know the criteria against which they will be evaluated, *not* a value judgment that is vague to those being evaluated.

3. It should be a reflection of the involvement of children, parents, and the rest of the staff in providing the best possible school, *not* something done to the staff by somebody higher in the system.
4. It should be based fairly on the programs, performance, and learning outcomes that are the objectives of the school, *not* on pretty bulletin boards or how popular the teacher is in community social activities. Evaluation is not a popularity contest.

If staff evaluation is viewed as an ongoing positive process, your role will include staff development through confirming behavior that supports your objectives. You can give positive rewards on the basis of such evaluations, perhaps a new plant for the science table of a teacher who has spent the weekend changing the classroom to suit a new emphasis for the children, or a word of appreciation to the janitor for the polished mirror in the restroom, or a pay raise for the aide who has completed a certificate program at night school. Related to this will be the assignment of extra responsibilities when you note that staff members are ready for them. Perhaps a teacher might give a report at a staff meeting on a special area of the curriculum or an aide might orient volunteer parents to their duties. Meaningful staff evaluation is not limited to a report filed under "personnel" in your office. Positive appreciation should be ongoing of course, and not only given after a formal process.

Many programs have forms that need to be used for the formal evaluation process. The actual forms used by a program should specifically relate to the program mission statement, goals, and objectives. Example 12.1 provides a sample evaluation form. As mentioned earlier in this text, *The Art of Leadership: Managing Early Childhood Organizations* (Neugebauer, 2003) is a good resource for specific examples of staff evaluation forms.

ENVIRONMENT OR PROGRAM EVALUATION

After you have completed evaluations on the children and staff, you need to consider the total environment or program. You have examined how you are meeting the needs of the children and staff, but what about the families and the program as a whole? You can address their needs through parent surveys or questionnaires. The NAEYC Accreditation process uses a survey that assesses communication procedures, policies, and the overall satisfaction of the parents with the program. Also you might develop your own survey tailored to your program's specific needs and services.

One way to evaluate the environment involves using a standardized system, such as the Environmental Rating System available through Teachers College Press. This system is designed with four different rating scales addressing infants and toddlers (Harms, Cryer, & Clifford, 2002), preschoolers (Harms, Cryer, & Clifford, 1998), school-agers, (Harms, Jacob, & White, 1996) and family child care programs (Harms & Clifford, 1998). Teachers, directors, and others can use these rating scales within the program. The scales address the total environment, including space and furnishings, personal care routines, language, activities and interactions, and parents and staff. The NAEYC Accreditation process also includes a classroom observation scale, to be completed by teachers, directors, or outside observers. This observation form can be used to examine child–staff interactions, classroom materials, and activities. You can also develop your own rating scale specific to your program. No matter what method you use, you should conduct periodic evaluations of your environment. Worksheet 12.1 gives you an opportunity to develop your own program evaluation tool.

worksheet

12.1
p. 197

ALTERNATIVE EVALUATIONS

You may find that other types of evaluation are appropriate for your program or are required by a funding source. These might include a community survey to measure whether you need to redesign your recruitment procedures or expand the enrollment, a self-study document in which the staff reexamines and appraises the objectives and the way they will be attained, a time–cost analysis or task-analysis to justify to an agency or corporation owner the cost of services and the efficiency of your operation, or other specialized evaluations. For most directors, however, the evaluation emphasis will be related to curriculum objectives and financial considerations.

Status Reports

Depending on the organizational structure of your program, you may find that reporting the results of evaluations constitutes a more difficult job than the evaluation process itself. The key question here is to ask who you are accountable to. Reports are an official communication between your center and the funding agency, the advisory board, the board of directors, or other groups to whom you are responsible. In some cases, the forms are provided for you, and it is simply a matter of filling in the blanks. The forms include financial reports (the annual budget report, a profit-and-loss statement), attendance records, progress reports, and any others that are specified. In addition, you will probably want to send other materials (parent newsletters, a new brochure, invitations to the Week of the Young Child open house) to individuals eligible for official reports so that they will have a more complete picture of what you are doing. This will make them more supportive of your objectives.

Perhaps you will also find that the report prepared for your board of directors is appropriate to send to others in your community. The early childhood education chairperson of the parent–teacher association, the local community college child development director, persons who have contributed time and money, interested alumni, and any referral agency or clearinghouse will be interested in them.

When writing the report, keep the audience in mind. Give a professional review but do not try to impress by including too much material or that which does not apply. Always include the dates of the period covered, the name and address of your center, the names of responsible officers and administrators, and a concise statement of your mission statement and goals. In writing the report, state the general purpose, define its scope, collect and analyze the information you want to include, organize the format, prepare a first draft, edit and edit again, then publish the final product.

CLASS DISCUSSION

Consider a published evaluation system, such as the Environmental Rating System by Harms, Cryer, and Clifford (1998, 2002) or another system appropriate to your program. Discuss what elements you would consider in your evaluation of the center or program.

SELF-EVALUATION

After you have evaluated all aspects of the program, staff, and children, it is time to evaluate yourself as the director. There are several ways to determine how well you are doing your job. One way is to use a standardized tool to assess how you handle the many aspects of the position. You can complete a self-evaluation assessment or ask your staff to provide feedback on certain aspects of what you do. You can also ask parents for feedback, especially if you prepare a program evaluation at the end of each year. The objective is to acknowledge your strengths and areas of growth. Do not expect yourself to be "perfect" in all aspects of the position. Everyone has areas to work on and as the director of a program you are no different. Worksheet 12.2 encourages you to consider the objectives for this guidebook to highlight your strengths and areas of growth.

worksheet

12.2 → *p. 199*

REFERENCES AND RESOURCES

Bloom, P. J. (2000). How do we define director competence? *Child Care Information Exchange, 132,* 13–18.

Bloom. P. J. (2004). *Leadership in action: How effective directors get things done.* Lake Forest, IL: New Horizons.

Bredekamp, S., & Rosegrant, T. (Eds). (1997). *Reaching potentials: Transforming early childhood curriculum and assessment: Vol. 2.* Washington, DC: National Association for the Education of Young Children.

Cohen, L., & Spenciner, L. J. (1998). *Assessment of children and youth.* New York: Addison Wesley Longman.

Culkin, M. (Ed.). (2000). *Managing quality in young children's programs.* New York: Teachers College Press.

Dodge, D. T., Heroman, C., Charles, J., & Maiorca, J. (2004). Beyond outcomes: How ongoing assessment supports children's learning and leads to meaningful curriculum. *Young Children, 59*(1), 20–28.

Gober, S. Y. (2002). *Six simple ways to assess young children.* Albany, NY: Delmar.

Guskey, T. R., & Sparks, D. (2000). *Evaluating professional development.* Thousand Oaks, CA: Corwin Press.

Harms, T., & Clifford, R. M. (1998). *Family day care rating scale.* New York: Teachers College Press.

Harms, T., Cryer, D., & Clifford, R. M. (1998). *Early childhood environment rating scale.* New York: Teachers College Press.

Harms, T., Cryer, D., & Clifford, R. M. (2002). *Infant/toddler environment rating scale.* New York: Teachers College Press.

Harms, T., Jacobs, E. V., & White, D. R. (1996). *School-Age Care Environment Rating Scale.* New York: Teachers College Press.

Kohn, A. (2001). Fighting the test: Turning the frustration into action. *Young Children, 56*(2), 19–24.

McAffee, O., & Leong, D. J. (2002). *Assessing and guiding young children's development and learning.* Boston: Allyn & Bacon.

McCutchen, W. (1998). *Franchising 101: The complete guide to evaluating, buying, and growing your franchised business.* Chicago: Upstart.

McDonald, S. (1999). *The portfolio and its uses: A road map for assessment.* St. Paul, MN: Red Leaf Press.

National Academy of Early Childhood Programs. (1991). *Accreditation criteria and procedures of the National Academy of Early Childhood Programs.* Washington, DC: National Association for the Education of Young Children.

Neugebauer, R. (2003). *The art of leadership: Managing early childhood organizations.* Redmond, WA: Child Care Information Exchange.

Nuttall, E. V., Romero, I., & Kalesnik, J. (1999). *Assessing and screening preschoolers: Psychological and educational dimensions.* Boston: Allyn & Bacon.

Sullivan, D. R. (2004). *Learning to lead: Effective leadership skills for teachers of young children.* St. Paul, MN: Red Leaf Press.

WEBSITE RESOURCES

Association for Supervision and Curriculum Development (ASCD):   www.ascd.org.

Culturally and Linguistically Appropriate Services of Early Childhood Research Institute: http://clas.uiuc.edu

Early Childhood Education Assessment (ECEA) Consortium: www.ccsso.org/projects/SCASS/Projects/Early_Childhood_Education_ Assesment_Consortium

Evaluation of Staff: http://daycare.about.com/library/weekly/aa0922009.

National Institute for Early Education Research: www.nieer.org/states

EXAMPLE 12.1

SAMPLE EMPLOYEE EVALUATION

Evaluator Name _____   Employee Name _____

Based on your experience with other employees with similar job duties and responsibilities, please indicate which best describes the employee:

A: Top performance

B: Meets standards

C: Improvement needed

CATEGORY	A	B	C
Attendance: The extent to which an employee is punctual, observes prescribed work break.			
Comments			
Reliability: The extent to which an employee can be relied on regarding task completion and follow up.			
Comments			
Job knowledge: The extent to which an employee possesses the practical/technical knowledge required on the job.			
Comments			
Independence: The extent to which an employee performs work with little or no supervision.			

EXAMPLE 12.1 *(continued)*

CATEGORY	A	B	C
Comments			
People skills: The extent to which an employee is willing and demonstrates the ability to cooperate, work, and communicate with co-workers, supervisors, subordinates, and outside contacts.			
Comments			
Adherence to policy: The extent to which an employee follows safety and conduct rules, other regulations, and adheres to company policies.			
Comments			
Initiative: The extent to which an employee seeks new assignments and assumes additional duties when necessary.			
Comments			
Communication: Communicates effectively, both verbally and in writing, with subordinates and superiors. Shares ideas, concepts, and knowledge with others. Listens to and understands others.			
Comments			

EXAMPLE 12.1 *(continued)*

CATEGORY	A	B	C
Organization/planning: Ability to assist in the development of goals and objectives (short and long range).			
Comments			
Team building: Promotes collaborative decisions, actions, and results with superiors, peers, and subordinates when appropriate. Promotes a spirit of good will and team building with other employees. A dedicated and committed team player.			
Comments			
Judgment: The extent to which an employee demonstrates proper judgment and decision-making skills when necessary.			
Comments			

CENTER EVALUATION

Name _____ Date _____

Objective: To develop an evaluation tool to critique a program.

Directions: Using the following areas, list what you would look for in your program.

Inside physical environment
  Routine spaces

  Curriculum spaces

  Children's interaction spaces: Individual, small group, and large group

  Parent space and resources

Staff space and resources

Outside physical environment

Other areas

SELF-EVALUATION

Name _____ Date _____

Objective: To use the knowledge gained through the completion of work-sheets to address the total job of a director.

Directions: Consider the objectives for the guidebook at the beginning of the text. Think about them one by one, and evaluate your strengths and areas of growth. Then analyze your assessment.

1. **Recognize your own personal administrative style.**

2. **Formulate and communicate to others the standards, purposes, and mission statement of early care and education.**

3. **Write and communicate to others the general, operating, and person-nel policies for a specific school or program.**

4. **Develop a teacher recruitment program and interview applicants.**

5. **Use differentiated staffing, including aides, parents, and other volun-teers, as well as teachers from varied backgrounds.**

6. **Plan and conduct meaningful staff meetings, including orientation.**

7. Set up and supervise a children's program that combines understanding from the past with recent research findings.

8. Participate meaningfully in professional organizations that act on behalf of young children and their welfare.

9. Develop an efficient and effective system for records and reports, including computer software programs.

10. Develop efficient and effective procedures for educational programs, including health, safety, and nutrition.

11. Apply common principles of communication when dealing with staff and the public; be aware of the principles of human relationships.

12. Plan effective parent orientation and educational opportunities, recognizing parents' diverse needs.

13. Understand basic dynamics of working with parents who have unique family values and expectations.

14. Appraise skills and techniques in evaluation of program staff and self.

TIMELINE OF EARLY CARE AND EDUCATION IN THE UNITED STATES

1840 Friedrich Froebel (1782–1852) officially opened his first kindergarten.

1856 First public use of term "Kindergarten" in Barnard's July issue of *American Journal of Education.*

1856 Margarethe Schurz taught German-language kindergarten in her Wisconsin home.

1860 First English-language kindergarten opened in Boston by Elizabeth Peabody.

1865 William Hailmann opened Froebelian kindergarten stressing parent involvement at German–American Academy, Louisville, Kentucky.

1868 Matilde Kriege established first U.S. kindergarten training school in Boston.

1869 Milton Bradley began the first large-scale manufacture of children's educational materials based on Gifts and Occupations of Froebel.

1873 Susan Blow directed the first public school kindergarten in St. Louis, Missouri, in 1880. NEA listed about 400 kindergartens in 30 states.

1882 Collegiate Alumni founded, later became the American Association of University Women (AAUW); helped establish preschools in the 1920s.

1884 National Education Association (NEA) formed a Kindergarten Department.

1892 International Kindergarten Union formed by women who believed men in NEA did not appreciate the value of kindergarten education.

1906 John Dewey established laboratory school at the University of Chicago.

1907 Congress of Mothers organized at a kindergarten conference; became National Congress of Parents and Teachers (PTA) in 1942.

1907 Maria Montessori opened *Casa dei Bambini* in Rome tenement; its success led to her developing a method of teaching.

1908 American Home Economics Association (AHEA) held organizational meeting; became American Association for Family and Consumer Studies in 1997.

1909 President Theodore Roosevelt held first White House Conference on Children and Youth.

1910 G. Stanley Hall, at Clark University, hosted psychoanalysts Carl Jung, Sigmund Freud, and Sandor Ferenczi; kindergarten leaders attended.

1911 U.S. Montessori school opened by Anne George in Tarrytown, New York.

1911 McMillan sisters established original "nursery school" near London, based on nearby Froebel kindergartens.

1912 Establishment of controversial U.S. Children's Bureau; published *Infant Care* in 1914 and *Your Child from One to Six* in 1918, with millions distributed at no cost to recipients.

1912 Children's Bureau Report said 7,557 kindergartens, up 133 percent in past ten years.

1914 Beginning of European military conflict now known as World War I.

1917   Smith-Hughes Act defined homemaking as a basic vocation for women; provided federal funds for child development laboratories.

1921   Patty Smith Hill brought Grace Owen, English nursery school teacher, to lecture at Teachers College in New York. The University of Iowa Child Welfare Research Station opened preschool center.

1922   Merrill-Palmer Motherhood and Home Training School in Detroit and Ruggles Street Nursery School in Boston established, both based on English nursery schools.

1923   Barbara Greenwood started laboratory school at the University of California, Los Angeles.

1933   Federally funded preschools began under Works Progress Administration (WPA).

1943   Federally subsidized Lanham Act Child Care Centers for children of women working in defense industry began; ended 1946.

1945   World War II ended in Japan on April 14; in Europe ended on May 8.

1946   First edition of Dr. Spock's *Pocketbook of Baby and Child Care* published.

1946   Twelve percent of mothers were employed, 3 million fewer than in 1944; beginning of baby boom generation.

1948   OMEP, World Organization for Preschool Education, founded.

1949   About one-third of five-year-olds were enrolled in kindergartens.

1950   Merrill-Palmer study showed 3,377 preschools in the United States.

1950   Midcentury White House Conference on Children and Youth.

1952   Francis Horwich started *Ding Dong School* as the first TV program for young children; it ran until 1963.

1952   U.S. Department of Education listed 254 cooperative nursery schools, with about one-third established in 1950–1951.

1953   President Eisenhower established the Department of Health, Education, and Welfare.

1954   *Brown v. Board of Education* desegregated public schools; protests followed.

1955   Martin Luther King, Jr., and others began nonviolent action to attain racial equality.

1956   Only one in ten doctoral degrees were granted to women, a lower ratio than in 1920. More than 18 million children were under age five, one-eighth more than in 1950.

1956   Public interest in Jean Piaget began; David Elkind began replication research.

1957   Launch of Russia's *Sputnik* started the space race; beginning of academic competition and emphasis on early literacy.

1960   National Defense Education Act recognized preschool importance as preparation for later schooling.

1960   Peak year for cooperative nursery schools, with about 1,000 in operation.

1960   White House Conference on Families convened in April.

1960   High/Scope Perry Preschool Project incorporated.

1961   C. Henry Kempe coined term *battered child syndrome* after doing national survey.

1961   John F. Kennedy became president; Jackie Kennedy started White House cooperative nursery school, which gave publicity to preschool education. Federal family support system initiated.

1961   United States entered Vietnam military conflict.

1963   Betty Friedan gave new focus to women's roles in *The Feminine Mystique*.

1963   Lyndon Johnson became president after Kennedy was assassinated.

1964   Federal Economic Opportunity Act provided Head Start funding.

1964   NANE reorganized to become NAEYC; *Journal* became *Young Children*.

1965   Project Head Start originated as a multidisciplinary program for children of low-income families, with 561 thousand attending hastily designed summer sessions that first year.

1966   U.S. Office of Education reported 97.8 percent of five-year-olds in public kindergartens.

1967   Educational Resources Information Center (ERIC) established.

1968   One out of every ten seventeen-year-old girls was a mother.

1969   First Kinder-Care Learning Center established in Montgomery, Alabama; became first large child care corporation with common stock sold on Wall Street; in its first ten years, 459 centers enrolled 47,000 children.

1969   Richard Nixon inaugurated as president; suggested "experimental" child care centers although 200 federal programs were already providing assistance.

1969   *Sesame Street* began broadcasting on public television stations.

1970   Office of Child Development was established, including Children's Bureau; was discontinued in 1977 because of federal reorganization.

1971   President Nixon vetoed popular Comprehensive Child Development Act (Senate Bill 2007).

1973   Marian Wright Edelman started Children's Defense Fund to advocate for family issues.

1973   Federal tax deductions authorized for employers providing child care services.

1974   Census found almost twice as many single-parent families as in 1960.

1975   Birthrate of 14.9 per thousand was lowest in U.S. history, but it was the first year to have more than 1 million divorces.

1975   First Child Development Associate (CDA) credentials awarded.

1978   Tennessee was first state to require children to wear seatbelts; others soon followed and further regulations were enacted.

1978   *Child Care Information Exchange* began publishing bimonthly journal for directors of preschools and child care centers.

1979   Congressional Budget Office said government had spent $1.7 billion on direct support of young children's programs and had given $500 million through parental income tax credits.

1980   About half (7.5 million) of American women with children under six were in the labor force. Falling birthrate began turning upward.

1980   White House Conference on Children and Youth cancelled because national conflict over definition of *family* could not be resolved.

1981   President Reagan signed Omnibus Budget Reconciliation Act that cut funding for many children's programs and related services.

1985   First congressional attempts to get federal legislation for family leave policy.

1990   Census found more than 10 million working mothers with children under six. National survey found that only 11 percent of those not employed outside the home had "substantial use" of preschool.

1990   President Bush signed P.L. 101–508 to help fund child care and Head Start but vetoed Family and Medical Leave Act.

1996   National attention aroused by "Stand for Children" in Washington, DC.

1996   "Welfare reform" legislation required low-income mothers to take employment and provided limited funding for child care.

2001   Bipartisan Congressional Caucus on Child Care is established, adopting Children's Defense Fund slogan of "Leave no child behind."

2003   U.S. Department of Education estimated that more than 5 million children were enrolled in child care centers or other preschool programs, about one-third operated on a for-profit basis.

FOOD Guide PYRAMID
for Young Children

A Daily Guide for 2- to 6-Year-Olds

Fats & Sweets — Eat LESS

MILK Group 2 servings

MEAT Group 2 servings

VEGETABLE Group 3 servings

FRUIT Group 2 servings

GRAIN Group 6 servings

U.S. Department of Agriculture
Center for Nutrition Policy and Promotion

January 2000
Program Aid 1651

USDA is an equal opportunity provider and employer.

FOOD IS FUN and learning about food is fun, too. Eating foods from the Food Guide Pyramid and being physically active will help you grow healthy and strong.

WHAT COUNTS AS ONE SERVING?

GRAIN GROUP
1 slice of bread
½ cup of cooked rice or pasta
½ cup of cooked cereal
1 ounce of ready-to-eat cereal

VEGETABLE GROUP
½ cup of chopped raw or cooked vegetables
1 cup of raw leafy vegetables

FRUIT GROUP
1 piece of fruit or melon wedge
¾ cup of juice
½ cup of canned fruit
¼ cup of dried fruit

MILK GROUP
1 cup of milk or yogurt
2 ounces of cheese

MEAT GROUP
2 to 3 ounces of cooked lean meat, poultry, or fish.
½ cup of cooked dry beans, or 1 egg counts as 1 ounce of lean meat. 2 tablespoons of peanut butter count as 1 ounce of meat.

FATS AND SWEETS
Limit calories from these.

Four- to 6-year-olds can eat these serving sizes. Offer 2- to 3-year-olds less, except for milk. Two- to 6-year-old children need a total of 2 servings from the milk group each day.

EAT a variety of FOODS AND ENJOY!

Source: Used with permission from the U.S. Department of Agriculture. Food Guide Pyramid. http://www.usda.gov/cnpp/KidsPyra/

CHILD CARE MEAL PATTERNS

CHILD CARE INFANT MEAL PATTERN: BREAKFAST

BIRTH THROUGH 3 MONTHS	4 THROUGH 7 MONTHS	8 THROUGH 11 MONTHS
4–6 fluid ounces of formula[1] or breast milk[2,3]	4–8 fluid ounces of formula[1] or breast milk;[2,3] 0–3 tablespoons of infant cereal[1,4]	6–8 fluid ounces of formula[1] or breast milk[2,3]; and 2–4 tablespoons of infant cereal[1]; and 1–4 tablespoons of fruit or vegetable or both

[1] Infant formula and dry infant cereal must be iron-fortified.
[2] Breast milk or formula, or portions of both, may be served; however, it is recommended that breast milk be served in place of formula from birth through 11 months.
[3] For some breast-fed infants who regularly consume less than the minimum amount of breast milk per feeding, a serving of less than the minimum amount of breast milk may be offered, with additional breast milk offered if the infant is still hungry.
[4] A serving of this component is required when the infant is developmentally ready to accept it.

CHILD CARE INFANT MEAL PATTERN: SNACK

BIRTH THROUGH 3 MONTHS	4 THROUGH 7 MONTHS	8 THROUGH 11 MONTHS
4–6 fluid ounces of formula[1] or breast milk[2,3]	4–6 fluid ounces of formula[1] or breast milk[2,3]	2–4 fluid ounces of formula[1] or breast milk,[2,3] or fruit juice[5]; and 0–½ bread[4,6] or 0–2 crackers[4,6]

[1] Infant formula and dry infant cereal must be iron-fortified.
[2] Breast milk or formula, or portions of both, may be served; however, it is recommended that breast milk be served in place of formula from birth through 11 months.
[3] For some breast-fed infants who regularly consume less than the minimum amount of breast milk per feeding, a serving of less than the minimum amount of breast milk may be offered, with additional breast milk offered if the infant is still hungry.
[4] A serving of this component is required when the infant is developmentally ready to accept it.
[5] Fruit juice must be full-strength.
[6] A serving of this component must be made from whole-grain or enriched meal or flour.

Source: Used with permission from U.S. Department of Agriculture. Child Care Meal Patterns www.fns.usda.gov/cnd/care/ProgramBasics/Meals.

CHILD CARE INFANT MEAL PATTERN: LUNCH OR SUPPER

BIRTH THROUGH 3 MONTHS	4 THROUGH 7 MONTHS	8 THROUGH 11 MONTHS
4–6 fluid ounces of formula[1] or breast milk[2,3]	4–8 fluid ounces of formula[1] or breast milk;[2,3] 0–3 tablespoons of infant cereal;[1,4] and 0–3 tablespoons of fruit or vegetable or both[4]	6–8 fluid ounces of formula[1] or breast milk;[2,3] 2–4 tablespoons of infant cereal;[1] and/or 1–4 tablespoons of meat, fish, poultry, egg yolk, cooked dry beans or peas; or ½-2 ounces of cheese; or 1–4 ounces (volume) of cottage cheese; or 1–4 ounces (weight) of cheese food or cheese spread; and 1–4 tablespoons of fruit or vegetable or both

[1]Infant formula and dry infant cereal must be iron-fortified.
[2]Breast milk or formula, or portions of both, may be served; however, it is recommended that breast milk be served in place of formula from birth through 11 months.
[3]For some breast-fed infants who regularly consume less than the minimum amount of breast milk per feeding, a serving of less than the minimum amount of breast milk may be offered, with additional breast milk offered if the infant is still hungry.
[4]A serving of this component is required when the infant is developmentally ready to accept it.

CHILD CARE MEAL PATTERN: BREAKFAST FOR CHILDREN
SELECT ALL THREE COMPONENTS FOR A REIMBURSABLE MEAL

FOOD COMPONENTS	AGES 1–2	AGES 3–5	AGES 6–12[1]
1 milk fluid milk	½ cup	¾ cup	1 cup
1 fruit/vegetable juice,[2] fruit and/or vegetable	¼ cup	½ cup	½ cup

1 grains/bread[3]
    bread or
    cornbread or biscuit or roll or muffin or
 	
    cold dry cereal or
    hot cooked cereal or
    pasta or noodles or grains
	½ slice
	½ serving
	
	¼ cup
	¼ cup
	¼ cup
		½ slice
		½ serving
		
		⅓ cup
		¼ cup
		¼ cup
			1 slice
			1 serving
			
			¾ cup
			½ cup
			½ cup

[1]Children age 12 and older may be served larger portions based on their greater food needs. They may not be served less than the minimum quantities listed in this column.
[2]Fruit or vegetable juice must be full-strength.
[3]Breads and grains must be made from whole-grain or enriched meal or flour. Cereal must be whole-grain or enriched or fortified.

CHILD CARE MEAL PATTERN: LUNCH OR SUPPER FOR CHILDREN
SELECT ALL FOUR COMPONENTS FOR A REIMBURSABLE MEAL

FOOD COMPONENTS	AGES 1–2	AGES 3–5	AGES 6–12[1]
1 milk			
fluid milk	½ cup	¾ cup	1 cup
2 fruits/vegetables			
juice,[2] fruit and/or vegetable	¼ cup	½ cup	¾ cup
1 grains/bread[3]			
bread or	½ slice	½ slice	1 slice
cornbread or biscuit or roll or muffin	½ serving	½ serving	1 serving
or cold dry cereal	¼ cup	⅓ cup	¾ cup
or hot cooked cereal or	¼ cup	¼ cup	½ cup
pasta or noodles or grains	¼ cup	¼ cup	½ cup
1 meat/meat alternate			
meat or poultry or fish[4] or	1 oz.	1½ oz.	2 oz.
alternate protein product or	1 oz.	1½ oz.	2 oz.
cheese or	1 oz.	1½ oz.	2 oz.
egg or	½	¾	1
cooked dry beans or peas or	¼ cup	⅜ cup	½ cup
peanut or other nut or seed butters or	2 tbsp.	3 tbsp.	4 tbsp.
nuts and/or seeds[5] or	½ oz.	¾ oz.	1 oz.
yogurt[6]	4 oz.	6 oz.	8 oz.

[1]Children age 12 and older may be served larger portions based on their greater food needs. They may not be served less than the minimum quantities listed in this column.

[2]Fruit or vegetable juice must be full-strength.

[3]Breads and grains must be made from whole-grain or enriched meal or flour. Cereal must be whole-grain or enriched or fortified.

[4]A serving consists of the edible portion of cooked lean meat or poultry or fish.

[5]Nuts and seeds may meet only one-half of the total meat/meat alternate serving and must be combined with another meat/meat alternate to fulfill the lunch or supper requirement.

[6]Yogurt may be plain or flavored, unsweetened or sweetened.

CHILD CARE MEAL PATTERN: SNACK FOR CHILDREN
SELECT TWO OF THE FOUR COMPONENTS FOR A REIMBURSABLE SNACK

FOOD COMPONENTS	AGES 1–2	AGES 3–5	AGES 6–12[1]
1 milk			
fluid milk	½ cup	½ cup	1 cup
1 fruit/vegetable			
juice,[2] fruit and/or vegetable	½ cup	½ cup	¾ cup
1 grains/bread[3]			
bread or	½ slice	½ slice	1 slice
cornbread or biscuit or roll or muffin or	½ serving	½ serving	1 serving
cold dry cereal or	¼ cup	⅓ cup	¾ cup
hot cooked cereal or	¼ cup	¼ cup	½ cup
pasta or noodles or grains	¼ cup	¼ cup	½ cup
1 meat/meat alternate			
meat or poultry or fish[4] or	½ oz.	½ oz.	1 oz.
alternate protein product or	½ oz.	½ oz.	1 oz.
cheese or	½ oz.	½ oz.	1 oz.
egg[5] or	½	½	½
cooked dry beans or peas or	⅛ cup	⅛ cup	¼ cup
peanut or other nut or seed butters or	1 tbsp.	1 tbsp.	2 tbsp.
nuts and/or seeds or	½ oz.	½ oz.	1 oz.
yogurt[6]	2 oz.	2 oz.	4 oz.

[1]Children age 12 and older may be served larger portions based on their greater food needs. They may not be served less than the minimum quantities listed in this column.
[2]Fruit or vegetable juice must be full-strength. Juice cannot be served when milk is the only other snack component.
[3]Breads and grains must be made from whole-grain or enriched meal or flour. Cereal must be whole-grain or enriched or fortified.
[4]A serving consists of the edible portion of cooked lean meat or poultry or fish.
[5]One-half egg meets the required minimum amount (one ounce or less) of meat alternate
[6]Yogurt may be plain or flavored, unsweetened or sweetened.

■ ■ ■ ■ ■ ■ ■ ■

DEVELOPMENTAL SKILLS CHECKLISTS FOR AGES ONE TO SEVENTY-TWO MONTHS

DEVELOPMENTAL SKILLS CHECKLIST: AGES ONE TO TWELVE MONTHS

Child's Name _____ Date of Birth _____

Consider the developmental skills for each child. Place the date that corresponds to the child's skill level at the time of the observations.

FINE- AND GROSS-MOTOR SKILLS	NOT YET	SOMEWHAT	INDEPENDENTLY
1–4 months			
Grasps with entire hand; not strong enough to hold items			
Rolls from stomach to back	_____	_____	_____
Can sit with support, holding head steady and keeping back fairly erect	_____	_____	_____
4–8 months			
Pincer grasp: finger and thumb to pick up objects	_____	_____	_____
Handles, shakes, and pounds objects	_____	_____	_____
Sits alone without support, holding head erect, back straightened, and arms propped forward for support	_____	_____	_____
May scoot backwards when placed on stomach; begins crawling forward	_____	_____	_____
8–12 months			
Manipulates objects, transferring them from one hand to other	_____	_____	_____
Stacks objects; also places objects inside one another	_____	_____	_____
Begins to pull self to standing position, stand alone, leans on furniture for support	_____	_____	_____
Creeps on hands and knees; crawls up and down stairs	_____	_____	_____

Source: Adapted from Allen, K. E., & Marotz, L. R. (2003). *Developmental profiles: Pre-birth through twelve.* New York: Delmar.

COGNITIVE–PERCEPTUAL SKILLS	NOT YET	SOMEWHAT	INDEPENDENTLY
1–4 months			
Watches hands intently			
Imitates gestures that are modeled: bye-bye, patting head			
Looks in direction of a sound			
4–8 months			
Uses hands, mouth, and eyes in coordination to explore body, toys, and surroundings			
Searches for toy or food that is hidden under a cloth			
Bangs objects together playfully			
8–12 months			
Reaches for toys that are visible but out of reach			
Shows appropriate use of everyday items, pretends to drinks from cup			
Begins to show an understanding of cause and effect			
Shows some awareness of the functional relationship of objects, for example puts spoon in mouth			

SPEECH AND LANGUAGE SKILLS	NOT YET	SOMEWHAT	INDEPENDENTLY
1–4 months			
Coordinates vocalizing, looking, and body movements in face-to-face exchanges with care giver			
Can follow and lead in keeping communication going			
Babbles or coos when spoken to or smiled at			
Coos using single vowel sounds *(ah, eh, uh)*			
4–8 months			
Responds appropriately to own name and simple requests, such as wave "bye-bye"			
Produces a full range of vowels and some consonants: b, m, p			
Babbles by repeating same syllable in a series: ba, ba, ba			
8–12 months			
Shakes head for "no" and may nod for "yes"			
Waves "bye-bye"; claps hands when asked.			
Says "da-da" and "ma-ma"			
Hands toy or object to an adult when appropriate gestures accompany the request			

SOCIAL/EMOTIONAL SKILLS	NOT YET	SOMEWHAT	INDEPENDENTLY
1–4 months			
Coos, gurgles, and squeals when awake			
Smiles in response to a friendly face or voice			
Recognizes and reaches out to familiar faces			
4–8 months			
Distinguishes among, and responds differently to, strangers and teachers			
Stranger anxiety, distress, or fear shown when approached by unfamiliar persons			
Becomes upset if toys or other objects are taken away			
8–12 months			
Exhibits a definite fear of strangers; clings to or hides behind teachers			
Shows need to be picked up by extending arms upward			
Carries out simple directions and request; understands "no"			

SELF-HELP SKILLS	NOT YET	SOMEWHAT	INDEPENDENTLY
1–4 months			
Begins fussing before anticipated feeding times; does not always cry to signal need to eat			
Begins to establish a regular time or pattern for bowel movements			
4–8 months			
Shows interest in feeding activities; reaches for cup and spoon while being fed			
Begins to accept small amount of pureed foods, such as cereal and vegetables			
Pulls off own socks; plays with strings, buttons, and velcro closures on clothing			
Takes two or three naps per day			
8–12 months			
Likes to drink from a cup, holding it alone			
Fusses when diaper needs changing; may pull off soiled or wet diaper			
Cooperates to some degree in being dressed; helps put arms in armholes, may even extend legs to have pants put on			
Takes one afternoon nap most days; length varies from infant to infant			

DEVELOPMENTAL SKILLS CHECKLIST:
AGES TWELVE TO THIRTY-SIX MONTHS

Child's Name _____ Date of Birth _____

Consider the developmental skills for each child. Place the date that corresponds to the child's skill level at the time of the observations.

FINE- AND GROSS-MOTOR SKILLS	NOT YET	SOMEWHAT	INDEPENDENTLY
12–18 months			
Repeatedly picks up objects and throws them			
Voluntarily releases an object			
Enjoys pushing and pulling toys while walking			
Most children walk unassisted during this period; falls often			
18–36 months			
Stacks two to four objects			
Grasps large crayon with fist; scribbles with whole arm on large piece of paper			
Enjoys pouring and filling activities			
Tries hard to balance on one foot			
Runs with greater confidence; has fewer falls			

COGNITIVE–PERCEPTUAL SKILLS	NOT YET	SOMEWHAT	INDEPENDENTLY
12–18 months			
Passes toy to other hand when offered a second object			
Enjoys object hiding activities			
Shows increasing understanding of spatial and form discrimination as through pegboards and puzzles			
18–36 months			
Exhibits eye–hand movements that are better coordinated			
Begins to use objects for purposes other than intended (may push a block around as a boat)			
Completes simple classification tasks based on one dimension (separates dinosaurs from toy cars)			
Shows discovery of cause and effect			
Recognizes and expresses pain and its location			

SPEECH AND LANGUAGE SKILLS	NOT YET	SOMEWHAT	INDEPENDENTLY
12–18 months			
Uses one word to convey an entire thought			
Follows simple directions: "Give mommy the doll"			
Identifies three body parts if someone names them			

SPEECH AND LANGUAGE SKILLS	NOT YET	SOMEWHAT	INDEPENDENTLY
Indicates a few desired objects and activities by name			
Acquires and uses five to fifty words	___	___	___

18–36 months

	NOT YET	SOMEWHAT	INDEPENDENTLY
Two- to three-word sentences	___	___	___
Uses 50 to 300 different words; vocabulary continuously increasing	___	___	___
Utters three- to four-word statements	___	___	___
Refers to self as "me" or sometimes "I" rather than by name: "Me go bye-bye"; has no trouble verbalizing "mine"; can call self by name	___	___	___

SOCIAL/EMOTIONAL SKILLS	NOT YET	SOMEWHAT	INDEPENDENTLY
12–18 months			
Helps clean up toys	___	___	___
Imitate adults' actions	___	___	___
Recognizes self in mirror	___	___	___
18–36 months	___	___	___
Identifies all materials as "mine"	___	___	___
Enjoys "helping" with household chores; imitates everyday activities	___	___	___
"Bossy"; makes demands and expects immediate compliance from adults	___	___	___
Watches and imitates the play of other children, but plays alone most of the time	___	___	___

SELF-HELP SKILLS	NOT YET	SOMEWHAT	INDEPENDENTLY
12–18 months			
Shows some control of cup: lifts it up, drinks from it, sets it down, holds the handle			
Helps with dressing: puts arms in sleeves, lifts feet to have socks put on, dress and undress self: takes off own shoes	___	___	___
18–36 months			
Likes simple, "recognizable" foods; dislikes mixtures; wants foods served in familiar ways	___	___	___
Feeds self with increasing skill; has good control of cup or glass, although spills happen often	___	___	___
Tries to help when being dressed; needs simple, manageable clothing; can usually undress self	___	___	___

DEVELOPMENTAL SKILLS CHECKLIST:
AGES THIRTY-SIX TO FORTY-EIGHT MONTHS

Child's Name _____ Date of Birth _____

Consider the developmental skills for each child. Place the date that corresponds to the child's skill level at the time of the observations.

FINE- AND GROSS-MOTOR SKILLS.	NOT YET	SOMEWHAT	INDEPENDENTLY
Uses vertical, horizontal circular strokes. Holds crayon or marker between first two fingers and thumb.			
Builds a tower of eight or more blocks.	_____	_____	_____
Jumps in place.	_____	_____	_____
Catches a large bounced ball with both arms extended.	_____		_____
Walks up and down stairs unassisted, using alternating feet; may jump from bottom step, landing on both feet.	_____	_____	_____
	_____	_____	_____

COGNITIVE–PERCEPTUAL SKILLS	NOT YET	SOMEWHAT	INDEPENDENTLY
Plays realistically:	_____	_____	_____
Feeds doll, puts down for nap	_____	_____	_____
Hooks truck and trailer together, loads truck, makes motor noises	_____	_____	_____
Places eight to ten pegs in pegboard.	_____	_____	_____
Attempts to draw; imperfectly copies circles, squares, and some letters.	_____	_____	_____
Sorts objects logically on the basis of one dimension, such as color or size.	_____	_____	_____
Names and matches, primary colors: red, yellow, blue.	_____	_____	_____
Counts objects out loud, begins to match numeral to number of objects.	_____	_____	_____
	_____	_____	_____

SPEECH AND LANGUAGE SKILLS	NOT YET	SOMEWHAT	INDEPENDENTLY
Talks about the actions of others: "Jessie is painting a picture."			
Joins in social interaction rituals: "Hi," "Bye," "Please."	_____	_____	_____
Comments about objects and ongoing events: "There's a house"; "The truck is pulling a boat."	_____	_____	_____
Vocabulary has increased; now uses 300 to 1,000 words.	_____	_____	_____
Recites nursery rhymes, sings songs.	_____	_____	_____
Answers "What are you doing?" "What is this?" and "Where?" questions dealing with familiar objects and events.	_____	_____	_____
	_____	_____	_____

SOCIAL/EMOTIONAL SKILLS	NOT YET	SOMEWHAT	INDEPENDENTLY
Seems to understand taking turns, but not always willing to do so.	_____	_____	_____
Joins in simple games and group activities, sometimes hesitantly.	_____	_____	_____
Uses objects symbolically in play: block of wood may be a car.	_____	_____	_____
Observes other children playing; may join in for a short time; engages in parallel play.	_____	_____	_____
Defends toys and possessions; may become aggressive at times, hitting another child or hiding toys.	_____	_____	_____

SELF-HELP SKILLS	NOT YET	SOMEWHAT	INDEPENDENTLY
Feeds self independently, uses spoon in semi-adult fashion.	_____	_____	_____
Pours milk and juice with fewer spills; serves individual portions from a serving dish with some help ("Fill it up to the line"; "Take only two spoonfuls").	_____	_____	_____
Takes care of own toilet needs during the daytime.	_____	_____	_____
Manages undressing better than dressing; is capable of putting on some articles of clothing.	_____	_____	_____
May begins to give up afternoon naps; continues to benefit from a midday quiet time.	_____	_____	_____

DEVELOPMENTAL SKILLS CHECKLIST: AGES FORTY-EIGHT TO SIXTY MONTHS

Child's Name _____ Date of Birth _____

Consider the developmental skills for each child. Place the date that corresponds to the child's skill level at the time of the observations.

FINE- AND GROSS-MOTOR SKILLS	NOT YET	SOMEWHAT	INDEPENDENTLY
Builds a tower with ten or more blocks.	_____	_____	_____
Paints and draws with an idea in mind, but may label the product something else.	_____	_____	_____
Threads small wooden beads on string/thread or lacing cards.	_____	_____	_____
Walks a tape or chalk line on the floor.	_____	_____	_____
Jumps over objects five inches high; lands with both feet together.	_____	_____	_____

COGNITIVE–PERCEPTUAL SKILLS	NOT YET	SOMEWHAT	INDEPENDENTLY
Stacks at least five graduated cubes from largest to smallest.	___	___	___
Names eighteen to twenty uppercase letters near the end of this age, children may be able to print several letters and write own name.	___	___	___
Understands the concepts of "tallest," "biggest," "same," and the picture that has the "most cars" or the "biggest dolls."	___	___	___
Rote counts to twenty or more.	___	___	___
Understands the sequence of daily events: "When we get up, we get dressed, have breakfast, brush our teeth, and go to school."	___	___	___

SPEECH AND LANGUAGE SKILLS			
Uses the prepositions "on," "in," and "under."	___	___	___
Produces elaborate sentence structures: "The big brown dog chased our cat up a tree."	___	___	___
Begins to correctly use the past tense of verbs: "Timmy closed the window," "Mommy went to work."	___	___	___
Refers to activities, events, objects, and people that are not present.	___	___	___
States first and last name, gender, siblings' names, and sometimes home telephone number.	___	___	___
Sings simple songs and rhymes.	___	___	___

SOCIAL/EMOTIONAL SKILLS	NOT YET	SOMEWHAT	INDEPENDENTLY
Holds conversations and shares strong emotions with imaginary playmates or companions.	___	___	___
Cooperates with others; participates in group activities.	___	___	___
Establishes close relationships with others, begins to have "best" friends.	___	___	___

SELF-HELP SKILLS	NOT YET	SOMEWHAT	INDEPENDENTLY
Able to use all eating utensils; can spread jelly or butter on soft foods like bread.	___	___	___
Likes to help in the preparation of a meal; dumping premeasured ingredients, washing vegetables, setting the table.	___	___	___
Takes care of own toileting needs; may begin to demand privacy in the bathroom.	___	___	___
Dresses self; can lace shoes, button buttons, buckle belts.	___	___	___

DEVELOPMENTAL SKILLS CHECKLIST: AGES SIXTY TO SEVENTY-TWO MONTHS

Child's Name _____ Date of Birth _____

Consider the developmental skills for each child. Place the date that corresponds to the child's skill level at the time of the observations.

FINE- AND GROSS-MOTOR SKILLS	NOT YET	SOMEWHAT	INDEPENDENTLY
Walks backward, heel to toe.	_____	_____	_____
Walks unassisted up and down stairs, alternating feet.	_____	_____	_____
Catches a ball thrown from three feet away.	_____	_____	_____
Rides a tricycle or wheeled toy with speed and skillful steering; some children learn to ride bicycles, usually with training wheels.	_____	_____	_____
Balances on either foot with good control for ten seconds.	_____	_____	_____
Builds three-dimensional structures with small cubes by copying a picture or model.	_____	_____	_____
Has good control of pencil or marker.	_____	_____	_____

COGNITIVE–PERCEPTUAL SKILLS	NOT YET	SOMEWHAT	INDEPENDENTLY
Understands concept of *same* shape, *same* size.	_____	_____	_____
Understands the concepts of smallest and shortest; places objects in order from shortest to tallest or smallest to largest.	_____	_____	_____
Identifies objects with specified serial position: first, second, last.	_____	_____	_____
Rote counts to twenty and above; many children count to one hundred.	_____	_____	_____
Recognizes numerals from one to ten.	_____	_____	_____
Recognizes and identifies penny, nickel, and dime.	_____	_____	_____
Knows alphabet; can name upper- and lowercase letters.	_____	_____	_____

SPEECH AND LANGUAGE SKILLS	NOT YET	SOMEWHAT	INDEPENDENTLY
Has vocabulary of 1,500 words or more.	_____	_____	_____
Identifies and names four to eight colors.	_____	_____	_____
Produces sentences with five to seven words; much longer sentences are not unusual.	_____	_____	_____
States the name of own city or town, birthday, and parents' names.	_____	_____	_____
Uses past tense of irregular verbs consistently: "went," "caught," "swam."	_____	_____	_____

SOCIAL/EMOTIONAL SKILLS	NOT YET	SOMEWHAT	INDEPENDENTLY
Enjoys friendships; often has one or two special playmates.	____	____	____
Shares toys, takes turns, plays cooperatively (with occasional lapses); is often quite generous.	____	____	____
Participates in group play and shared activities with other children; suggests imaginative and elaborate play ideas.	____	____	____
Follows directions; generally does what teacher requests.	____	____	____

SELF-HELP SKILLS	NOT YET	SOMEWHAT	INDEPENDENTLY
Likes familiar foods; prefers most vegetables raw.	____	____	____
"Makes" breakfast (pours cereal, gets out milk and juice) and lunch (spreads peanut butter and jam on bread).	____	____	____
Takes full responsibility for own toileting needs.	____	____	____
Dresses self completely; learning to tie shoes.	____	____	____

RESOURCES IN EARLY CARE AND EDUCATION

This guidebook is designed to coordinate your investigation into management principles as they apply to the administration of early care and education programs and related family support systems. We can only sample the vast array of appropriate printed materials. Selection is based on availability and lasting value, which means that many current pamphlets and books are omitted because they may be difficult to find or soon will be out of print. A few select journal articles are listed; there are simply so many of them that there is not space in this guidebook to list all of them. Remember that there are also dozens of publications in business management, educational supervision, and social service administration. Daily newspapers frequently carry articles dealing with personnel and other topics that apply to any business, including your center.

ASSOCIATIONS/AGENCIES/ORGANIZATIONS

Alliance of Work/Life Professionals, 515 King Street, Suite #420, Alexander, VA 22314; phone: 703-684-8396; www.awlp.org.

American Montessori Society, Inc., 150 Fifth Avenue, New York, NY 10011; phone: 212-924-3209; www.amshq.org.

Association Montessori International, 161 Koninginnewege, 1075-CN Amsterdam, The Netherlands; www.montessori-ami.org. (Founded in 1929 by Maria Montessori and with family involvement it is still operating at the present time.) A free-book introduction to the Montessori system is available at ww.michaelolaf.net.

Association of Waldorf Schools of North America (www.awsna.org/education) includes D. Mitchell and D. Alsop, *Essays on Business Practices within Waldorf Schools*; E. Limbret, *Music and Eurithmy*; R. Steiner, *Understanding Young Children* (2003 reprint); and *Renewal Magazine*. This site also includes a listing of member schools in the United States.

Center for Early Childhood Leadership National-Louis University Director: Paula Jorde Bloom, 6310 Capitol Drive, Wheeling, IL 60090-7201; phone: 800-443-5522, ext. 7703; www.nl.edu/cecl.

Child Care Aware, 2116 Campus Drive, SE, Rochester, MN 55904; phone: 800-462-1660; www.dhc.com/targetwww/html/child01.html.

Child Care in Health Care, Bryan Memorial Hospital Child Development Center, 1600 South 48th Street, Lincoln, NE 68506; phone: 402-483-8624.

Children's Defense Fund, 25 E Street, NW, Washington, DC 20001; phone: 202-662-3544; www.childrensdefense.org.

Council for Early Childhood Professional Recognition; phone: 1-800-424-4310.

Ecumenical Child Care Network, 8765 West Higgins Road, #405, Chicago, IL 60631; phone: 773-693-4040; www.eccn.org.

Families and Work Institute, 330 Seventh Avenue, New York, NY 10001; phone: 212-465-2044; www.familiesandwork.org.

Forest T. Jones & Co., Inc.: toll-free phone: 1-800-265-9366; www.ftj.com.

Generations United, 122 C Street, Suite 820, Washington, DC 20001; phone: 202-630-1263; www.gu.org.

High/Scope. An interactive website, www.highscope.net, provides assessment tools that chart children's progress over the period of their enrollment. Information and materials are available at www.highscope.org or by phone at 1-800 40 PRESS, including *High/Scope ReSource* magazine.

Instructional Systems materials from Science Research Associates, Inc., 259 East Erie Street, Chicago, IL 60611.

International Food Information Council Foundation,1100 Connecticut Avenue, Suite 430, Washington, DC 20036; phone: 202-296-6540; http://ific.org.

Montessori Education Centers Associated, 5728 Virginia Avenue, Clarendon Hills, IL 60514; phone: 630-654-0151; www.MontessoriECA.org.

National Association for the Education of Young Children, 1509 16th Street, NW, Washington, DC 20036-1426; phone: 1-866-naeyc-4u; www.naeyc.org.

National Association for Family Child Care, 525 SW 5th Street, Suite A, Des Moines, IA 50309; phone: 515-282-8292; www.nafcc.org.

National Association of Child Care Resource and Referral Agencies, 1319 F Street NW, Suite 810, Washington, DC 20004-1106; phone: 202-393-5501; www.naccrra.org.

National Black Child Development Institute, 1023 15th Street, NW, Suite 600, Washington, DC 20005; phone: 202-387-1281; www.nbcdi.org.

National Center for the Early Childhood Workforce, 733 15th Street, NW, Suite 137, Washington, DC 20005-2112; phone: 202-737-7700.

National Center for Montessori Education, PO Box 1543, Roswell, GA 30077; www.montessori-ncme.org.

National Coalition for Campus Children's Centers, University of Northern Iowa, 119 Schindler Education Center, Cedar Falls, IA 50614-0605; phone: 319-273-3113; www.campuschildren.org.

North American Reggio Emilia Alliance, phone: 770-552-0179.

OMEP-USNC Child Care Information Center, 2109 South Stoughton Road, Madison, WI 53716; www.omep.usnc.org.

The Center for Career Development in Early Care and Education, Wheelock College, 200 The Riverway, Boston, MA 02215-4176; phone: 617-734-5200; http://ericps.ed. uiuc.edu.ccdece/ccdece.html.

PUBLISHERS OF PERIODICALS, BOOKS, AND MANAGEMENT FORMS

Child Care Information Exchange, published by Exchange Press, PO Box 2890, Redmond, WA 98073, www.ccie.com, is devoted entirely to management topics for early childhood program administrators. Since 1977, Roger and Bonnie Neugebauer have expanded from this bimonthly magazine to publish books, organize a director's network, and conduct workshops. Free publications list.

Educational Resources Information Center (ERIC): www.eric.ed.gov

Gryphon House, Inc., PO Box 275, Mount Ranier, MD 20712, is distributor for hard-to-find materials from several sources.

Humanics, Ltd., 1389 Peachtree Street, and Save the Children, 1340 Spring Street, Suite 200, both in Atlanta, GA 30309, have varied offerings but can be particularly recommended for personnel materials and moderately priced books that are specific to administration of early childhood programs. Free lists.

Redleaf Press has resources for early childhood care and education as well as web-based courses (information available at www.rcclearningcenter.org). 450 North Syndicate, Suite 5, Saint Paul, MN 55104-4125; phone: 1-800-423-8309; www.redleafpress.org. Available books include Tom Copeland's *Family Child Care Record Keeping Guide* and *Family Child Care Contracts and Policies.*

School-Age Notes, PO Box 40205, Nashville, TN 37204-0205, publishes extensive "how-to-do-it" books for administrators and teachers, a monthly newsletter, and audio CDs. Free catalog: phone 1-800-410-8780 or www.afterschoolcatalog.com.

Teachers College Press, 1234 Amsterdam Avenue, New York, NY 10027, specializes in early childhood education books and has a free catalog for convenient mail order service; www.teacherscollegepress.com.

The American Management Association, AMACOM Publishing Division, PO Box 1026, Saranac Lake, NY 12983-9986, has books and both audio and video cassettes about business management.

The Center for Early Childhood Leadership, National-Louis University, 6310 Capitol Drive, Wheeling, IL 60090-7201.

Toys 'N Things Press, a division of Resources for Child Caring, Inc., 906 North Dale Street, Saint Paul, MN 55103, publishes record keeping forms, curriculum books, posters, and other materials; www.allbookstores.com.

GOVERNMENTAL SOURCES

Consumer Information Catalog (www.pueblo.gsa.gov) from the Federal Citizen Information Center was developed to distribute consumer information to the public. Phone 1-888-8PUEBLO, or write FCIC-03B, PO Box 100, Pueblo, CO 81002.

Local or regional offices of the Small Business Administration, Internal Revenue Service, Department of Agriculture, Department of Health and Human Services, and other federal agencies often list toll-free numbers in the local telephone directory.

The Foundation Center publishes *The Foundation Directory, Grants for Children and Youth,* and other materials available in many public libraries.

U.S. Department of the Treasury; Internal Revenue Service, Tax-Exempt Status of your organization, publication 557, catalog 46573C, Washington DC.

ACRONYMS IN EARLY CARE AND EDUCATION

AAUW	American Association of University Women
ACEI	Association for Childhood Education International
AFSC	American Friends Service Committee (Quaker service program)
AHEA	American Home Economics Association (became American Association of Family and Consumer Sciences [AAFCS] in 1993)
CFR	American Council on Family Relations
ECE	Early Care and Education, formerly Early Childhood Education
IEA	International Association for the Evaluation of Educational Achievement
IKU	International Kindergarten Union (precursor to ACEI)
ISGHE	International Standing Group for the History of Education
LSRF	Laura Spellman Rockefeller Fund
NAEYC	National Association for the Education of Young Children
NCBA	National Cooperative Business Association
NEA	National Education Association
NSSE	National Society for the Study of Education
PCPI	Parent Cooperative Preschools International
PLA	Preschool Learning Alliance (Great Britain)
SRCD	Society for Research in Child Development
UNICEF	United Nations International Children's Emergency Fund

INDEX